Adult Section:
Coping for Capable Kids

by
LeoNora M. Cohen and Erica Frydenberg

With Contributions by:
Christine Badawy, Christine Durham, Jane Gleeson, Carol-Anne
Hammond, Ken Jamieson, Elaine Johnson, Efstratios Karakitsos,
Lynne Kelly, Catherine Lauffer, Karen McAsey, Pam Matters,
Helen Rimington, and Glenice Thomas

Illustrations by Ginny Bates

PRUFROCK PRESS

©1996 Hawker Brownlow Inc.
Melbourne, Australia

Published by Prufrock Press, P.O. Box 8813, Waco, TX 76701

ISBN 1-882664-23-X

Contents

Acknowledgments

Writing a book requires help from many sources. We would first like to thank our husbands, Mickey and Harry, for their patience and support during the long birthing of this book. Special thanks also to Mickey for his help with the section on humor and his assistance with proofreading and pagination.

Special thanks go to a dear friend and colleague, Joan Smutny, director of Project '95 at National Louis University, for generously collecting data on coping from her very capable kids. Thanks also to Ellen Tomchin at University of Virginia who arranged for scoring of the Adolescent Coping Scales in the US and shared her own research with us. Thanks to Ron Breyne, director of the Phoenix School of Roseburg, a special school for underachieving gifted students, for his research on alcoholism and drug abuse. Special thanks to Reva Friedman, whose wisdom about resilience, self-concept, and families of gifted students, as well as feedback on the book were invaluable. We value the many useful ideas provided by Melva and Darci Boles and Ben and Emmy Ryon on the contents and structure of the book.

We would also like to thank Douglas McClenaghan, creative writing teacher at Eltham High School, for encouraging his students to share their works with us. Thanks to each of these students, Tom Harvey, Scott Lascelles, Romney Shuttleworth, Stuart Pritchard, and Phoebe McGuiness-Thomas for their excellent contributions of poetry.

The information on mentors was written by Pam Matters, coordinator, Gifted Students Program P-12 and Tertiary, Directorate of School Education, Quality Assurance Division, Victoria. Pam's master's and doctoral work involved research on mentoring the gifted.

Students in the masters program in the Department of Educational Psychology and Special Education at the University of Melbourne in the Social, Emotional, and Moral Development of the CHIP course are especially to be thanked for their literature searches on the different topics, their collection of research data with adolescents, teachers, and parents, and their varied and creative projects. The materials they developed or reported have been woven together into the various chapters. Specifically, the following contributions were made:

Tannenbaum's Definition of Giftedness, Information Parents Want, and Appendix—Resources for Parents: Jane Gleeson;

Self-concept and Stereotyping: Lynne Kelly

Emotional Development: Glenice Thomas;

Family Influence, Goal Setting, and Time Management Worksheets: Carol-Anne Hammond;

Friendships and Peer Relationships, Affective Skills, and Using Thinking Strategies: Karen McAsey;

Moral Development: Christine Badawy;

Ethnic Gifted and Disabled Children: Ken Jamieson;

Perfectionism: Helen Rimington and Elaine Johnson;

Helping the Perfectionist Do's and Don'ts and the "What to Do" Sheets: Helen Rimington and Cathy Lauffer;

Boredom and Underachievement: Elaine Johnson and Lynne Kelly;

Anorexia: Lynne Kelly and Elaine Johnson;

Coping with Change and Parents of the Gifted, Talented, Can You Read the Writing on the Wall? and A Memo from Children to Parents: Christine Durham;

What the Kids Discovered about School: Collated by Christine Durham from class interviews with adolescents;

Metacognition: Efstratios Karakitsos; and

Case Studies of 10 Capable Students: Ken Jamieson and Glenice Thomas from materials collected by class through interviews and questionnaires.

Many thanks to the wonderful parents and teachers who shared what they learned about helping young people cope. And finally, thanks especially to all the young people who opened their hearts and our eyes to how capable kids cope.

Introduction

The need for this book became apparent when one of the authors of this book gave her 13-year-old daughter *The Adolescent Coping Scales*. She wanted to determine whether this measure of coping developed by Frydenberg and Lewis (1993a) might be useful to help graduate students understand the social and emotional development of able adolescents. She was appalled at the limited "coping vocabulary" of this intense, sensitive and creative young person. This gifted young woman basically used four strategies to deal with most of her problems and some of these strategies were not productive in overcoming her difficulties. But what has been even more disturbing, found through research with over 90 highly able adolescents, is that gifted students were reliant on fewer coping strategies than their normal peers.

In fact, gifted young people rely on only about six strategies to help them cope (although these are most often the most productive strategies), while their normal peers typically use about nine. This difference can either be explained as use of more efficient strategies by gifted students — that is, use of fewer strategies that work for most situations; or it can be explained as lack of flexibility in coping with personal concerns among the gifted.

If efficiency were the best explanation, then we would expect gifted young people to experience fewer difficulties coping, for they would generally be successful in dealing with problems in their personal worlds. While it is true that many of these students are successful, particularly in the academic arena, a fair percentage of capable kids suffer much pain in coping with their stresses. In addition, we would expect them to use productive strategies rather than non-productive or avoidance strategies. Although research finds that more capable kids do use productive strategies that are effective in dealing with difficulties, other capable young people do not.

On the other hand, lack of flexibility might seem surprising, as gifted students are often so flexible when it comes to solving academic problems. For instance, when the same young woman was asked how she learned French verbs, she provided a whole range of strategies, from thinking about words that share the same root in English, to saying the word several times, to envisioning it, to thinking up rhyming word clues and several others as well. Apparently for her and for many other bright young people, strategies for learning are easy, but when it comes to coping with personal difficulties, the various options available are not considered.

There are also those young people who thrive on opportunity, blossom through experience and enjoy their passage through adolescence. It is these young people who best learn from others and attempt to maximize opportunities. They too will find that by reflecting on coping and examining their experience, it is possible to broaden their coping repertoire to achieve personal goals in the diverse arenas where adolescents interact.

This book was written to help capable kids, their parents and teachers consider a variety of coping strategies for dealing with their concerns. It also explains why having a range of strategies available maximizes the outcomes and increases a sense of control and adequacy. It details the problems and needs of bright young people and the unique patterns of personality, social, emotional and moral development that typify this group. True stories of bright kids and how they cope told from varied perspectives — their own, their teachers and/or their parents — offer a glimpse of the differing viewpoints on common problems. The book also includes reference lists for further help.

Coping for Capable Kids is really two books. One is written specifically for adolescents and preadolescents; the other is written for teachers and parents. However, we believe that capable kids can understand complex ideas, and we also believe that we don't tell adults one thing and kids another; therefore, both groups should read both books. We have divided it simply because the material sort of organized itself that way.

We can all examine our behavior and find things we would like to have done differently in dealing with a problem. It is possible to expand our effective coping repertories and reduce the use of less effective strategies. By examining our coping actions and consciously embarking on developing and employing other options, we can direct our own behavioral change. We as individuals make choices and can learn and even create new strategies. This book should help us and the capable kids with whom we live and work to enhance performance and optimize outcomes. It can help us all do what we do better.

This edition of the book grew out of a graduate class on Social, Emotional and Moral Development of the Gifted at the University of Melbourne and research collected in the United States. From summaries of the literature; research involving interviews, discussions, and questionnaires with bright adolescents, their parents and teachers; and from synthesis projects, the materials for chapters evolved. In fact, many of the ideas came directly from the wise words of able young people. If these students could only talk with each other and share strategies, they could encourage growth or lessen the pain. And if teachers and parents could understand how hard it can be to grow up in an increasingly troubled and violent world for bright, sensitive kids — if teachers and parents could reach out to these young people and offer assistance—some of the tragic loss of potential and some of the pain might be avoided. This book, then, is a group effort on the part of graduate students, adolescents and pre-teens, parents, teachers and university faculty to help capable kids cope more effectively.

The next three chapters are summaries of the research literature on a variety of topics related to coping and are necessarily brief. For greater depth, the reader should look at the End Notes, then the References and follow up with further readings. The final two chapters of this section for adults are suggestions for teachers and parents. In "Some Definitions," we begin with some definitions related to coping and capable kids. We first look at the period of adolescence in order to set the context. Next, we discuss what we mean by the terms "coping" and "capable." The chapter concludes with a discussion of self-concept, a central issue in coping.

SOME DEFINITIONS

What is Adolescence?

Life is the passage through a series of phases. Some phases of development are experienced by all, and are associated with a life-long process of learning and adaptation, accompanied by cognitive and emotional growth. Adolescence is one such period that spans the interval between puberty and adulthood. For many capable young people, some of the changes typically associated with adolescence begin considerably earlier. While some young people experience this passage with calm and tranquility, for others it is a period of turbulence. How to challenge this passage effectively is the purpose of this book. Preadolescents may also find the book helpful in anticipating and preparing for this journey into adulthood.

Adolescence occurs within a variety of environmental or contextual locations which can be classified under four major spheres of influence: the school, the home, the peer group and the broader community with its specific characteristics. Development is influenced by the context in which it takes place.

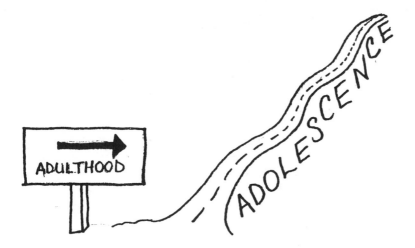

The period of adolescence is highlighted by developmental changes in all facets of the individual that are different from other periods of the life span. Biological changes are generally thought to be complete with the attainment of puberty. However there are aspects of maturing body shape which continue with growth in body size. These bodily and hormonal changes influence self-image which in turn exerts an impact on a host of psychological variables. The sum total is the self-concept or how the individual feels about the self. The period is highlighted by the search and possible resolution of identity issues. This has been summed up as attempts to answer the question "Who am I?".

Capable adolescents don't always "know themselves" as well as we might believe, given their advanced cognitive development. Additionally, it is a time when sexual needs and sexual identity issues come into prominence. Cognitive or intellectual development is another area of major change which takes place during adolescence. During this phase, abstract thinking develops. While abstract thinking typically first appears during adolescence, many adolescents or adults never manifest the capacity to think abstractly. Gifted young people are likely to have accelerated development in that regard. Moral reasoning advances during adolescence to involve concerns about society. Capable adolescents or those who are identified as gifted have usually developed the capacity for abstract thinking and often display heightened sensitivity to issues of social justice well in advance of their peers. Thus during this phase, there is the development of principles, conscience and moral judgments.

The commonly perceived signs of adolescent development can be summarized and grouped into the following four broad areas:

1. Biological maturation, sexual development and the achieving of adult stature. In all these areas there is a great deal of variation in the rate of development. The early bloomers, especially girls where there are clear changes in body development, often feel self-conscious about being different from their peers in that regard. The late bloomers, especially the boys who display delayed growth spurts, can find it difficult to believe that they will ever grow.

2. Relationships and uncertainty about meeting adult and

peer expectations. There may be a shift from intimacy within the family to intimacy with peers. This transition may not be straightforward and it may be painful for both the adolescent and the parents, as adolescents attempt to separate and differentiate themselves from their parents, but at the same time stay connected to the family. Sometimes there is attending family turmoil and conflict. There is accompanying uncertainty about friendships and possible loneliness.

3. The questions relating to identity and purpose: "Who am I and what am I about? Where am I going with my life? How do I get there? Where do I fit in? Who can I be friends with?" There are also issues of organization and time management that relate to achieving goals and purposes.

4. Cognitive development, and the different rates at which it happens, especially as related to abstract reasoning and the management of moral dilemmas. Gifted adolescents can develop high expectations of themselves and feel impatience at not being able to solve problems, or they can be impatient with others who do not see the solutions or perspectives which they perceive.

The strength to cope with these changes appears to be influenced by previous adjustments, particularly before the age of 5; consistency of family support prior to adolescence; and the adolescent's aspiration to move to a more balanced state.

Although gifted adolescents demonstrate advanced reasoning in academic areas, they may progress far more slowly in social maturity. In fact, although all young people go through a regressive period during adolescence, the gifted may appear to do so more noticeably. On the other hand, they bring certain strengths to the age period, including increased capacities to relate to and learn from others, increased ability to observe the self and verbalize (rather than act out) strong feelings; use of logical and deductive reasoning; expansion and intensification of interests and skills; increasing need for autonomy and greater ability to cooperate; and realistic perceptions of self that include integration of ideals.

Areas of particular difficulty for gifted adolescents include:

1. *Identity diffusion*—Young persons are out of contact with their past and have doubts about their abilities and talents.

2. *Worries about being different*—They perceive that their talents make them noticeably different and equate different with inferior.

3. *Perfectionism*—(discussed in depth in "Coping with Problems Common to Gifted Kids).

4. *Premature identity*—Impatience with lack of clear cut answers to their own identity and difficulties experiencing ambiguity and confusion related to identity, which leads to foreclosing on an identity before it has "ripened."

5. *Jolting separation-individuation process*—Finding out how one is different from parents, siblings and other intimates, which often involves severing attachments, not only to family, but including halting the development of talents, to affirm selfness and abilities on their own.

6. *Problems of perseverance*—The flashes of success previously experienced in one or more areas of endeavor now require patient honing to achieve results. In other words, gifted young people may not realize that years of practice are required to become really good at something. Postponing fun for disciplined hard work may not be considered worthwhile.

What is Coping?

Generally, coping implies a range of behaviors such as adaptation, mastery, defense or realistic problem solving. The conceptualization of coping used in this book deals with coping as adaptive functioning, where the individual and the environment are interactive. The individual perceives the world in a unique way and these perceptions make up that person's reality. The individual then responds to the environment according to his or her perceptions.

All people have concerns that worry them; youth are no exception. Whether the concerns relate to personal matters or to matters of social consequence beyond the subjective, personal world of the individual, they are important at a given time to the person. In recent years we have become increasingly aware of stress and its consequences. "Stress can be regarded as an interference with the normal and full functioning of mental abilities that assist individuals to cope with their problems." Mild stress of short duration may improve performance, activity and learning, but continued over a long period, may lead to breakdowns. Under intense stress,

particularly of long duration, performance deteriorates, and collapse and breakdown occurs. When the stresses become so great that a person is not able to cope, in extreme circumstances the individual may resort to suicide. Suicide is on the increase in our communities and around the world. Twice as many teens attempted or committed suicide in 1990 as in 1970 in America. The rate of actual teen suicides went from 8.0 per 100,000 in 1970 to 13.2 between 1987-1990. In Australia, Norway, Canada, and Switzerland, teen suicide rates were even greater. For example, Australia's was the highest teen suicide rate, with 16.4 suicides per 100,000. In Australia, the incidence of female suicide doubled between 1970 and 1990 (World Health Organization, 1994). Gifted young people are too often represented in these statistics. Issues such as the destruction of the environment, threat of nuclear war, genocide, unemployment, depletion of natural resources, hazardous wastes, the changing family structures with increase in the incidence of divorce, violence and crime may induce a sense of hopelessness and helplessness.

There are anticipated stresses that involve transitions through life phases such as going through puberty, getting a driver's license, passing the final year of high school, and so on. There are also unanticipated stresses like having an accident, getting a particular illness, dealing with the divorce of parents or experiencing a death in the family. In addition there are stresses that individuals put on themselves because of their personality, feedback that they have received from others, their theories and beliefs, or extreme sensitivity that make coping difficult. These self-stresses are the messages that we give ourselves (the *shoulds, musts, have tos* and *can'ts*), negatives about ourselves that allow emotions to block effective actions. The resources that one has, such as those based on previous experience and learning along with specific skills and personality dispositions, influence what one does or how an individual copes. The way we manage our concerns depends upon the resources we have available to cope and how we utilize the resources.

Recently there has been a growing interest in how people cope with their different concerns. What is clear is that young people manage their concerns in different ways. Some of these differences may be manifestations of an individual's coping style, others are specific to groups. Distinctions are generally found by gender, cultural group and level of ability.

For a long time psychologists have been preoccupied with stress and the individual's response to stress. This is a deficit approach to examining behavior that looks at what is going wrong and whether the individual is maladaptive. This deficit approach is reflected in the body of literature relating to the measurement of stress and anxiety. These approaches have in common notions of human failure and inadequacy. They focus on behavioral deficit rather than on behavioral competence. However, in recent years there has been a shift to approaches which examine an individual's capacity to cope, or adaptive behavior. The focus on coping represents the emergence of interest in "ability" models for the understanding of human behavior.

What concerns young people and how they cope with their concerns can be addressed in each of the many contexts within which young people must function. These settings include school, home, peer groups, the community and the workplace. Both the individual and the social context are determinants of human behavior. In keeping with that view, the individual is considered to be a part of the social context, a relational view of the person and the environment. Essentially the relationship is based on a complex set of interactions between the human and the environmental factors. How one acts depends not only on the particular event, for example being told that a piece of work has to be done by a specific time, but also, the circumstance—who is doing the telling and what else is happening for the individual. How the person responds, for example with acceptance or with protest, then influences the response from the requester: will there be negotiation or will there be a determined stand, and so forth.

Since many adolescents spend much of their time in the company of other adolescents, whether it be at school or in after-school leisure or sporting activities, the peer group represents a significant context that influences the individual. However, the family and other significant adults play an important part in determining the development of adolescents. Parents, and the expectations they place on children, continue to exert an overriding influence on many adolescents. Contexts or systems such as the family, school and peer group, while in some sense separate, often represent a system of interlinking nets which exert an effect on the individual simultaneously.

The theory of coping provides a framework within which behavior can be investigated according to how an individual adapts. Thus coping is the set of cognitive and behavioral strategies used to deal with the demands of everyday living. Frydenberg and Lewis have identified 18 distinguishable coping strategies, described with exemplars on pp. 25-27. These make up the thoughts, feelings and actions which individuals are able to call upon in particular circumstances to manage their concerns. There are two distinguish-

I JUST NEED TO FIND SOME REAL OPTIONS.

able modes of dealing with life problems. These modes are in the cognitive (thinking) and affective (feeling) domains and have been described as problem-focused coping (attempts to deal with the problem directly) and emotion-focused coping (attempts to reduce the stress felt by the individual). These two domains can be further differentiated into other coping modalities.

Coping as Psychosocial Competence

The person exhibiting psychosocial competence has an active coping orientation. This person is characterized by high initiative, realistic goal setting, substantial planning, forbearance, and effort in the service of attaining goals. He or she demonstrates capacity for both enjoying successes and learning from failures and can build from both.

One aspect of psychosocial competence is *resilience*, the ability of the individual to bounce back or even thrive when facing difficulties or traumas. To Rutter, one of the foremost researchers on the topic, "resilience is characterized by some sort of action with a definite aim in mind and some sort of strategy of how to achieve the chosen objective." The achieving of the objective has several elements including a sense of self-esteem and confidence, an ability to deal with change and adaptation, and a repertoire of social problem-solving approaches. These cognitive sets are likely to be fostered by stable affective relationships, experience of success and achievement. Generally success needs to be defined by the individual in the area that is valued.

But Rutter points out that it is not the quantity that counts. For example one good relationship can mitigate the effect of other bad relationships. Another protective feature is the ability to emotionally distance oneself from an unalterable, bad situation. The ways parents deal with stresses themselves and the use of inductive disciplinary techniques to appreciate the consequences of their actions are important, for example, acting rather than reacting.

Resilience provides protective factors to situations or events that might commonly result in maladaptive outcomes. Such hardiness of a personality is related to control and the assessment of choices in the situation, challenge (how do I use the problem to improve myself?), commitment to school, and commitment to self. It also relates to social competence and a sense of purpose and future. Resilience is apparently influenced by emotional support provided during crises or trauma. Of course, resilience depends on the severity of the stress—the frequency, intensity, duration, kind or type, timing, and whether the stress is isolated or combined with other stresses. Young people who are resilient seek new situations, are not fearful, play hard, and are self-reliant. They typically have characteristics of independence; use creative hobbies, interests, and extracurricular activities as havens from stressful environments; and have effective social skills. They ask for help from adults, are well-liked by peers, use positive role models, and have active, friendly natures. When they are faced with severe adversity, they do experience nose dives, but they don't stay down and they get out faster. Several of these are coping strategies that are aspects of psychosocial competence.

How we cope is determined by a host of factors including what we have learned; the role models that we have had among parents, teachers and other significant adults as well as peers; and the experiences that we have had throughout our lives. Recently, researchers such as Martin Seligman have focused on how we learn to be optimistic rather than hopeless, wherein a person distances him or herself from failure. Another researcher, Rick Snyder, finds that being hopeful is the key to being successful at facing challenges. Hopeful children learn to think of alternatives when they are blocked. They tackle difficulties and find other pathways to get what they want. They tend to have multiple "stretch goals"—that is, the goals are difficult and demand effort. They view these goals as challenges, anticipate problems and build back up systems, and work at reaching their goals. They are "smart investors who can switch goals when they are tired or blocked." In fact, they are often delighted when they encounter blockage, consider the difficulty a challenge, and enjoy the "trip" of working on the challenge as much as "getting there." Low hope kids, on the other hand, usually have a single goal and have difficulty articulating what they would like. They perceive their goals as being threats, and select safe, easy goals to ensure success. Low hope kids find goal blockages a nightmare. They understand life as a goal game, but can't seem to play it. Snyder found that intelligence does not relate to hope, nor does gender.

Carol Dweck and her colleagues have demonstrated that we carry around with us theories of the mind. Like Snyder, she finds that how we cope is determined by the goals we set for ourselves. However, for her, the goals are determined by the theory of intelligence that we carry around with us. According to Dweck, there are *mastery-oriented* individuals who have unflagging optimism because they see situations as opportunities in which outcomes depend on effort. Mastery-oriented individuals hold the theory that intelligence is a potential and increases through hard work. *Helpless* individuals, on the other hand, focus on ability required and subsequently they experience inadequacy. Their theory is that intelligence is a thing, an *entity*, and therefore you shouldn't have to work at something if you have a high intelligence. They are performance, rather than process-oriented and feel that they constantly must test how smart they are. Mastery-oriented individuals seek challenges that foster learning and the see their minds as malleable and able to develop incrementally. There is no limit to the challenges that can be met and the way these challenges can be tackled.

Fortunately, it appears that adults can do several things to help young people become mastery-oriented, instead of helpless. For example, parents and teachers can emphasize development of, not display of abilities. Rather than praising speed and perfection, they might apologize if a young person gets a perfect paper, because the task was not challenging enough! Adults can model enjoyment of challenges and help young people to learn a variety of approaches to meet challenges, so students can learn to cope with difficulties. Social comparison and competition should be minimized. Praise should not be given for minimal effort in the name of self-esteem. Finally, the emphasis should be on intellectual growth and that intelligence is cultivated through learning.

Depending on these personality factors, people have a relatively fixed repertoire of coping strategies (a *coping vocabulary*) which they call upon according to the context. These strategies can be conceptualized as a limited range of coping styles. There is no right or wrong coping, just strategies that work effectively or ineffectively for the individual in a particular circumstance. The broader the coping repertoire, the more flexibility the individual has in being able to call on resources as the need arises. An important aspect of this conceptualization of coping is that individuals not only use a set of strategies to cope but they can assess for themselves the effectiveness of their coping. By analyzing one's coping strategies, the basic data is provided for self-directed behavioral change. Thus it is possible to expand one's repertoire or make changes in the use of one's coping strategies.

Investigating Coping Strategies

For over eight years, Frydenberg and Lewis have been involved in investigating how adolescents cope with their concerns. They have developed an instrument, the *Adolescent Coping Scale* (ACS), to assess these tactics. The 80 items of the ACS were generated from over 2000 descriptions of coping strategies provided by over 600 secondary students. Their responses were grouped into 18 key areas. The scale was constructed on a population that represented the full range of intellectual functioning and was tested on thousands of young people. However, no such list is ever complete. Thus we find that when we go to a particular group of young people such as the gifted, they describe additional strategies they use in particular circumstances.

The major objective in developing an adolescent measure of coping was to facilitate the development of psychosocial competence in young people. The underlying philosophy behind the development of the ACS is the belief that we can all take a long hard look at what we do and modify aspects of ourselves that we would like to improve—ways that we would like to act, strategies we would like to abandon or use less and strategies that we would like to enhance. This is also the philosophy underlying this book. By reflecting on one's coping and armed with some ideas from others, a young person or an adult can embark on a journey of personal development.

The following are the key areas of coping with examples for each. In the young people's section are examples of coping collected from a wide population of capable young people.

1. **Seek Social Support**—an inclination to share the problem with friends or relatives and enlist support in its management,
   e.g., I talk to somebody as I have discovered it really helps.
2. **Focus on Solving the Problem**—a strategy which tackles the problem systematically by learning about it and taking into account different points of view or options,
   e.g., I look at all the possible ways I could overcome this worry, then I work out a plan to cope with it.

3. **Work Hard and Achieve**—describes commitment, ambition and industry,
   e.g., I am working hard to the best of my ability at school.

4. **Worry**—indicates a concern about the future in general terms or, more specifically, a concern with happiness in the future,
   e.g., I worry about school, and I worry about the behavior of kids.

5. **Invest in Close Friends**—engaging in a particular intimate relationship,
   e.g., I spend as much time as I can with my boyfriend or girlfriend.

6. **Seek to Belong**—indicates a caring and concern for one's relationship with others in general and, more specifically, concern with what others think,
   e.g., If I talk to people about what they like, they accept me.

7. **Wishful Thinking**—having hopes and anticipations of things turning out well,
   e.g., I daydream a lot.

8. **Social Action**—letting others know what is of concern and enlisting support by writing petitions or organizing an activity such as a meeting or a rally,
   e.g., I got people to sign a petition and sent a letter to the government.

9. **Tension Reduction**—is characterized by items which reflect an attempt to make oneself feel better by releasing tension,
   e.g., If something bad has happened I go and write it down, I have a cry and then I feel lots better.

10. **Not Coping**—consists of items which reflect the individual's inability to deal with the problem and the development of psychosomatic symptoms,
    e.g., I don't have any strategies—I just battle on, taking each day as it comes.

11. **Ignore the Problem**—characterized by items which reflect a conscious blocking out of the problem,
    e.g., I try to forget about my concerns.

12. **Self-blame**—indicates that individuals see themselves as responsible for the concern or worry,
    e.g., It's my fault so I feel bad.

13. **Keep to Self**—characterized by items which reflect the individual's withdrawal from others and wish to keep others from knowing about concerns,
    e.g., I don't show others my feelings, instead I deal with things myself.
14. **Seek Spiritual Support**—characterized by items which reflect prayer and belief in the assistance of a spiritual leader or God,
    e.g., I pray to the Lord to take care of all my problems.
15. **Focus on the Positive**—represented by items which indicate a positive and cheerful outlook on the current situation. This includes seeing the "bright side" of circumstances and seeing oneself as fortunate,
    e.g., It helps if you look at positive things.
16. **Seek Professional Help**—denotes the use of a professional adviser, such as a teacher or counselor,
    e.g., I go to the teacher or counselor to get help.
17. **Seek Relaxing Diversions**—relaxation in general rather than sport. It is characterized by items which describe leisure activities such as reading and painting,
    e.g., I escape with music, either by listening to it or playing it.
18. **Physical Recreation**—characterized by items which relate to playing sports and keeping fit,
    e.g., I play sports or just keep fit.

The 18 coping strategies can be usefully grouped into three styles of coping. First there are those strategies that represent an attempt to remain positive while solving the problem. Sometimes this may mean use of relaxation. These strategies are: Focus on the Positive, Focus on Solving the Problem, Physical Recreation, Seek Relaxing Diversions and Work Hard to Achieve. The second group of strategies relates to interacting with other people and remaining socially connected. These strategies are: Seek Social Support (from friends and family), Invest in Close Friends (a strategy which involves engaging in an intimate relationship), Seek to Belong, which denotes a concern for others and in particular what others think, Seek Spiritual Support, the use of Professional Help and the recourse to Social Action. The third group of strategies are less productive in reaching a solution. They also have an emotional focus, rather than an action-oriented one.

These strategies are Worry (in particular about the individual's personal future), Wishful Thinking, Ignore the Problem, the use of Tension Reduction strategies such as smoking, eating or drinking, Keep Problems to Oneself, Self-blame, and Not Coping, which is a declaration of an inability to cope. Although this last group of strategies may appear to be ineffective to the observer, they may actually be an appropriate solution to a particular problem. For example, when John (aged 12) says, *"I ignore the problem. There is nothing I can do to prevent fighting in other countries,"* he may be using a strategy that is appropriate for him under the circumstances. Other young people may choose to write letters or read about the concern, but there is no right or wrong prescription for all individuals. However, some of the emotional coping strategies, such as using drugs or drinking, are not only less effective, but are harmful to the individual.

How Adolescents Cope

By using the ACS over a number of years and with different groups of young people, Frydenberg and Lewis found that the strategies used most frequently by adolescents were Seek Relaxing Diversions, Work Hard to Achieve, Focus on Solving Problems and Physical Recreation. The three least used coping strategies were Seek Spiritual Support, Seek Professional Help, and Social Action. These findings indicate that young people in the general community see themselves as being industrious, able to deal with problems that arise, but at the same time they relax and engage in physical recreation.

There are both similarities and differences in how boys and girls cope. In one study, Frydenberg and Lewis found that boys are likely to take more risks and they resort to physical recreation more than do girls. In contrast girls generally use more talking to friends and relatives, daydreaming, and tension reduction strategies than do boys.

In summary, the pattern of usage of different coping strategies, for students participating in the investigations to date, indicates that young peoples" foremost response to their general concerns comprises attempts to deal directly with the causes of concerns while attending to both their own physical and social well being. The gifted tend to employ the latter strategies less, however, as will be seen shortly.

It is important to note that while researchers gather their data carefully and are able to describe behavior according to averages across groups or populations (such as gifted and non-gifted, girls and boys) there are important variations according to individual circumstances. That is, not all boys resort to physical recreation more than girls and not all gifted girls avoid fitting in with the peer group. Educators need to obtain information about groups of young people so that they can plan teaching and learning environments accordingly, but they must also respond to the unique features of the individual. Teachers are taught to do this and parents often do so intuitively. The case studies in the young people's section of this book describe stories and coping actions of a sample of young people and give a flavor of these individual differences.

In addition to obtaining information about groups of young people such as those middle and high school students in Australia and the United States who participated in the studies, we can describe how a specific group of young people cope; for example, those in a particular grade level or class, or those in particular settings, such as hospitalized young people, or those who are studying a particular subject. Furthermore, an individual student can plot his or her own coping profile. For example the profile of Jason, a high school junior who was living at home with his parents and a younger sister when he completed the ACS, shows that the most frequently reported strategies he used were Solving the Problem directly, Physical Recreation, Turning to Friends of the opposite sex, and at the same time Keeping Problems to Himself. The least used strategies were those that involve the Seeking of Spiritual Support, turning to Social Action and turning to Professionals for Help. Jason's is quite a typical profile for boys.

In contrast, Sarah, who has lived with her divorced mother since she was eight, and was in eighth grade at the time of completing the ACS, used strategies that relate to Working Hard and Focusing on the Positive side of things while turning to others for Social Support, Investing in a Close Friend of the opposite sex, and seeking Relaxing Diversions. Sarah's least used strategies involved Seeking Spiritual Support, Not Coping and Ignoring her Problems.

Adolescent Coping Scale

Individual Profile of Coping Strategies

©1993 Erica Frydenberg and Ramon Lewis

Name: *Jason and Sarah* Date: ____ Form: ☐ General ☑ Specific

#	Scale	Description
1.	SocSup	**Seek Social Support**—sharing my problem with others; enlisting their support, encouragement and advice.
2.	SolvProb	**Focus on Solving the Problem**—tackling my problem systematically by thinking about it and taking other points of view into account.
3.	Work	**Work Hard and Achieve**—Being conscientious about my (school) work: working hard, and achieving high standards.
4.	Worry	**Worry**—worrying about the future in general and my personal happiness in particular.
5.	Friends	**Invest in Close Friends**—Spending time being with close friends and making new friendships.
6.	Belong	**Seek to Belong**—being concerned with what others think, and doing things to gain their approval.
7.	WishThink	**Wishful Thinking**—hoping for the best, that things will sort themselves out, that a miracle will happen.
8.	NotCope	**Not Coping**—not doing anything about my problem, giving up, feeling ill.
9.	TensRed	**Tension Reduction**—making myself feel better by letting off steam, taking my frustrations out on others, crying, screaming, taking alcohol, cigarettes or drugs.
10.	SocAc	**Social Action**—enlisting support by organizing group action to deal with my concerns and attending meetings and rallies.
11.	Ignore	**Ignore the problem**—consciously blocking out the problem, pretending it doesn't exist.
12.	SelfBl	**Self-Blame**—being hard on myself, seeing myself as being responsible for the problem.
13.	KeepSelf	**Keep to Self**—keeping my concerns and feelings to myself, avoiding other people.
14.	Spirit	**Seek Spiritual Support**—praying for help and guidance, reading a holy book.
15.	FocPos	**Focus on the Positive**—looking on the bright side of things, reminding myself that there are others who are worse off, trying to stay cheerful.
16.	ProfHelp	**Seek Professional Help**—discussing my problem with a professionally qualified person.
17.	Relax	**Seek Relaxing Diversions**—taking my mind off the problem by finding ways to relax such as reading a book, watching television, going out and having a good time.
18.	PhysRec	**Physical Recreation**—playing sports and keeping fit.

Coping and Giftedness

In "Giftedness" we will learn more about specific aspects of giftedness that relate to how young people cope. In this section, the research on coping and gifted adolescents is reviewed.

The gifted are not represented on any one personality type or value profile. Current research indicates that there is a great variety in personality type, intellectual focus and behavioral style among this group. Individual differences are the likely critical predictors of success. For example, in one study that looked at early entry into a university setting, it was clear that each of the students had a different technique for coping, such as approaching instructors, taking comprehensive notes or not interacting with their peers.

Betts and Niehart identified six profiles of the gifted based on behavior, feelings and needs: the successful (teacher pleasers), the divergently gifted (creatives), the underground (mostly gifted females who hide their talents), the dropout (academic failures and social misfits), the double labeled (physically disabled or learning disabled and gifted) and the autonomous learner.

Buescher's research found that coping with one's gifts and talents and feelings of being different depended on individual personality factors. Gifted adolescents who were sensitive, independent and flexible used a small number of positive strategies. Those who were more rigid, conforming and apprehensive used a narrow range of negative strategies. They also found that more boys than girls "arrived at age 16 with their talents intact and development well under way."

The danger for gifted young people, particularly girls, is that giftedness can be made into an entity. The child is considered to be endowed with intellectual abilities, rather than having potential for accomplishment through learning. Such young people may fear not meriting the label and thus choose to focus on performance goals, rather than process goals. Because they don't want the world to find their flaws, they choose safe, well-known tasks, and won't take challenges, thereby limiting their performance. These patterns can start as early as preschool and are compounded by perfectionist standards, with bright girls being particularly vulnerable. Such young people hold a fixed theory of intelligence, question their ability in the face of difficulty, and show impairment under stress. Dweck found that the highest IQ girls were most thrown when faced with a confusing passage that they had difficulty mastering. If passages were not confusing, there was no problem. She posits three reasons for these beliefs among the gifted (particularly for girls): 1) the child is esteemed for abilities, rather than for taking challenges; 2) boys get taught that lack of effort causes problems, while girls may not get the same lessons; and 3) girls become perfectionistic in grade school and can "do it all" correctly, but later, the work becomes more complex and socialization becomes an issue. Since perfection is difficult to maintain, endeavors become limited.

On the other hand, the characteristics that mark resilient individuals are also often descriptive of gifted young people, such as task commitment, reflectiveness, school achievement, verbal ability, love of learning, risk-taking, self-understanding, and intelligence. Both resilient and gifted young people frequently have families that encourage academic achievement and cultural activities, model successful behaviors, provide time and support for positive interactions, and offer unconditional love. Often, these families offer a safe haven for the child to express emotions. Although some gifted young people do experience social and emotional difficulties, gifted children or adolescents may also have resources that help them develop psychosocial competence. They may possess the ability to discuss their problems with adults due to high verbal skills. They also have the ability to use *cognitive appraisal* (ability to evaluate the environment and change their behaviors to make it work for them, or modify the interpretation of the environment), that is more characteristic of adults, even as young as age 9. One result here, is that the gifted young person may adjust to a situation without actually choosing to adapt to it. For example, a student who is teased or harassed by peers may decide to read during recess, rather than deal with the peer problem. Such a strategy may actually perpetuate a myth that the gifted are not adjusted, but sometimes gifted young people are caught "between a rock and a hard place" by the dilemmas they face. For example, this same child may be taunted by peers to share homework and may feel doubly tortured because the teacher has told the class that doing someone else's work is cheating. Opting out of the harassment by reading may be the best strategy at the time for that child. Clearly, the particular environment is very important in this cognitive appraisal as well as in how the coping strategy is judged.

There may be mixtures of resilience and vulnerability within an individual. For example, the child described above may exhibit many resilient characteristics, but have difficulties dealing with age peers in the particular school setting. Or there may be cultural or environmental factors at work that have not been appropriately understood. In one study of a 13-year-old Chinese-American student, the characteristics of self-reliance, creative interests, willingness to ask for help, inclination to play hard, and use of extra-curricular activities to deal with stress were indicative of resilience. At the same time, this young boy tended to use a resignation strategy, defer to adults, lose his temper, get bored easily, and generally lack positive peer relations. While these aspects may appear to be maladaptive, the cultural influences must be carefully considered. For example, deferring to adults or passivity might be a cultural positive in the child's ethnic context, but considered maladaptive in his school culture. Likewise, Black youth may use somewhat different strategies to help them cope with some problems some of them face, such as poverty, racism, or fear of violence. They may be overwhelmed by anti-achievement messages, have difficulties with social identity, and find that cultural expectations are different. Role models, strong school-family relations, mentors, and counseling may be needed, specific to this population. In a study of an exceptionally bright child whose emotional development was far less mature than his intellect, certain resiliencies were evident, but social interactions were difficult, particularly forming real friendships. This child used withdrawal from peers as a major coping mechanism, but found a haven in his family and received their support to improve the school situation. It may be possible for gifted students who are experiencing difficulties to learn to become more resilient through capitalizing on their intellectual, reflective, and verbal strengths. Alternative coping strategies can also be considered.

In another study, 12- to 15-year-old gifted adolescents were asked to prioritize coping strategies that young people like themselves might use. The following were the top six strategies in priority order recommended by these young people:

1. Accept abilities and use abilities to help peers.
2. Make friends with other students of exceptional talent.
3. Select classes/programs designed for gifted/talented students.

4. Build more relationships with adults.

5. Achieve in areas at school other than the academic.

6. Develop in talent areas outside the school setting.

This advice to peers can be added to one's "bag of coping strategies." Other groups of students might wish to debate the merits of this list, enlarge it, or come up with their own.

The coping strategies used may be more or less "expensive", depending on the energies required for dealing with the situation. Sometimes, the cost is so high that breakdown occurs, or creative needs may be suppressed. The young person may conform on the outside, and appear obedient and dependent. By so doing, healthy feelings about the self may be sacrificed, and the young person may develop anxiety or other emotional problems. Creative energies are blocked. When this occurs, aggressive behaviors may result, due to the inability to use these creative energies to overcome tensions.

Gifted young people go through predictable crises as part of their development. They also have somewhat different social and emotional experiences than their general peers. Gifted adolescents were found to be most lonely and vulnerable when rejected, alienated, isolated and not in control of the situation. Strategies used most by these young people were engaging in individual pursuits, extending social contacts, using cognitive reframing (telling themselves how things can be seen differently), and keeping busy. The less frequently used strategies were: engaging in religious activities, seeking adult help, and using negative escape routes.

On the face of it, this composite picture indicates that many gifted young people are dealing in a satisfactory way with difficulties. Of course that is not the case for all individuals in all circumstances.

Our research using the Adolescent Coping Scale on a broad range of gifted students in the Melbourne region of Australia, found that these young people use a more limited range of strategies than their normal counterparts, just as Buescher had discovered. However, like other groups of adolescents, their most commonly used strategies were: Work Hard to Achieve and Focus on Solving the Problem. They also used Seek Relaxing Diversions and Physical Recreation. Strategies used least by this group of gifted students were getting involved in Social Action, declaring that they had an Inability to Cope, Tension Reduction, Seeking Professional Help, Ignoring the Problem, and Seeking Spiritual Support. When the two groups of young people are compared, that is the general population and the gifted, it is clear that gifted young people Work Hard to Achieve and Focus on Solving the Problem more than their regular counterparts. This group of young people was further distinguished from the general population by the fact that they engaged less in Wishful Thinking or Investing in Close Friends (intimate relationships or friendships), resorted less to negative Tension Reducing strategies (e.g. smoking or alcohol use), and were also less inclined to declare their inability to cope (Not Cope).

Compared to the general population of girls, able girls in Australia focused more on Solving the Problem and were less likely to Seek Relaxing Diversions, Invest in Close Friends, use Wishful Thinking, or declare they do Not Cope. Able boys were found to declare they could Not Cope less than the general male population. Mirroring the general student community, able boys were more inclined to engage in Physical Recreation than able girls.

These findings were largely replicated in a study of US adolescents by Tomchin and her colleagues. The study also used the Adolescent Coping Scale with students who were participants in a summer enrichment program for gifted young people. When these young people were compared to the general school-age population, it was found that the gifted students were less likely to relax, worry or daydream, blame themselves, ignore problems, release tensions, or declare that they did not cope than the general group of students. On the other hand, they were more likely to work hard, focus on solving problems, seek social support, seek professional help, use spiritual support, and become engaged in social action. These findings are not altogether surprising. However, what the Tomchin study found was that the gifted girls and boys coped in much the same way. This is in contrast to most other studies which almost always find a striking difference between the ways in which boys and girls cope, implying that gifted young people are more similar than dissimilar in the ways in which they manage their concerns. Indeed they may share similar issues of concern.

In a study comparing gifted students ages 10-15 from an impoverished metropolitan environment in the United States to those of more affluent urban and suburban communities, many more children from low income environments expressed worries about violence in their communities and were more concerned about their futures. Concerns about violence were particularly high among the African American population, especially in low income communities. These young people used more seeking of spiritual support, worrying, and wishing than their more affluent counterparts. Young people in more affluent communities were more concerned generally with education and school issues and somewhat more concerned with peers.

The profiles of two young gifted adolescents, Jane and Steve, show some unique features of their coping and present a contrast to Sarah and Jason's profiles presented earlier. Jane engages in Work to a great extent but also uses Tension Reduction strategies substantially (unlike many of her gifted peers), Self-blame and Keeping to Herself. Unlike girls who generally use Social Support she uses it to a minimal extent. Like Jane, Steve engages in Work but he also Solves the Problem, Focuses on the Positive, and also resorts to Self-blame a great deal. Both Jane and Steve engage in Physical Recreation less than their regular peers. While each young person's profile is different from the other and represents his or her unique pattern of coping, gifted young people resort to coping actions in ways that are somewhat different from the general population of young people.

Adolescent Coping Scale — Individual Profile of Coping Strategies

©1993 Erica Frydenberg and Ramon Lewis

Name: _Steve and Jane_   Date: ____   Form: ☐ General ☑ Specific

Scale	Adjusted Score Gen.	Adjusted Score Spec.		Description
1. SocSup	20		30 – 40 – 50 – 60 – 70 – 80 – 90 – 100	**Seek Social Support**—sharing my problem with others; enlisting their support, encouragement and advice.
2. SolvProb	20		30 – 40 – 50 – 60 – 70 – 80 – 90 – 100	**Focus on Solving the Problem**—tackling my problem systematically by thinking about it and taking other points of view into account.
3. Work	20		30 – 40 – 50 – 60 – 70 – 80 – 90 – 100	**Work Hard and Achieve**—Being conscientious about my (school) work: working hard, and achieving high standards.
4. Worry	20		30 – 40 – 50 – 60 – 70 – 80 – 90 – 100	**Worry**—worrying about the future in general and my personal happiness in particular.
5. Friends	20		30 – 40 – 50 – 60 – 70 – 80 – 90 – 100	**Invest in Close Friends**—Spending time being with close friends and making new friendships.
6. Belong	20		30 – 40 – 50 – 60 – 70 – 80 – 90 – 100	**Seek to Belong**—being concerned with what others think, and doing things to gain their approval.
7. WishThink	20		30 – 40 – 50 – 60 – 70 – 80 – 90 – 100	**Wishful Thinking**—hoping for the best, that things will sort themselves out, that a miracle will happen.
8. NotCope	20		30 – 40 – 50 – 60 – 70 – 80 – 90 – 100	**Not Coping**—not doing anything about my problem, giving up, feeling ill.
9. TensRed	20		30 – 40 – 50 – 60 – 70 – 80 – 90 – 100	**Tension Reduction**—making myself feel better by letting off steam, taking my frustrations out on others, crying, screaming, taking alcohol, cigarettes or drugs.
10. SocAc	20		30 – 40 – 50 – 60 – 70 – 80 – 90 – 100	**Social Action**—enlisting support by organizing group action to deal with my concerns and attending meetings and rallies.
11. Ignore	20		30 – 40 – 50 – 60 – 70 – 80 – 90 – 100	**Ignore the problem**—consciously blocking out the problem, pretending it doesn't exist.
12. SelfBl	20		30 – 40 – 50 – 60 – 70 – 80 – 90 – 100	**Self-Blame**—being hard on myself, seeing myself as being responsible for the problem.
13. KeepSelf	20		30 – 40 – 50 – 60 – 70 – 80 – 90 – 100	**Keep to Self**—keeping my concerns and feelings to myself, avoiding other people.
14. Spirit	20		30 – 40 – 50 – 60 – 70 – 80 – 90 – 100	**Seek Spiritual Support**—praying for help and guidance, reading a holy book.
15. FocPos	20		30 – 40 – 50 – 60 – 70 – 80 – 90 – 100	**Focus on the Positive**—looking on the bright side of things, reminding myself that there are others who are worse off, trying to stay cheerful.
16. ProfHelp	20		30 – 40 – 50 – 60 – 70 – 80 – 90 – 100	**Seek Professional Help**—discussing my problem with a professionally qualified person.
17. Relax	20		30 – 40 – 50 – 60 – 70 – 80 – 90 – 100	**Seek Relaxing Diversions**—taking my mind off the problem by finding ways to relax such as reading a book, watching television, going out and having a good time.
18. PhysRec	20		30 – 40 – 50 – 60 – 70 – 80 – 90 – 100	**Physical Recreation**—playing sports and keeping fit.

Column headers across the scale axis: Not Used at All, Used Very Little, Used Sometimes, Used Frequently, Used a Great Deal

In a study of coping strategies among female high school students, one of the contributors to this book, Elaine Johnson, examined the coping strategies of a group of high ability adolescent girls in years 9 and 10 at a girls" school in metropolitan Melbourne. She found that gifted girls used two strategies more than a similar group of non-gifted girls: Focus on Solving the Problem and Work Hard to Achieve. The gifted girls were less likely to seek intimate relationships with friends and used physical recreation less than the regular group of adolescent counterparts. Below are some comments by parents and teachers about coping difficulties for gifted girls:

Susan's Mother

"Susan's major difficulty at school lies in the way the girls relate to each other. I think she is aware that I don't like girls who are nasty to one another, and if she thinks that nastiness comes into it she won't share her problems with me. What I find difficult to understand is that teachers are not aware of children's interactions, of problems that occur in the classroom. I feel that teachers are concentrating too much on the teaching rather than on the social behavior of children. Maybe these issues should be sorted out by an independent person, perhaps someone with psychological expertise, who would come to the school and talk to the children—preferably on a regular basis.

Academically, I believe there should be enrichment for students like Susan who need it. I am fortunate in that Susan will go out of her way to look for work, whereas her younger sister, who is equally bright in my opinion, will do only as much work as is required, and that's it. I believe the classes should be ability grouped so that those who are capable of working at a higher level are encouraged to do so."

Susan's Teacher

"I really think that in lots of ways by the time they reach sixth grade these students who have special abilities need some extra help in terms of their emotional needs. Something like inter-grade counseling or group therapy, or

someone who can lead a session like "we've noticed this behavior in the playground (or this particular problem)" and the students can put their name on a list and come in and talk about it. Counseling. You know, those youngsters that are always fighting could maybe come in and sit down as a group. We try it often (teachers, that is), but we don't really know how to help. You see, teachers try to be a bit of everything, but we don't really have the skills in this area. Once I get to a point where I've tried everything that I know—every strategy I've ever used or been taught—then my bank of knowledge is just used, and I don't know where to go."

Jenna's Mother

"Concerning Jenna's problem about the lack of challenge in the classroom, I think there is a major problem for those "brighter" children. The difficulty with problem solving and cooperative group work (which are currently in vogue in educational circles), which should in theory allow all children to operate at their best potential, doesn't work out that way in practice. Part of the problem is that peer pressure tends to hold these students back. Because your friend isn't quite as bright, you tend to follow them in group work sessions and hold back a bit so as not to make them feel bad. This is particularly so with girls, I think. I think, too, that in this system, children are not encouraged to excel in the early years, with the problem that the children become lazy. I had this problem with an older daughter. She was a very bright student in elementary and middle school, and didn't need to do any work. By the time she got to high school, things started to change, and by grade 10, they really changed. She was used to coasting because she was never pushed or challenged, and suddenly she was challenged and she didn't know how to cope with it. So she had to make some major changes in her behavior and her study habits which she hasn't made very easily. In those early years, she was so used to writing an essay in 10 minutes and getting an A for it. She had never been told that she was bright and she could do things. She's always been held back."

The Adolescent Coping Scale:
Uses and Availability

The Adolescent Coping Scale (ACS), along with the accompanying manual for practitioners, is available from the Australian Council for Educational Research (ACER). To order in the United States and Canada contact Psychometrics Canada, Ltd., 3rd Floor Students Union Building, University of Alberta, Edmonton, Edmonton, Alberta, Canada T6G 2J7; (403) 469-2268 or fax (403) 469-2283.

Teachers or counselors can use it as a self-help instrument with which students can come to understand their own coping behavior and subsequently make self-initiated changes. It can be used as an instrument of research to establish the ways in which a population of students or an individual young person copes, in different contexts and in different circumstances. It provides the data to assist with the development of programs for cognitive behavioral change. It can be used by counselors to develop programs, or to meet an individual's needs. The ACS can be used by educators to enhance their understanding of student behavior in a class or group setting. By collecting data from a class or group of students, a teacher can obtain a profile of student coping behavior which could include such information as frequently and infrequently used strategies. Subsequently, that information can be used to encourage change in identified directions.

Who Are Capable Kids?

There are three types of capable kids. Some are combinations of these types:

1. Capable kids are those who believe themselves to be capable because they have a strong self-concept.
2. Capable kids are those whose experiences in coping give them confidence and competence in dealing with ordinary stresses without serious difficulty.
3. Capable kids are intellectually, academically or creatively gifted kids, or those with talents in visual or performing arts, spatial thinking, leadership or other valued areas of

human endeavor who may or may not be successful in handling problems in their worlds.

Because each child interacts with the world in a unique manner, there is no recipe that can guarantee that a child will have self-confidence and a positive attitude. As a parent, you may have tried very hard to instill a sense of worth, autonomy and self-respect in your son or daughter. You may have been consistent in expectations and in setting limits. You may have encouraged your child to try new things, fostered interest development, praised the small accomplishments, ignored mistakes or suggested that in time your child would be able to handle them. You may have tried to find compatible peers, encouraged friendships, helped your child to relate to others by your own example as a friendly, supportive person. As a teacher, you may have tried to nurture budding talents and abilities, helped a young person to grasp difficult concepts, worked on being a good role model, avoided put-downs or too much praise, tried to make your lessons interesting and engaging and provided for the individual needs of students.

There are so many influences on a child and so many ways of interacting with the world that even under the best of circumstances and with the greatest of good intentions on the part of parents and teachers, a young person may develop difficulties coping. Peers, the school setting, the media, family stresses or world events are only a few of these influences. Even the subtlest nuances can make a difference. Added to the external influences is the marvelous uniqueness of each individual personality. What we are trying to say is that *it's not your fault* if you have tried to be a good parent or teacher and a young person is having difficulty coping with a particular situation. Often very bright youngsters develop coping difficulties because they become aware that their interests and feelings are different from the others. This awareness can begin even in the early elementary years and can be severely exacerbated as the child moves into adolescence.

On the other hand, if parents are overly protective, give mixed messages, have unrealistic expectations, overemphasize having a high IQ, are inconsistent in handling limits and discipline, or if the family situation is dysfunctional, young people may develop chronic problems in coping.

We cannot protect children and shield them from all difficulties in the world. In fact, if we try to do so, we cause them to become less able to cope with the problems that necessarily come their way, as they have not had experiences in dealing with obstacles. We can, however, help them to develop more effective strategies for coping. By providing information about coping, guiding students to reflect on their own behaviors and helping them to consider options, they can develop an increased repertoire of coping strategies to employ when they face difficulties. In addition, we can respect and value each child to encourage a sense of self-worth.

This section of "Some Definitions" will focus on self-concept, one of the three types of capabilities described above. Competence in coping, the second type of capability, has already been described in this chapter. "Giftedness" will focus on giftedness and the specific factors related to coping that may lead to difficult for gifted young people.

Self-concept and Self-esteem

The self-concept is a powerful system of beliefs, both good and bad, that a person holds true about him or herself. These beliefs mediate how a person interprets and responds to events or behaviors directed towards the self. The self-concept is both a complex structure and a dynamic organization. Related to structure, the self-concept is an integration of all the individual's experiences which form the images held of self. Although there are many views of self-concept and images of self, Abrom's distinctions are useful because of how the definitions relate to capable kids. She proposes four types of images of self:

1. Physical self—one's body and how it functions;
2. Social self—how one thinks others see and respond to oneself;
3. Real self—how one compares with others;
4. Ideal self—the abilities, attributes and relationships one values and aspires to.

The self-concept develops and changes over time and is therefore dynamic. Its formation depends on many external and internal forces, particularly early intimate relationships with key caregivers and other family members. Other factors for a healthy self-concept include having needs met; positive relationships with peers; school achievement; experiences of "flow," productivity and satisfaction with accomplishment; and successful risk-taking. A solid self-concept involves living with one's self comfortably and requires development of stress-management procedures ... in short, successful coping strategies.

The self-concept can change depending on circumstances, as much of it is derived through interactions with others. While a solid grounding through development of a positive self-concept in infancy and early childhood can assist over a lifetime, it does not guarantee that the self-concept will always be positive. However, a positive self-concept generally means the individual feels capable which leads to more productive coping.

When an individual has a favorable opinion of and acceptance of the self, he or she is said to experience *self-esteem*. The two terms, *self-concept* and *self-esteem*, are often used interchangeably by teachers and some professionals. However, a distinction generally drawn by psychologists is that there are two aspects of the self: *self-description* and *self-evaluation*. Self-concept is generally regarded as self-description and relates to the total organization of the perception that the individual has of the self. Self-esteem is the evaluative component and is the value or the judgment that the individual places on the self. Self-esteem involves valuing one's worth as a person and having positive feelings about one's self-image. It is risked by too large a disparity between the real and the ideal self. Discussion of self-concept, self-esteem and the gifted will be dealt with in the next chapter, which focuses on giftedness.

GIFTEDNESS

Although high levels of cognitive ability are usually what is thought of in discussing giftedness, this chapter will focus on other aspects of the developing young person that have more to do with coping. Of course, a good mind can be an asset when facing difficulties, as will be discussed in the sections on Thinking and Metacognition in "Teaching for Coping." In fact, because both intelligence and coping have a common relationship through their connection to adaptation, we might expect that gifted children cope better than their normal counterparts. In this chapter, explanations for why this may not always be the case will be provided. Giftedness will be defined and the child considered in a systems context. Next, personality patterns common to the gifted that can be either great assets or serious liabilities will be addressed. Although general aspects of self-concept and self-esteem have been discussed as being central to one's coping abilities, research findings specific to self-concept and the gifted will be described, with a section on stereotyping, a problem for many gifted young people. Emotional development and emotional giftedness are treated next. The research on social development and the influ-

GIFTS COME IN ALL SHAPES AND SIZES.

ences of family, peers and friends, and mentors on gifted young people is described. The chapter concludes with a discussion of the moral development of the gifted.

Definition of Giftedness

For the context of this book, we take a very broad view of what giftedness is. Our view, like that of Tannenbaum (below) is that giftedness is potential for, or a capability for high levels of production or performance in many different areas of human endeavor. It is our belief that we should be casting a wide net in looking at giftedness. As parents and educators, we should be finding the gifts and capabilities in every child. Although the most common views of giftedness involve intellectual and academic ability, many extraordinary individuals are missed by so narrow a focus. Omitted are those whose effort and/or passionate interests are not measured by standardized tests. What about the creative thinkers, superb mechanics, exquisite dancers or musicians? Do we overlook the peace-makers, the organizers, the individuals who make us laugh or those who touch us with their gentleness and caring, and so, so many more talents and gifts needed for the survival of ourselves and our fragile planet? The more narrow view, which is too often represented through popular stereotypes of the gifted but really represents only a fraction of the many and varied types of capabilities, is described in the section on stereotyping in "Self-concept and the Gifted."

According to Tannenbaum, giftedness in young people is the potential to become outstanding in production or performance in any culturally valued area of human endeavor. For potential to be actualized, he says, five factors need to interact. Each one of these factors is necessary for fruition, although the minimal threshold for the five factors vary, depending on specific talent areas. These factors are:

1. *Superior general intelligence*—One major view of intelligence is the ability or capacity to adapt to the world through learning, solving problems and interacting with the environment; to modify the self in order to deal with events discordant to it, according to the famous Swiss psy-

chologist, Jean Piaget. Coping strategies are the cognitive and behavioral mechanisms or techniques through which one does so, related to dealing with the demands of daily living that assist the individual to regulate the self in relationship to environmental demands. Intelligence cannot be directly observed, as it is characteristic of certain behaviors. There are four conditions required to define behavior as intelligent: awareness (consciousness of what one is doing and why); goal-directedness (purposeful and directional); rational (capable of being logically deduced, consistent, relevant); and worthwhile. Therefore, classifying a person as highly intelligent is a value judgment.

Individuals with high general intellectual ability are frequently characterized by the following: They learn faster, better and somewhat differently. They are curious and investigative, able to deal with complex concepts and abstractions, frequently have high verbal ability, perceive relationships and patterns, and reflect on their mental processing. General intellectual ability is usually identified through tests of general intelligence. However, a recent theory of intelligence by Howard Gardner of Harvard University, suggests that there are actually seven distinct, biologically-based intelligences (verbal, figural/spatial, logical/mathematical, musical, bodily/kinesthetic, interpersonal and intrapersonal) and that very high ability in any of these areas would indicate giftedness. Such a view opens the concept of giftedness to a much broader population and recognizes that it is reflected widely in the community. If we considered that 3 to 5 percent of the population would be gifted in each of these intelligences, the gifted population would be approximately 15 to 35% of the total population (some individuals may be gifted in more than one area so there is overlap). Another contemporary theory that underscores a broad view of intelligence is that of Robert Sternberg of Yale University. His Triarchic Theory suggests that a person might demonstrate one or a combination of three types of intellectual giftedness: *memory/analytic giftedness* which is marked by the ability to dissect a problem and consider the parts, make comparisons, use analogies, or makes judgments and is typically measured by conventional tests of intelligence; *synthetic giftedness*, which is characterized by behaviors that are insightful, intuitive, creative, and adept at coping with novel situations; and *practical/contextual giftedness,* which involves the ability to apply one's skills to every day experience, to "read the hidden curriculum", and to benefit from instruction. These types of intellectual giftedness are built on three loci of intellectual functioning: componential, experiential, and contextual. If we add to these recent theories the notions of capable kids as we defined them earlier, as well as creative thinkers, and those who are developing optimally in specific talent areas, the percentage of potentially gifted individuals would be considerably higher.

2. *Distinctive special abilities/aptitudes*—Outstanding aptitudes or talents in one or more areas. A combination of hereditary potential and appropriate environmental support leads to transformation of aptitudes into talents. Talent development requires appropriate instruction at the right point in time to reach very high levels.

3. *Supportive non-intellectual traits*—Many non-intellective factors combine to achieve success, such as energy, effort, motivation, willingness to take risks, task-commitment, health, immersion in an interest, self-concept and "metalearning" (sensing the "rules of the game').

4. *A nurturing environment*—Giftedness requires appropriate social environments that enhance its maturity. The environments most likely to have a significant influence on a child are the family, school, the peer group and the community. Society determines the types of talents that are valued and is a major force in propelling the gifted child in the pursuit of excellence. Talent therefore needs to fit in with the cultural and social values of the time and place, in order to be recognized and appreciated. The environment also includes the physical world and the world of ideas. The things or ideas the child encounters affect which interests or talents develop. For example, if a child is not given the opportunity to play a musical instrument, it is unlikely that a talent in this area can develop.

5. *Good fortune, at critical periods of life*—The influence of chance factors on great achievement has not been widely researched. Yet, the unexpected and unpredictable in life can mean the difference between seeing one's goals achieved or not. There are four kinds of chance factors: a) Good or bad luck that befalls a person in the context of

their daily lives—for example, being in the right place at the right time; b) When a person increases the likelihood of good luck by being in a state of constant motion; c) When luck is experienced by a person who is prepared to understand the significance—for example, Fleming's discovery of penicillin; d) When good fortune besets an individual because of his or her own highly unique action. Of course, heredity and environment, one's birth and environment, are the biggest chance factors in any individual's life.

All of these factors affect the coping of gifted children. A highly intelligent student (factor 1) forced to sit through instruction in math that she mastered two years ago must cope with boredom and frustration, for example. The other four factors will affect how she copes with this situation. Perhaps she will be able to "read" the rules of the game easily and can sense that the teacher is overwhelmed with too many students and too little time to plan for an individual's needs. This student might find a more advanced math book at the library and ask if she can work independently instead of doing classwork, thus alleviating the teacher's burden and her own boredom.

Returning to Tannenbaum's five factors, it is useful to think of the individual as having several interacting internal systems as well as functioning within several external systems. The value is that we can examine each system separately, yet see how it interacts with other systems as part of the whole—a focus on the relationships between and among systems. A second reason is that changes in one system may inhibit or encourage development in another, and by holding each system as separate, the nature of that interaction can be seen. Gaps or lags that cause *asynchrony*, or lack of synchrony from one system to another are called *dysplasias*. Conversely, one system can exert a positive pull on another, allowing it to *escalate* to a higher level. A third reason is that systems theories allow for "equifinality'—that the same goal or end state may be reached under different conditions and by different paths. Finally, systems theories recognize that destructuring is required in order to transform to higher levels of understanding or function. This notion is particularly important in understanding emotional giftedness (pp. 77-79).

The internal systems related to Tannenbaum's starfish are: 1) a system of general intelligence (universal cognitive system); and 2) a system of specific aptitudes or talents (the non-universal cognitive system). There are also several non-intellective factors: 3) a system of affect (includes emotions, values, ethics); 4) a system of purpose (deals with effort, task commitment, motivation, interest); 5) physical and 6) perceptual systems; and perhaps 7) intuitive and 8) spiritual systems. These internal systems may develop in concert with other systems, there may be pulls or pushes from one system to another, or there may be severe gaps, lags or dyssynchronies among and between the systems.

External to the individual are several systems with which the individual interacts: 1) the physical system (world of objects); 2) the social system (world of intimate others); 3) the cultural system (world of the social group); and 4) the geo-political system (geography, economics, politics, history and time). These are the environmental and chance factors from Tannenbaum. Other chance factors cross these systems, such as particular events that have meaning to a specific individual at a certain point in time. Reading a passage from a book, meeting a person or finding something, for example, may have tremendous impact on one individual and not another. Thus, the internal systems must be prepared to accept chance events as influential or catalytic.

We can think of the child's internal systems as vines of a plant growing towards light. Sometimes, one vine grows much faster than another, or diverges and grows up a different support. Sometimes, an affected vine may destroy or severely constrict another; for example, when a child is sexually or emotionally abused, the talent vine may wither. The external systems are the lattices upon which the vines grow, providing the support needed to flower. The gardener's pruning and weeding, fertilizing and watering are also part of the external systems, as is the sun. Sometimes when there is a weaker vine, for example, the perceptual or physical system in the case of severe hearing loss, additional supports may be needed for the systems to bloom. If the individual has great emotional sensitivity, the gardener may need to tend very gently to encourage flowering. All of these internal vine systems and the external systems affect the coping of the individual.

Most academically and intellectually gifted students cope well with academic work. After all, that is what they are usually good at (with the exception of underachievers, but it is not usually the difficulty of the material that causes the problem, as will be discussed later). They usually have excellent cognitive strategies for learning about the world. Often, their internal and external systems work in harmony and they are well balanced, with a positive self-concept. But the unique personality of the gifted individual may cause considerable problems in coping with their world, particularly if they are creative. "The incidence of serious psychosocial problems among gifted youth is at least as prevalent as in the general population" with not less than 7 percent-10 percent tending towards maladjustment. There are also probably another 10 percent who experience some difficulties or temporary problems in the psychosocial area. Often, because of the obstacles of finding appropriate companionship and acceptance among age peers, those who are exceptionally brilliant may suffer such difficulties.

Although there is a strong interrelation between the affective, social and cognitive systems of development, programs for the gifted (if, indeed they are provided) have too frequently neglected the emotional and social areas, as well as the other systems. Unfortunately, a range of options for able students is often not provided, so a "one-size-fits-all" program must suit moderate to extreme levels of ability as well as the varied areas of strength and interest. The complexity of the gifted student's potential and the greater attention given to their intellectual adjustment has often obscured their emotional and social needs. Some professionals have argued that gifted adolescents have a unique set of affective needs compared with their non-gifted peers. The vast emotional range and intensity of feelings that gifted adolescents experience may make them seem quite contradictory: mature and immature, arrogant and compassionate, aggressive and timid. Outer composure and self-assurance often mask deep feelings of insecurity in gifted adolescents. In the next sections, we will look at these other aspects that strongly affect the coping of capable adolescents and preadolescents. It is important to note that most of the research on these aspects of gifted individuals focuses on the more traditional views of giftedness, that is, individuals with high intellectual or academic ability.

Personality

IT'S JUST THE WAY I AM.

In personality patterns, gifted children tend to have broad and mature interests, high standards of quality, willingness to wait for deferred rewards and self-sufficiency. In interpersonal relationships, they tend to be fairly positive with the ability to engender trust and cooperation. Some individuals have resiliency, a non-intellective factor which empowers them to overcome great barriers, and which also enables them to achieve as successful adults.

Linda Silverman, a psychologist and counselor particularly known for her work on the emotional aspects of gifted students, states that the complex and intricate thought processes of gifted individuals are mirrored in their emotional development. She describes three "emotional tributaries" of the gifted, qualities which "combine to create a unique personality structure governed by a vision of the ideal ... and a capacity to bring one's ideals into fruition." These three qualities are both great potential strengths and potential areas of difficulty. They are:

1. *Intensity*—The hallmark of passion; but intensity can lead to depression due to inability to reconcile the emotional

life with what is expected in the normal world. "I should-n't have such strong feelings, be so sensitive, be such a dork."

2. *Perfectionism*—The driving force behind pursuit of excellence; but perfectionism can lead to a paralyzing inability to do anything because it is never good enough. The big difference in perfectionism leading to healthy desires to excel and be deeply involved in one's work and feelings that one *must* excel is based on believing the "shoulds," wherein unrealistic expectations and feelings of inadequacy are produced.

3. *Heightened sensitivity*—The basis of compassion; but heightened sensitivity can lead to excruciating pain. "Sensitivity refers to an awareness of one or more of the following: thoughts, feelings, and behaviors of self or others. This awareness has the potential of promoting a greater understanding and/or increased emotional responsiveness to the feelings of self and others. A person's experience of sensitivity is not necessarily expressed directly to others. Thus, sensitivity can be intrapersonal or extrapersonal and can be expressed in cognitive or affective areas that lead to self-awareness and perspective taking, empathy, and emotional experience.

Dabrowski, a Polish psychologist known for his work on emotional development in the gifted, suggests that a richer psycholog-

ical endowment in the form of psychic overexcitability may be at the root of these personality characteristics; the stronger the degree of overexcitability, the more difficult for others to understand. He describes five types of overexcitability that both contribute to enhancing mental activity and indicate greater developmental potential:

1. *Psychomotor*—active, energy, drive; for example, the infant who does not sleep, or the youth who is involved in every after-school activity.
2. *Sensual*—differentiated and alive sensual experience; for example, intense sensitivity to color, smells or music.
3. *Intellectual*—search for knowledge and truth—a love of ideas, patterns, theories; curiosity; for example, playing with the relationship of millions and billions at the age of 5; trying to find a pattern in data.
4. *Imaginational*—thought creation, vivid imagery, fantasies, dreams, inventions; for example, the youngster who rigs up an elaborate contraption to turn off his alarm; another who writes extraordinarily rich poetry.
5. *Emotional*—depth and intensity of feelings, compassion, responsibility, self-examination, self-criticism; for example, the 12-year-old who gives his coat to a homeless man huddled on a steam vent because he cannot bear the pain of suffering.

These overexcitabilities may also be at the base of other personality characteristics that can affect coping. Some, like the three emotional tributaries already described, can be either great strengths or vulnerabilities. In addition, certain environmental factors lead to greater vulnerability. This notion of vulnerability has been described by Horowitz and O'Brien to help explain why some children "make it" in spite of extraordinarily harsh environments and others, with a rich genetic endowment and given every opportunity, become very ordinary or even non-productive. It is almost impossible to determine why a particular individual is more vulnerable than another. However, as a generalization, we believe that the developmental outcome is more likely to be optimal when the organism is unimpaired and the environment is facilitative.

What personality characteristics, vulnerabilities and environmental-mental factors do we see reflected in this set of teachers" reports on Tom, a 14-year-old boy?

Following are some extracts from Tom's report cards from kindergarten to grade 8. It is a sad reflection on Tom's living and schooling experiences to read the progress of one bright, bubbly little boy through nine years of school and to observe the shade gradually being pulled down.

Kindergarten

Tom's interest in, and knowledge of, volcanoes and the universe has led him to become a resource for the class and myself. Tom tends to put pressure on himself to get things "correct," which inhibits his confidence, although throughout the year he seems to have eased this pressure. Tom is a happy and cheerful child who enjoys his peers" company.

Grade 1

Tom enjoys being the center of attention and will disrupt the class to this end. He is rather self-indulgent. He becomes very indignant if someone does to him something he deems unpleasant, yet is thoughtless in his verbal and physical actions to others. He is a high achiever and pretends not to pay attention when a new concept is introduced, preferring to wait until he completely understands it, and will succeed, before participating. He resents help or advice. Tom is popular with his classmates.

Grade 2

Tom is well liked by his peers and is beginning to form some strong relationships. In class he can produce work that lacks effort, although he is capable. He has difficulty coping with peer problems, and always seeks the teacher to solve the problem. This term he is more relaxed and happy, but he is a serious child.

Grade 3

Tom says he hates school but his manner and behavior doesn't seem to back this up. He likes to be on his own often in the playground and doesn't seem to desire strong friendships within the class. Work has been a bit ordinary in recent times.

Grade 4

Tom says school is okay at the moment. His work, although it doesn't look neat, is completed accurately. He claims to hate PE and often comes unprepared in order to avoid it. He still has problems in the playground on occasions. Sitting up the front has helped his confidence.

Grade 5

Tom is rather eccentric in his manner. He needs to be pushed to greater challenges otherwise he is quite content to stay on his level. Socially he appears happier. Mother has a lot of influence over his thoughts.

Grade 6

Tom is a very serious boy. He questions why he is here, why the world is like it is, and that there can't be a God. He became very depressed. He was referred to counseling and also taught time management skills. Tom scored on the 99th percentile on the Peabody Test [a language-based measure of intelligence]. Tom has severe social problems. He does not enjoy sports, and the boys tease him about this and other matters.

Grade 7

Tom has poor social skills. He sometimes lashes out when provoked and must learn to control his temper. Although he is capable, he does little of the required classwork and is failing science and health education. However, he seemed interested and did most of the work for a research project on black holes for his English class, but failed to put it in final form. I believe he is capable of more.

Grade 8

Tom has withdrawn from classmates. He becomes sullen and refuses to work with others in cooperative learning groups. Tom sits and daydreams most of the time and any work done is of *minimal quality. He has missed all but seven homework assignments this term. He appears to be obsessed with war and draws battle and death scenes on assignments. He must become more serious about school to pass into high school.*

Tom's Mother

"Tom is no longer working to obtain his teacher's acceptance. He doesn't think what he "puts in" is good enough nor does he think assignments are relevant or of interest. He is not at all satisfied with school. However, I feel that he is coping. He is not overwhelmed by these feelings."

Other Personality Characteristics: The Effects of Internal Systems

From Tom's story, we can see additional characteristics of gifted young people that can either be assets or a vulnerabilities, exacerbated by intensity, perfectionism and heightened sensitivity.

1. *Power / Control*—Gifted individuals want to be in charge of themselves and their environments. This quality is especially evident in young children and is actually a healthy and adaptive characteristic. We all want some measure of control, as anyone knows who has experienced skidding on an icy road, lost a job, encountered serious illness or death in the family, or had a love relationship broken up. Gifted young people often prefer leadership roles, opportunities for choice, independent work and self-management of time. This can be a problem in some school settings where even the most basic self-management is denied (having to ask permission to use the bathroom, for example). Sometimes, these powerful young people may challenge authority and get into struggles for control. From his teacher's reports, we see that Tom no longer feels any sense of control in the school setting and has abdicated power, becoming passive and withdrawn rather than challenging authority.
2. *Concern about the world*—Perhaps because gifted children are so aware of their world and have heightened moral

development, they often are profoundly concerned about their world. They feel that they must DO something to make it better, to preserve it, to alleviate suffering. This energy, commitment and compassion needs to be focused on making a difference—a harnessing of "child power." Otherwise, disillusion, cynicism and depression can take over because of a sense of helplessness and hopelessness. Young people concerned about world hunger could set up a food drive, aid in a class adoption of a child through such agencies as Save the Children, fast for a lunch and donate money to a charity, or assist in a soup kitchen at a mission, for example. Tom's concerns for the world do not seem to have been supported. He appears to have become bitter and cynical.

3. *Holistic experiencing of the world*—Gifted children, especially those who are very highly gifted, experience the world as a whole, the gestalt, the big picture. They find patterns and relationships, and can grasp the essences, the themes, the generalizations. These youngsters find the lock-step classes, and the highly sequenced, concrete, repetitive curriculum not only boring but stifling. This is a problem for Tom, particularly in years 6 and 7.

4. *Introversion*—Some gifted individuals are reflective, inward looking, quiet, reticent, withdrawn and slow to participate. Their introversion is a style of being that may prevent identification as gifted, as the evidence is not immediately obvious. Sometimes, as with Tom, a serious lowering of self-esteem may lead to introverted behavior as a way of coping.

5. *Perceptiveness*—Often, gifted young people demonstrate the ability to see several points of view at the same time, understand multiple layers of feeling and meaning, be insightful and intuitive, and get to the heart of things. They are amazingly perceptive in the way they grasp patterns and find hidden meanings. They may even become frightened by their sense that they can read minds or have psychic abilities or they may be overly aware of others" attitudes towards them, even when not directly expressed. Tom was clearly very perceptive about his teachers" attitudes towards him, perhaps too much so.

6. *Entelechy*—Goal-directed behavior, in which gifted young people create their own destiny, illustrated in inner strength, self-motivation, desire to become all they can be, and the need for self-determination. It is a "will to be", a strength of spirit, which may make them appealing to adults and unusual friends because they are inspiring. It can also be viewed negatively, wherein the young person can be humiliated or given a hard time, especially when the will is very strong. Tom's spirit was broken in his early school experience.

Environmental factors

1. *Peer relationship conflict*—One of the biggest difficulties for some gifted children is dealing with peers, particularly those less able or with different interests and values. Sometimes children are very cruel to each other and may tease or embarrass a bright child. While many can take it (and give it back with good humor), the heightened sensitivity may make the pain intense. Gifted young people may feel different, weird or that there is something wrong with them. More than anything, they want to be accepted for who they are. They want to be liked and, especially in early adolescence, they don't want to be singled out for being different. The higher the degree of giftedness, often the greater the gap between intellectual and social skill confidence (and academic and social self-concept). This is really a problem of location, as when the child is grouped

with other gifted students, compatible peers are found. Tom's relationship difficulties appear to have begun in first grade, perhaps because the teacher did not acknowledge his unique qualities or know how to help the little boy relate more successfully.

2. *Inappropriate environment*—Some environments are nurturing of talent, others could be called "toxic." The more a gifted child's abilities differ from the "norm" the more inappropriate the program in the regular classroom becomes. This is particularly a difficulty when students are extraordinarily gifted. Such young people may make simple things complex (they see the multiple possibilities) and, conversely, make complex things simple as they comprehend patterns rapidly, grasp the heart of an issue promptly, and reason abstractly. They have a need for precision, immerse themselves in interests, have extraordinary memories, and are highly empathetic, in addition to having difficulties relating to average age peers and to standard school fare. Inhospitable environments may result in the gifted child becoming withdrawn or displaying behavior problems or psychosomatic symptoms. The school environment is clearly a problem for Tom.

3. *Adult expectations*—Research tells us that high expectations by parents and teachers are essential for high levels of achievement. For the gifted, however, unrealistic expectations may arise because the young bright child seems so much more mature. A tantrum by a two-year-old who can explain all the instruments in the orchestra and who uses words like "fantastic," "especially," or "uvula" seems uncharacteristic. The child may also have an internalized set of unrealistic self-expectations that may or may not come about from expectations of others. Sometimes, masking of difficulties occurs because the student is afraid of not meeting expectations. Tom is not meeting adult expectations.

Although in our example Tom clearly has serious difficulties that need immediate attention, as well as a very poor concept of himself, most gifted children have healthy self-concepts.

Self-concept and the Gifted

Conflicting results have been found in varying studies of self-esteem and the gifted. Several studies indicate that gifted children average higher self-esteem scores than the norms for the given test. Other studies show that the gifted have comparable or a lower self-esteem than the average. Some researchers find that self-concept varies amongst the gifted population, due, in part to whether students are in special classes, degree of acceptance by significant persons in their lives and a willingness to take risks. In an overview of the research that has been conducted on self-concept and the gifted thus far, Hoge and Renzulli conclude that the direct comparisons of gifted and non-gifted students reveal that the gifted students as a group showed no major deficits in self-esteem. Some indirect evidence exists that labeling a child gifted has a positive impact on self-esteem, but the direct evidence is lacking. There is also some support for a social comparison type of process; that is, moving a child from a regular classroom to a homogenous, highly gifted group, may have a negative impact on self-concept. In spite of the generally positive nature of the conclusions regarding self-concept and giftedness, the limitations of the types of research done to date, as well as a host of difficulties with definitions (both of giftedness and of self-concept), study designs, instrumentation, and lack of longitudinal research were acknowledged. The authors also recognized that social self-concept of the gifted needs considerably more research. It is this aspect of self-concept that appears to be particularly vulnerable. However, there is no doubt of the importance of positive self-concept on academic achievement.

Self-concept and School Achievement

A clear link exists between positive self-esteem and academic achievement. Gifted students construct their perceptions of self through the "lens" of their intellectual functioning. For intellectual functioning to flow smoothly, the concept of self-as-student (including intrinsic motivation, self-efficacy, and self-esteem) needs to be positive, or cognitive activity can be short-circuited.

Although self-esteem appears to drop when students are placed in homogeneous programs for the highly gifted, this is likely a temporal adjustment to becoming a "small fish in a big ocean" and no longer having one's abilities stand out. In fact, self-concept was found to rise again over a longer duration in gifted programs.

The need for positive self-esteem for students to reach their potential is universally recognized. When self-esteem improves, school performance is markedly improved. In *Self-concept and School Achievement*, William W. Purkey states that the role of the teacher is critical in this regard: "Six factors seem particularly important in creating a classroom atmosphere conducive to developing favorable self-images in students. These are 1) challenge, 2) freedom, 3) respect, 4) warmth, 5) control and 6) success."

Poorer school achievement is found in students with a lower self-esteem. For those with lower self-esteem, one reason may be the "frustration of never living up to your own standard and expectations [which] can be very self-defeating and interfere with mental and emotional growth." Apparently, gifted students, particularly those who suffer dysfunctional perfectionism, judge themselves more sharply than others, weighing everything and being very self-critical. But many factors other than giftedness affect self-concept and self-esteem. An issue is whether teachers (and parents) should invest effort to enhance children's feelings about themselves and should help them find an "affective regulator" for their self-critical evaluative mechanisms to assist both underachievers and paralyzed perfectionists.

Problems with the Social Self

Gifted students scored significantly higher on tests of academic self-concept than on tests of social self-concept. In fact, the most serious difficulty with self-concept experienced by gifted young people is related to how they believe they are perceived by others. Children's own view of their giftedness shows mixed attitudes, but generally, if they are negative, they are in areas of social self-concept. One study indicated that children whose parents use the term "gifted" were consistently less well-adjusted on both self-report and peer-report measures. Warnings are offered in interpreting these results, indicating the relationship may be with parents overemphasizing the child's giftedness at the expense of healthy child adjustment, or the use of the term to compensate for other problems. In another study, over half the gifted students used the coping mechanism of hiding their abilities and not commenting about them to avoid social stigmatization for being different. But additional research indicates that gifted students also have positive views about being labeled "gifted," particularly in affirming views of themselves and in relating to people who know them best—parents, teachers, and friends.

Self-concept, particularly social self-concept, moderately predicts peer status. Self-concept appears to be lower for high IQ students who consider themselves "different" compared to those who don't. Although the students may see this difference positively, there seems to be a greater problem with peer relations among such children. An overview of the research on peer relationships indicates that children who have poor peer affiliations, particularly those with aggressive behaviors, rather than those who are shy or withdrawn, are at risk for difficulties later in life, such as dropping out, crime, or psychopathology. However, most gifted young people are socially competent. For example, in one study, most gifted students evidenced significantly higher levels of social skills and less antisocial behavior than average students, although there was a subgroup who demonstrated poor social competence and antisocial behavior. Children who experience difficulties with peers may need emotional support and assistance in learning to relate to others if they are to optimize their personal and social development.

Gender Differences

In some studies, a gender difference was reported with gifted boys scoring more highly on the tests of self-concept than girls. Gifted girls are faced with conflicting social messages about academic success and cultural stereotypes. The typical feminine ideal of being well behaved, conscientious and obedient contradicts the assertive pursuit of ideas or ideals. Trying to be "superwoman," being dependent and socially manipulative, having self-doubts, not being planful, and the desire to conform may also result in lowered future achievement for some girls. Other researchers claim giftedness seemed to be an advantage for girls but not for boys. In one study, gifted girls appeared to have a more positive self-concept and more internal locus of control than did non-gifted girls. Gifted boys gave some evidence of lower self-satisfaction when compared to control (non-gifted) boys, particularly when comparing their ideal to real self in areas of physical strength and aggressiveness. With boys, the traditional ideal male is supposedly aggressive, self-reliant and individualistic. Intensity, sensitivity and perfectionism in a gifted boy may cause role conflict and lower self-esteem. Athletic self-concept relates to social self-concept, particularly for boys. Expressing emotion can be a problem in a "macho" environment, or fear of failure can make a paralyzed perfectionist not try at all in a success- and achievement-focused environment. The shift from the female-dominated elementary education to more male teachers in secondary grades may have a positive effect on boys. It appears that gender is an issue in self-esteem, affecting both boys and girls differently.

School Interventions

Gifted young people need affective education to help them deal with their sensitivity and vulnerability to distortions of self-esteem. Teacher awareness and sensibility coupled with learning activities can be used to enhance students" sense of self. It may be necessary, for example, to assist students in the lower end of the gifted range who are placed in a specialized class for the highly able, as the change in the structure of the group with which they now compare themselves may cause a lowering of self-concept.

Tuning into one's "center core," one's essence of self is not a problem in infancy and early childhood, but doubts begin to grow as discordant messages are received from outside. "A shell begins to build around this lovely, real center, and it is made up of all the "crummy" stuff we feel and believe about ourselves after such encounters." Between 10 and 13, the "crummy" self can no longer be presented to the world and the inner core is forgotten. A search for desirable qualities in others is made and a second shell is formed from these images, a phony self. Others must be kept away from this false self to ensure they do not find out about the "real" self, the inept, crummy, incompetent person we are. This process of shell-building is intensified in gifted individuals, because self-imposed and external expectations are greater and, too often, mental abilities are not valued.

Teachers and parents need to recognize this shell-building phe-nomena and attempt to support the inner core. One way is to value young people as persons rather than just for their achievements. Another is to talk about one's inner core and the importance of "being yourself ". Some schools even offer courses to young adolescents on such topics, but English and Social Studies are also natural subjects for discussions about the self. Assisting young adolescents to focus on and celebrate their successes instead of worrying about their mis-takes can also help. "You got 24 right out of 25," not "you got one wrong"; or "Five years from now, will it make any difference if you made a few mistakes on your math homework?" In fact, for some young people, it may be valuable to practice mistake-making.

Teachers can also encourage and model the principle "dare to dream'—i.e. to have lofty ideals and challenging standards that are seemingly unattainable but which serve as motivators. In such a climate and with such teachers as mediators of the environment, students can attempt to actualize their ideal image of self and integrate it with their inner core, gaining control of achieving their goals (See also "Teaching for Coping"). A major difficulty, however, appears to be stereotyping.

Stereotypes

Because an important aspect of self-concept is derived from how others see us, stereotypes of gifted individuals shape young people's views of themselves. The stereotypes which are commonly accepted influence both children and their parents. Stereotypes derived from a tiny fraction of gifted students are too often applied to the entire population. But these stereotypes are so prevalent that educators, parents, the general community and the young people themselves express anti-gifted sentiments and view giftedness as undesirable. In England, for example, parents may fear having a gifted child who may be "odd." It is very important that gifted young people feel accepted as individuals rather than as gifted stereotypes. In some cases, gifted students do not want to be so recognized or singled out. In other cases, they do not recognize themselves as gifted. Yet a broad view of giftedness as meaning capable with potential for accomplishment or outstanding in a particular domain might well help to overcome the stereotypes as described below.

On TV shows, gifted children are often portrayed as "dorks." For example, the popular show, *Family Matters,* has a character, Steve Urkel, who is scrawny, with big glasses on a chain, a weird voice and behavior and dress sense, who is a social outcast. Perhaps an attempt to break this stereotype is the character of

Doogie Howser, who is a fairly sociable and likable kid, but the giftedness shows as gaining a medical degree at 14 or so. This is a common concept of giftedness extremes. Hence, tell children they are gifted and they will often reject the notion on these grounds. Neither stereotype is realistic.

In the recent film "Little Man Tate", a very able little boy is portrayed as capable of feats in a very broad range of domains that only the most extremely gifted prodigies might demonstrate and then, usually in just one area. His differentness is highly accentuated, and although attention was drawn to the needs of the highly gifted child, too much was stereotypic.

In contemporary children's literature, there are often such stereotypes. For example, in *Hating Alison Ashley* Robin Klein has her sixth grade narrator describe her reaction to the new, perfect, very clever Alison, as follows:

> *"The questions were so hard she received blank looks from everyone. But when she asked Alison, Alison answered correctly. And it was like that right up until lunch break. Alison Ashley knew all her tables and got all her math right. She turned out to have a reading age of 14.6 years. She knew all the rivers of northern New South Wales in perfect order.*
>
> *My feelings of inferiority swelled into dislike, and the dislike into absolute loathing. I was so sick with jealous resentment..."* (Klein, 1984, p. 20)

Again the unpopular stereotype, but with an interesting perspective. Adults" negative attitudes towards gifted children are portrayed in the sympathetic story *A Wind in the Door* by beloved author, Madeleine L'Engle. On the first day of first grade, the teacher has asked the children to tell something about themselves. Charles Wallace stood and said:

> *"What I'm interested in right now are the farandolae and the mitochondria."*
> *"What was that, Charles? The mighty what?"*
> *"Mitochondria. They and the farandolae come from the prokarycocytes—"*
> *"The what?"*

(Charles then launches into a lengthy explanation of their evolution and their symbiotic relationship with humans).

"Now Charles, suppose you stop making silly things up, and the next time I call on you, don't try to show off."

Because Charles Wallace repeatedly comes home bloodied and battered as a result of being beaten up by other boys, his older sister, Meg, decides to talk to her former elementary principal, Mr. Jenkins on her way to high school.

"Oh, please, Mr. Jenkins, I know people have thought Charles Wallace isn't very bright, but he's really—"

He cut across her words. *"We've run IQ tests on all the first-graders. Your little brother's IQ is quite satisfactory."*

"You know it's more than that, Mr. Jenkins. My parents have run tests on him, too, all kinds of tests. His IQ is so high it's untestable by normal standards."

"His performance gives no indication of this."

"Don't you understand, he's trying to hold back so the boys won't beat him up? He doesn't understand them, and they don't understand him. How many first-graders know about farandolae?"

"I don't know what you're talking about, Margaret. I do know that Charles Wallace does not seem to me to be very strong."

"He's perfectly all right!"

"He is extremely pale, and there are dark circles under his eyes."

How would you look if people punched you in the nose and kept giving you black eyes just because you know more than they do?"

"If he's so bright"—Mr. Jenkins looked coldly at her through the magnifying lenses of his spectacles—"I wonder your parents bother to send him to school at all?"

Considering these stereotypes in the media, an eleventh grade physics class at a school with a reputation for academic excellence was asked to complete a description of gifted young people. At least 20 percent of the students in this class would be considered gifted by usual definitions. The question was: "What do gifted kids look like and behave like? What are they like socially?" The results were fascinating. The stereotypical response (small, glasses, withdrawn, no friends, not into sports, etc.) was produced by about one third of the students—in all cases boys! Most of the girls were willing to accept an appearance of normality. Many students referred to gifted kids trying to act "normal." In most cases, the authors were not identifiable, but some made a point of discussing their response, or were proud of it and identified themselves.

AVERAGE GIFTED STUDENTS

Some responses were:

> *"Intellectually gifted people look "dorky" and are socially incompetent. Most hang around by themselves and get teased, and as a result are unhappy. Some play sports but not football or ice hockey."* (Male, 16)

A very capable male, who is the school's greatest troublemaker and achieves poorly despite general recognition of his abilities responded with the statement below. He is happy to be a very successful member of the ski team, but rarely uses his ability academically. Herein may lie the explanation—but not the solution:

> *"The talented people who use it [the term gifted] look like geeks. They are weird dudes that don't flow with the go. Cool dudes like me look great, act bad and have excellent talent in many fields."*

A gifted girl responded:

"I think intellectually gifted children look much like others but they are usually quieter than others, first because their peers might perceive them as being intelligent and therefore a threat, and they are intimidated. Secondly, they probably have better things to think about! Gifted kids may also be really disruptive because they are bored. But generally I think they appear to be much the same as other people."

It was interesting to note the response of a boy who is above average intelligence, the younger brother of a gifted girl:

"First: I can't say too much because I'm not gifted. They are goons that wear thick glasses, have stupid hair cuts and hang their mouths open going, "What?" They look like bald apes and are smart. They think too much. They are upper class snobs. They don't have many friends of their own sex, if any. They try to play pingpong. They are only happy in their family. They don't care much about clothes and appearance."
"They look like themselves." (Female, 16)

"No particular traits, but there is usually something which makes them different." (Female, 17)

"They don't necessarily have to look "dorky" because a lot of so-called "dorks" are just people who cannot or do not want to mix in with the crowd. This is an individuality, not just an intellectual gift." (Female, 16)

"Look like: usually frail, wear glasses, have few friends, don't engage in physical activity. Think like: think in terms of computers, teachers, scientists, etc. Behave like: usually very well-behaved, quiet, don't cause trouble, usually have no friends, don't like sports, if so fairy games like pingpong, badminton." (Male, 16)

"Intellectually gifted kids often wear glasses, they are

usually thin and many have black hair. They usually keep to themselves and are very quiet. They think they have to go it alone and no one will talk to them so they never try to communicate with others. They don't have many friends, mainly the friends they do have are other intellectuals. They're not very good at sports and don't appear very happy, even though they might be they don't show it." (Male, 16)

A favorite, from a gifted male, age 16:

"Noticeable differences to the naked eye are detailed in the box below."

In talking to children about their giftedness we must be aware of the stereotypes which they may associate with giftedness, and which will almost certainly differ enormously from their concept of themselves.

Emotional Development

Gifted children can be expected to be as happy and well balanced as other children. The psychosocial adjustment of gifted children is at least comparable with the non-gifted except possibly in adolescence, when more adjustment problems are sometimes noted. They are found to be superior in ability in making certain social judgments and having an emotional life more compatible with older children, although the research here is sparse. For example, gifted children's fears have been found to be similar to those of older, "normal" children. They are often highly productive people who have a healthy self-concept as a result of emotionally supportive relationships with significant other people, such as parents, peers, mentors or a favorite teacher. These intimate relationships produce a secure sense of self which engenders innovation and productivity.

One aspect related to emotional development is whether gifted children should be labeled as "gifted." The effects of such labeling are uncertain. Many children were found to be ambivalent about the label, and some found the label disabling, affecting relationships with others. For example, some gifted children tend to over generalize their feelings of superiority and focus on their differences from rather than similarities to other children. These children need help in gaining a balanced view of their self-worth.

On the other hand, understanding giftedness appears to be beneficial, as young people realize that their personality characteristics are not peculiar to them alone.

As was described in "Some Definitions," some gifted children are characterized by resilience, the ability to get back up on one's feet after taking a few knocks. Factors in resilient individuals include temperament, maternal conditions (positive role models), behavior based on self confidence and awareness, and talent. Others may be more vulnerable to the effects of environment and their own interpretations of it.

Cultural factors

The culture into which an individual is born determines how giftedness is viewed. In some cultures, recognition of outstanding abilities is perceived as promoting elitism. In other cultures, extraordinary abilities are thought to be divinely given, and the individual so endowed is respected as the vehicle for the workings of a higher power. In some cultures, one's gifts are to be enhanced for personal happiness and benefit to the individual. In other cultures, the values are egalitarian, and to have one's gifts recognized detracts from the group. Yet children's outstanding abilities may be identified and enhanced through special programs, justified as contributing to benefit the state rather than the individual. In some cultures, the thrust in education is on excellence for all without special recognition for individual achievement. Every child is expected to strive toward optimal potential, so that special programs for the gifted are not deemed necessary. In other cultures, the importance of individual excellence and optimal development of potential is recognized through many different options for the gifted. In certain material cultures, having a gifted child is almost like having two cars and a boat in the driveway. Thus, the experience of having extraordinary abilities may be desirable in one setting and problematic in another.

A useful exercise would be to consider what the cultural values are of a given group and think about how these values might impact on services for gifted children (or on attitudes toward them). An American class might review the list below and then discuss what is valued in their own context. They could extend the discussion by conducting a survey on attitudes and values among students or community members as an exciting and authentic learning experience.

For example, in discussions with two graduate classes at the University of Melbourne, the following values were proffered for the general Australian culture:

♦ Mateship: Stick by your mate; males only
♦ No worries; she'll be right mate; laughing at yourself—not taking life seriously
♦ Cutting down tall poppies; anti-intellectual attitudes; anti-elitist; arts/entertainers/performers are okay and respected, as are skills, e.g.. fixing a car well or being an excellent carpenter, but not being an entrepreneur for big bucks. Others can push you, but don't brag about yourself.
♦ Love of the underdog. Classless society, but there are big gaps between rich and poor. Rags to riches is okay.
♦ Tough on the outside for males
♦ Outdoor focus; sporting culture
♦ Owning one's own home
♦ Education is the route up; but message is mixed: education is a pill, not a gift.

Of course, sub-groups within that broad context might have quite different values and these must be taken into account as well.

Difficulties

In the section in this chapter on personality, we learned that gifted children are often highly sensitive, perfectionistic and intense, as well as exhibiting overexcitabilities in a variety of areas. In some cases, these aspects which can be indicative of greater potential can also lead to difficulties with self-concept as well as conflict with the environment. Other problems with which gifted young people may have to cope include:

1. *Uneven development*—Young gifted children often have gaps or lags between their systems of cognition and their physical and emotional systems. For example, the six-year-old can visualize precisely how she wants to draw a horse, but screams in frustration when her hand cannot make the pencil do what she wants. This unevenness can also be beneficial, in that conflicts due to gaps or lags may stimulate growth. For example, a young child afraid of earthquakes and other natural disasters may learn everything he can about volcanoes. By becoming an expert, he both overcomes his fear and he grows cognitively. There is a pulling effect, a displacement from emotional and perceptual systems to the cognitive systems. Knowledge is power. Adolescents often develop in a patchwork fashion. They may internalize adult aspirations for them without developing their own values. For example, a young person may be encouraged to study law, take the subjects, but drop out because

her own values lie in working in the "green" movement. They may also be advanced emotionally in their ability to empathize with others, but may act like a little kid when teased by a peer or sibling.

2. *Multipotentiality*—Most gifted young people are very good at some things, but not at everything. Some, however, have an "abundance of riches" and are capable of outstanding work in almost any field they might encounter. Multipotentiality or overchoice can be overwhelming for adolescents when so many options are available. A major difficulty for these students is deciding on careers, as they are pulled in many directions. A key issue is what the individual values and holds dear and important.

3. *Alienation*—Gifted children often realize when quite young that they are different from their age mates, particularly in their interests. They find that friends or others to talk to are hard to find and they may become socially isolated. When they become disillusioned with their peers, their teachers and themselves, when they cannot cope with the social world and its pressures, they feel alienated. A change of setting to a class with other bright students often helps. This is best done before the damage is too severe.

4. *Role conflict*—Gifted students experience role conflict when they get double messages from parents, peers or teachers. Girls often get the double message to be achievers and to be popular and feminine. Frequently, they lose IQ points in an attempt to do the latter, hiding their abilities and not exercising their talents. Age 14 appears to be a critical period for girls, as choices they make at that time may affect their later careers and their lives. Boys get double messages as well. They are supposed to be achievers, yet be brawny (and therefore not brainy) athletes. If they are interested in music or poetry, but not sport, they may suffer considerable teasing or ostracism, especially if they are small or thin.

5. *Impostor syndrome*—Some gifted young people, frequently girls, do not believe they are really gifted and are certain that the world will find out how stupid, foolish or bad they really are. They fear success because they fear they cannot

keep up the false front. Others will continue to expect top work and the judge of the work may just be trying to be nice.

6. *Non-success*—After a lifetime of high achievement, young people may encounter a difficulty that cannot be solved or they may experience failure for whatever reason. For example, a very able student with a fear of a particular teacher may actually fail a subject. This can be a devastating experience for children who have never developed flexibility, learned through overcoming earlier failure.

7. *Emotional over-control*—Being in control was described as a personality characteristic of the gifted. When young people experience a loss of control, their self-concept may be diminished. Sometimes, the need for control may lead to emotional over-control, particularly when messages that "it's not okay to be angry" are received. These angry feelings may later erupt, perhaps during adolescence through a particularly rebellious period. Some highly intelligent girls may be perceived as being bossy and domineering but collapse when criticized, owing to deep control conflicts and a less than sturdy self-concept. Some younger adolescent boys may experience significantly high levels of discouragement and feelings of hopelessness than older boys at secondary school. This may be due to earlier feelings of lack of control or placing emotional relationships at a much lower level of priority as they get older, and beginning to emphasize career success.

8. *Difficulties at school*—Gifted students may have problems at school with boredom, quantity of work, inappropriate pedagogy for their unique learning patterns, parent/teacher expectations and personal high standards. These difficulties may add to the emotional stresses of able learners. Stress is often caused by an imbalance between what is expected and what the child can do. For

example, sometimes before young gifted boys are developmentally ready for the traditional education system they have been labeled as difficult, immature, hyperactive, etc. owing to their excessively creative and eager minds and bodies working overtime, while the visual/motor development is typically delayed behind girls" development. Other gifted young people may attempt to do things in a nonconforming way or express thoughts of a divergent nature, and therefore experience difficulties, both with teachers and with peers.

When emotional stresses become overwhelming, some gifted young people may become underachievers, drop out of school or even drop out of life. Some investigators found that gifted underachievers display negative, antisocial, self-defeating attitudes. Such young people should be acknowledged for even the slightest movement in the right direction towards "successive successes" to motivate achievement. The most extreme difficulties in the emotional area for gifted young people sometimes result in suicide. This topic will be discussed later.

Being Emotionally Gifted

An individual may be emotionally gifted, that is, have the potential to reach levels of self-actualization or transcendence. Piechowski describes five levels or regions of emotional development. Transcending each level requires self-judgment, effort, "positive disintegration" or tearing down in one's inner core of the earlier way of being. The levels, from highest to lowest, are:

Level 5: Inspiration by powerful ideals, such as world peace, universal compassion, self-sacrifice, total dedication to serving others.
Examples: Mahatma Gandhi; Mother Theresa.

Level 4:   Self-actualizing—A deepening understanding of universals coupled with a strong sense of responsibility in which one's actions agree with one's ideals.
Examples: Eleanor Roosevelt; Abraham Lincoln.

Level 3:   Fight for one's principles—vulnerable, yet autonomous; trying to live up to one's inner ideals, but unable to attain them. Conflict between the higher and lower self.
Examples: Marcus Cicero; Martin Luther King, Jr.

Level 2:   Inner fragmentation and lack of inner direction—mainstream and relativistic values.
Examples: "Do your own thing." "There is no absolute truth." "I feel split into a thousand pieces."

Level 1:   Self-serving motivations, pre-occupation with self-protection and survival. Others are instruments to serve you.
Example: Dog-eat-dog mentality.

Very few individuals reach the top two levels, perhaps because the struggle for one's principles in Level 3 is so difficult and the destructuring or disintegration is frightening but required to reach Level 4. However, extraordinary emotional sensitivity and overexcitability in childhood could indicate developmental potential in this area. Piechowski suggests that a focus on feelings and frustration with feelings of being misunderstood are a hallmark of potential for emotional giftedness in adolescence. Characteristics include awareness of one's growth and changes; awareness of many developmental paths; awareness of and attending to feelings; feelings of unreality; inner dialogue and self-judgment; questing, searching, finding problems; and awareness of one's real self.

Romney Shuttleworth's poem indicates his potential for emotional giftedness. He is a year 10 student.

Inside
Inside of me is eternal sleep
For time is always.
Pockets of eternity suffocate,
In eternity will drown.

Inside of me is the blinded fool,
Laughing, a hideous sound.
This mirth conceals fear,
On his journey hellward bound.

Inside of me dwells the wise man,
No knowledge does he hold,
But for the knowledge that,
In time all things unfold.

Inside of me is the madman,
He's pulled his life to shreds,
Shrieking bitter pathos,
To the world that fear pretends.

Within all of us is fear,
The fear of finding ourselves.
In fear we run from each other,
Into our separate hells.

Interventions

Although emotional giftedness is found only in a few individuals, gifted young people often need support for their emotional well-being as well as for their cognitive growth. Personal and social responsibility and social and emotional growth should be emphasized in school provisions for the gifted, as well as development of the intellect. An important requirement is to offer opportunities to work with like peers in order to find acceptance. Because so much of a person's feelings about self depend on how he or she is perceived by others, gifted young people need opportunities to experience relationships and apply their capacities for developing friendships. Also reality affirmation with others (or thoughts, perceptions) assists in distinguishing reality and fantasy.

Related to emotional growth, gifted students may require guidance which varies significantly from that required by other students. Current guidance programs emphasize underachievement and inadequate emotional adjustment rather than prevention of the problems. Instead, strong affective bases need to be constructed for optimal development. Crisis management is too late a stage for intervention programs. More will be discussed about affective education in "Teaching for Coping."

Social Development

The most important single influence on the gifted child (or any child) is the role of the significant caregivers and the family. Other social influences include peers, friends, the school, mentors and others in the community. In this chapter, we will focus on the roles of the family, friends and peers, and mentors in the development of gifted young people.

Family Influences on Gifted Young People

"Researchers have consistently found parenting to be the most potent factor in the development of giftedness, creativity and eminence." While being a parent of a gifted child may be a joyful and stimulating experience, it may be also be a challenge, especially if the child has very high levels of overexcitability or is having difficulties coping. At times, "it is no easier to be a parent of a gifted child than it is to be a gifted child."

Research on the family patterns of gifted children has focused on family systems—the structural characteristics, family climate and family values.

Family Structural Characteristics

✔ *Birth Order*—Research shows a tendency for gifted children to be first born, perhaps because adults are language role models. There are more opportunities for verbal interaction. Older children perform parent-surrogate roles and talk for younger siblings. The ordinal position is the position of organizer, giving structure to family relationships. Close age (2 years and less) spacing is negatively correlated to academic achievement. Special family position (i.e., eldest son, eldest surviving son) has been found to be characteristic of many eminent individuals. Specialness should be based on effort and accomplishment in talent areas. For underachievers, there was early discovery of giftedness

and then the specialness was withdrawn and given to another family member. Loss of specialness was sometimes due to school adjustment (causing the child to feel "attention neglected').

✔ *Parental Education*—There is a tendency for both parents to have tertiary education. This may contribute to financial stability of the family, capability of parents to facilitate education and value educational achievement.

✔ *Parental Age*—Parents of gifted tend to be older than average: over 30 years. Older parents are more financially established and better able to give a psychologically stable tone.

✔ *Parental Loss*—Amongst eminent individuals, a high incidence of parent, especially father loss, was found. This reduction of parent-child affiliation may lead to early psychological maturity, the disruption to parent-child identification, and possibly cognitive freeing from family relationships.

Family Climate

This includes attitudes of parents to children, relationships, parental child-rearing practices and structuring of family life.

✔ *Parenting*—is child-centered. Reasonable standards of family organization appear important for all achievement.

Children of authoritarian mothers were found to get better marks and teacher ratings but were less original. Less conventional parenting, i.e. more freedom and greater respect for the child, was more in evidence with creative children. Parents feel ambivalent about the gifted label (a burden). Consistency between parents is more critical than any particular style of parenting especially for underachievers, who were found to manipulate one or both parents. Gifted children are more cynical about family relationships than other family members (perhaps as a defense for special abilities).

✔ *Parent self-concept*—Where parents perceive themselves as highly able, potential problems are reduced. The larger the discrepancy between parent self-perception and ability, the greater the need for counseling.

Values Espoused and Enacted by Parents

✔ *Achievement orientation*—Parental emphasis on cultural and intellectual pursuits—success, ambition, persistence, doing one's best—was found to be conducive to achievement in children. Parents expected their children to be successful and were vigilant in monitoring practice time, checking homework and communicating with teachers. Achievers developed abilities to handle their own homework independently and typically learned beyond school requirements. In families with underachievers, although parents espoused values of achievement, their own lives modeled more of the frustrations than the satisfactions of that value. Parents were also involved in some opposition to school for 90% of children. In some cases, the problems were more related to parents, in other cases, to inappropriate classroom arrangements. Often, unfinished and incomplete work was characteristic.

Several researchers have found parents often feel inadequately prepared to meet the needs of their gifted children. This is due to myths and misinformation about the gifted; blatant or covert hostility; lack of societal support for identification and nurturing; limited financial resources of parents; the child's uneven development; unclear or conflicting expectations of the gifted child; and confusion about the gifted child's role in the family.

The following issues related to gifted children have been identified as being of particular concern to parents:

- ◆ Observing that a child is different;
- ◆ Desiring assessment;
- ◆ Feeling inadequate to raise a gifted child;
- ◆ Determining school placement;
- ◆ Needing assistance with unsympathetic school staff;
- ◆ Determining appropriate home stimulation and develop-
ment of special talents;
- ◆ Desiring information about resources, e.g.. enrichment
programs;
- ◆ Coping with underachievement and non-motivation;
- ◆ Dealing with the child's intensity, perfectionism, height-
ened sensitivity, introversion or depression;
- ◆ Helping the child develop better peer relations;
- ◆ Experiencing increased tension in family as a result of
needs of the gifted child; and
- ◆ Understanding their own giftedness.

Friendships and Peer Relationships

Peer status and peer relations have been recognized as important factors in general child and adolescent development, and successful peer relationships enable children to develop cognitively, socially, emotionally and morally. In fact, the social adjustments of gifted youngsters are often of greater concern to parents than their scholastic development. Unpopularity and poor peer relations may lead to maladjustment and social problems in adulthood. Many longitudinal studies have found a moderate positive correlation between early peer acceptance and various measures of adult adjustment. The pattern of normal friendship development in adolescence is apparently mercurial, with friendship groups forming and reforming. But young people who are experiencing constant social problems need to be identified and helped so that they will have fewer problems in the future.

Early studies reporting peer relations of gifted students found that highly gifted students experience social problems with their same-aged peers. This was due to difficulties in relating and communicating effectively as well as feeling alienated and isolated because of advanced vocabulary and different interests. It may also be related to an ability to understand, intellectually and communicatively, what is required in a friendship, but not be able to put it into practice. But one of the major problems for the gifted is that the inability to get along with age peers is seen as a deficit in these young people. Many of the more recent studies have focused on "refuting the stereotype that they are social misfits rejected by their classmates". Researchers have examined pre-school children to university entrants ranging from moderately gifted to profoundly gifted children. These studies have found that although gifted children generally are popular with their peers, there is a significant minority that have problems with peer relations. Often, however, as soon as gifted young people are put into groups with others like them by ability or interest, the difficulties end. Gifted students usually develop social skills more easily with mental age peers than chronological peers.

Through use of sociometric techniques, such as peer nominations, or peer rating scales, observations, role play methods, parent and teacher ratings and self-report scales, the following has been found by various researchers at each age level.

Preschool
- Gifted preschoolers display high levels of social knowledge but not necessarily high levels of social behavior.
- They prefer to play with older children and adults.
- They are no more popular than their average ability peers.

Primary School
- Gifted children are generally popular and well accepted by their peer group.
- Giftedness is not a social liability—it tends to be an asset.
- A small minority of the gifted were not popular, but may have had older friends. A significant minority of highly gifted children (about twice the proportion of average ability and moderately gifted children) do have some social problems and experience loneliness and isolation. This is due to: advanced language and different interests, parental pressure to develop intellectual skills rather than social skills and an awareness that they are different. A majority of these children achieve successful social development later.
- Gifted children have similar play interests as other children, but are not as interested in competitive and vigorous physical play; play more alone; and prefer activities that involve reading and a sense of humor.
- Gifted children prefer other gifted children as friends and classmates.

Secondary School
- High academic achievement did not affect the social status for gifted boys through secondary school, although prominent athletes were the most popular students.
- Gifted girls lose social status in secondary school and tend to hide their abilities so that they will be popular with members of the opposite sex.
- Gifted boys were found to be the most popular sub-group and gifted girls the least popular sub-group in the popular status category in one study. Gifted girls are at risk of decreasing their academic achievement due to conflicting messages and peer pressure.

Tertiary Level

♦ Girls can get smart and breathe a sigh of relief as they enter university and mix with peers who value achievement. They can finally "come out of their shell," become open to challenges and do as well as males. They realize that they can "have it all," being free of restrictions and peer group pressure.

Reasons for Popularity and Unpopularity

♦ Unpopular students differed from average and popular students in family social status, social self-concept and academic self-esteem.

♦ Unpopular students have behaviors that do not endear them to peers—they constantly require social attention, do not co-operate well with others, are not quiet in class, do not like failing or being criticized and do not become leaders.

Most young people will experience friendship difficulties at one time or another. For those students experiencing chronic problems coping with peers, assistance from family members, teachers and/or counselors may be necessary. One intervention may involve helping young people reflect on their own behaviors that might cause the problem. For example, a 13-year-old asks peers at school for feedback and guidance to help her avoid "being a geek" and gain acceptance. But it may be that the location needs to be changed to one where others accept academic interests, moral concerns and individual differences. It is an issue of adaptation. Why should a capable kid have to always be the one who does the adapting? A common statement by gifted young people who are grouped for special services is, *"At last, I can finally be myself."*

Sexuality

Sexuality is one of the major developmental hurdles, generally associated with intimacy, that is traversed by adolescents. It is the final stage of several major adolescent tasks on the road to finding one's identity. Sexuality is one of the least-researched areas on able adolescents, according to Buscher, an expert on gifted teens. However, it may be that there are a wide range of adaptations and developmental milestones that are not specific to gifted adolescents, and consequently they have not come under the researchers" microscope.

In America, dating begins typically at about age 13. Although more than half of teenagers begin to have sexual relations by age 17, gifted young people more typically delay sexuality and focus on the long-term goal of a career after college and before marriage. Postponement of intimacy and sexuality may result in conflicting feelings for some able young persons who have competing desires to have a boyfriend or girlfriend like many of their peers, but who also want to attain goals. On the other hand, some gifted students who are ready for all things early, may be precocious sexually, do not delay gratification, and are able to think their way through to early sexual encounters.

The sexual standard is different for boys and girls in spite of sociological changes in the last 30-40 years, at least in certain cultural contexts. Sexually active boys are still likely to be viewed favorably as studs, while sexually active girls are often seen unfavorably as sluts. However, discussion with a group of bright teens reveals that there are qualifiers to this idea: Girls in a steady relationship who have sex with their boyfriend are not considered sluts, although girls who engage in sex with multiple partners without caring relationships are. Boys who have multiple partners but have a relationship with each girl in turn are OK, but boys who use girls and sleep around a lot are considered unethical and gross.

Some 26 percent of American gifted youth age 16-17 had gone steady and felt pressured to have sexual intercourse. More than 90 percent of the girls said the pressure came from their boyfriends, while over half the males said the pressure came from their buddies. Besides sports, the other "playing field" for boys is proving their masculinity by "making it" with girls. In a traditional macho role, the boys are expected to be aggressive and make the first move. They are supposed to be aloof, cool, strong. Gifted boys who are sensitive may feel they must conform to a "tough guy" stereotype and go against their own nature, setting up internal conflicts. Alvino points out that the language is very much like that of sports ('did you score?"). Gifted boys may also be stressed about having relationships with girls who, according to media stereotyping, are supposed to be "10s". Because boys typically develop later than girls and may already suffer alienation because they are gifted, attractive girls may be threatening. Often, becoming a "jock" is the way to fit in and avoid being labeled a "nerd" if one is not ready for sexual encounters. With gifted boys, a host of additional personal attributes may come into play. There is persistent curiosity, independence, and lack of self-assessment. Because of heightened sensitivity, sex education should be directed at social responsibility. According to Reichart, some gifted boys may demonstrate aggressiveness, competitiveness and manipulation, and need to be curbed for responsible interpersonal behavior to occur. They cannot run with their sexual urges in ways that they may with their intellectual capacities. But boys who postpone sexuality may find it difficult in the "scoring" culture.

Girls suffer from the double standard as well as from peer pressure to have romance and boyfriends. Girls who like to be in charge may have to passively wait for the boys to do the conquering. Their heightened sensitivity may make them feel like they are too weird or something is the matter if they haven't been pursued. They want to affiliate, to be close to someone, to have emotional commitment, as well as to achieve. In addition, they must be the "perfect 10" to attract the opposite sex. It is probable that the relationship would be of greater significance, so finding someone they can talk to rather than score with would be important. However, from their statements, it would seem that they would be very pressured into delivering to the boys. Sex education and social responsibility, along with help in asserting their true feelings would be needed for girls.

The competing wishes for both peer acceptance and for being distinctive make estrangement sometimes necessary but painful. Feeling different is sometimes so stressful that even risky behaviors may be used to reduce feelings of separation, including the denial of abilities. For many able young people, however, much time, perseverance, and effort is put, instead, into the development of talents. This delay of sexual intimacy does not apparently cause difficulties in such relationships in later years. Late adolescent and young adult intimate relationships were found to enhance self-esteem and support release of talents and abilities through creative and excellent productivity, as well as contributing to healthy, sustained intimate relationships. On the other hand, when girls have certain role expectations, such as anticipated age of marriage, their occupational achievement may be constrained. Able young people do not typically engage in sexual experimentation with many partners, preferring intimate connections with partners who provide both feelings of safety and promise.

Mentors

The mentoring process refers to the natural tendency of a person (mentor) with power, status, knowledge and skills to establish a relationship with a relatively inexperienced person (mentee). The mentee is perceived as having potential. The mentor derives professional and personal fulfillment from helping the mentee to develop his or her potential. The benefits of successful mentoring partnerships are reciprocal.

Types of Mentorships

Mentorships can be organized around the type of mentor used or the types of skills developed and exchanged. There are two major categories of mentoring: informal and formal. Informal mentoring passes on skills, awakens mentees to the world around them, provokes, fills them with enthusiasm. Failures are not important because the mentor and mentee try to succeed for their own ends. Formal mentoring incorporates commitment to an organization. Success or failure must be evaluated in terms of organizational goals as well as those of the individual.

The essence of mentoring relationships requires intense devotion to an area of interest. One must be fascinated with something—in fact, love it! The mentee must be willing to pursue fact acquisition and involvement in a defined area with passion, requiring constant practice of even very simple operations over a long period of time. This necessitates absorption and concentration to the exclusion of other things. Generally, it involves an intensive, long-term (more than one year), one-to-one relationship with a mentor.

Value of Mentorships for the Gifted

For gifted students, mentoring provides the opportunity to combine ability with creativity and wisdom. Mentoring is a strategy that permits full exploration of a dominant interest area and cognitive integration of many related aspects. The mentee possesses intellectual potential that needs to be developed. The mentor provides knowledge of a specific domain. Making explicit the mistakes that have occurred, presenting a long term view, listening and advising, the mentor is of prime importance in assisting the mentee to translate theory into action while permitting a freedom to explore without being limited by conventional thinking. There is room to take risks and test ideas. Mentoring helps to promote the mentee's innate drive for accomplishment and/or recognition.

Successful mentors to women have been noted to have access to the highest levels of their own profession to be able to bring mentees into contact with powerful networks that allow them to develop personal resources and appropriate career paths.

Coping mechanisms to contend with peer pressure are consistently described by gifted adolescents. Informal mentoring relationships are nominated as main strategies to escape, temporarily, the intense pressure to conform to a designated social group. Both males and females detail gender imperatives that force them to deny specific interests and potential at this developmental stage.

Of the various types of mentoring relationships, three are particularly suitable to the development of gifted students:

Informal mentoring passes on skills, but guides, counsels, provokes and criticizes, within the context of close friendships. By sharing ideas and experiences, the mentee is initiated and sustained in the pursuit of a special area of interest. The mentor gains personal satisfaction from helping a future generation. The mentor may be a grandparent, teacher, community leader, professional leader or an acknowledged expert in a particular field.

Formal mentoring incorporates a commitment to a purpose. Goals, skill training, planned outcomes and tangible indicators of success are an integral part of the process. These programs are usually of short duration (maximum 1 year, but usually 2-3 months) and have a definite focus.

Partial mentoring where the prime mentor cannot provide all the information required occurs when she or he asks another colleague in the field to mentor a student or students in a specific and highly specialized component or topic of the interest area for a brief period of time.

The benefits of successful mentoring relationships to gifted students are:

1. One-to-one contact with an expert in a chosen field of endeavor.
2. The defusing of negative influences that may arise from peers.
3. Provision of positive emotional environments which create opportunities for challenge, enthusiasm and success.
4. Establishment of a close emotional relationship with a significant mature person outside the immediate family.
5. Awareness of how to find appropriate mentors at critical developmental stages through life.
6. Facilitation of the building of a network of professional friends who may become future colleagues.
7. Provision of information on their chosen subjects which is not available to them elsewhere.

Mentors and mentees comment upon the knowledge, expertise and enjoyment to be gained from these shared, competency-based learning partnerships. These factors are essential in fast-paced, accelerant gifted, mentoring relationships where evidence of similarities in pacing and learning style provide intense excitement, stimulation, productivity and creative responses to previously acquired knowledge.

For the creatively gifted mentee, the access to new knowledge, benign emotional atmosphere and encouragement to take risks with high tolerance for unconventional solutions to problems refines the abilities of mentees and facilitates the development of their potential.

Mentoring relationships can be described as a form of reflective learning. It is the ability of the mentor to understand and anticipate the mentee's understanding and offer just enough information, support and questioning to move the student into more complex areas of reflection and practice. Successful mentors manage this transition smoothly because they share a similar style of thinking with the mentee. The mentee encounters ideas which appear to come from within themselves. In reality they have, but the mentor has been the catalyst, revealing to the mentee what was already known but not developed.

Finding a Mentor

There are two major ways of obtaining mentors. The first is through formal mentoring programs that exist in some schools, departments of education or businesses. The second (far more common for gifted students) is informally, through the mentor-to-be recognizing the potential of the future mentee or the mentee recognizing the eminence of the mentor. Chances to meet potential mentors becomes extremely important. Schools can become conduits for such opportunities by inviting interesting speakers to visit classes; suggesting that students seek out individuals that share their interests through use of university speakers" bureaus, the yellow pages, or letters or calls to individuals whom they have learned about and admire; and developing resource files of parents and community members who are willing to share their expertise.

Moral Development

Parents and teachers of gifted children often comment on the effects of gifted children's heightened sensitivity and high moral development. Older children and adolescents fume and/or worry about injustices they see all around them: at home and school, in religious and social organizations, and in society.

"It's so unfair. The party has been canceled just because a few kids acted up!"

"What's the use of going to church when people in the Third World are dying from starvation? Why don't churches do something useful?"

"You keep saying each person is unique but then you treat me like all the others."

"At school everyone is supposed to do their best, but in reality only certain activities or people are acknowledged and rewarded."

Gifted young people tend to be highly sensitive to moral issues in their everyday lives. They typically demonstrate advanced moral awareness, but may not be able to behave accordingly. Because they can understand moral issues cognitively does not mean they can cope with the issues emotionally. Their judgment, emotional maturity and tolerance for rapid change or long-term solutions may lag behind their intellectual abilities. A major dilemma is that gifted young people are not yet able to solve many moral dilemmas, but adults want them to care enough to develop special talents to potentially resolve world problems.

By the age of 5 to 7, gifted children may begin to worry about moral, social, humanistic and religious concerns and may feel: 1) burdened by unrealistic attempts to assume adult responsibility; 2) unable to cope with human fallibility; 3) unable to accept readily-available solutions; and 4) that being gifted means being responsible for solving problems. Gifted youth may have problems tolerating ordinary aspects of society: the inconsistencies, loopholes, socially expedient and hypocritical facades, adult weaknesses and games, and power structures.

Gifted adolescents raise many moral issues concerning friendships, love relationships, self-concept, search for identity and purpose, self-evaluation, family relationships and concerns for the preservation of the world and the people in it. The difference between the gifted child's moral and intellectual views and those of peers can be a major stressor as there may be differences in perception of reality and concerns with more serious issues. Particularly in early adolescence, age peers may tend to magnify differences.

One moral dilemma faced by young able adolescents is maintaining friendships with others who are looked upon by peers as "nerds" or "dorks." Young people describe the social cliques that form in school as being a series of circles from those on the outside, the social outcasts, to those very popular students in the inner circle, the "trendies." In order to gain peer status and ascend to a higher circle of peers, they must choose between old friends and the aspired-to new group which demands disassociation with the former group. *"I feel really badly about leaving Lisa, but Christie said she's pulling me down. I'd like to be part of Christie's group, but I don't want Lisa to feel bad."*

Despite their sensitivity to moral issues, it cannot be assumed that moral reasoning will develop unaided, or that high intellectual ability will naturally lead to a high level of moral development. Positive role modeling and discipline which focuses on spirit and intent allows young people to see the limits being imposed. Through exploration and observation, children build their own ethical system based on the behavior observed. From watching how members of the family treat each other and how they interact with the general community, children gradually accumulate a value system. Thoughtful reflection by parents about their own values and discussion with their adolescent children helps to make explicit a sense of values.

Appropriate models for moral education are those which resist moral indoctrination or authoritarian teaching of values. Role models that are involved in the community are recommended. By allowing students freedom and autonomy to explore moral issues, teachers provide a climate in which students can construct their own system of values. At the same time, curriculum design in moral education needs to provide future leaders with appropriate models and methodologies for re-establishing values at the center of consciousness, such as a national and international conscience, a concern for the preservation of our planet, a sense of propriety and a pursuit of excellence. Ethics need to be integrated as a core component of the curriculum.

Many gifted children and adolescents worry about world concerns. They feel burdened by their own unrealistic expectations that somehow they are personally responsible for finding solutions. Appropriate moral education allows gifted students to recognize that while they do have the potential to change and improve the world, they must learn about themselves first. Then they can go on to devote themselves to developing their special talents and, possibly, to contribute to resolving world problems.

Coping with Problems Common to Gifted Kids

Certain difficulties are encountered by gifted students who come from underserved populations, such as the ethnically different or physically disabled. There are also specific problems experienced particularly by gifted young people. They include perfectionism, boredom, underachievement, drug and alcohol abuse, anorexia and bulimia, depression, and suicide.

The Ethnic Gifted

Most of the reported research on this topic comes from the United States, dealing with minorities peculiar to the American experience—African Americans, Native Americans, Hispanics/Latinos and Asians. Problems central to the question of ethnic identity, experience, cognitive style, and so on, can be extrapolated from this material and generalized (with caution) to other contexts. Much of the literature subsumes concepts and questions that come from the observations and findings of cross-cultural-psychology, cultural anthropology, sociology and linguistics. It is probably more productive to explore this literature in order to come to terms with major ethnic groupings and their incidence within specific school communities, their specific problems and needs.

The processes that underlie educational achievement are considered to be culture dependent—for instance the attitudinal and motivational obstacles of the passive recipient of information who may see no need for mastery, who lacks curiosity and even may have an expectation of failure by attributing success and performance to factors external to the self. Such attitudes and values must be understood in order to identify and provide appropriately for able young people from diverse backgrounds.

Identification

Identification of high ability is a problem given the number of variables influencing behavior and performance. Inevitably there are ideological disputes, including the status and reliability of psychometric measures. In addition, difficulties occur in identifying giftedness among special groups—indigenous populations, refugees, females in particular cultures, children of color, as well those groups whose values, cognitive or personality styles may inhibit the demonstration of gifted behaviors as defined in the literature. In addition, gifts recognized in a given culture may be different from those recognized in western society and thus not acknowledged. The failure to take account of these differences can compound the problems of underachievement, motivation and self-concept. Injustices are done by failing to perceive and nurture potential, thereby perpetuating disadvantage. Added to this is the prevalence of the multi-cultural school in low socio-economic (SES) areas, parents who may have little education and political know-how, and schools with low expectations and little contact with parents. These factors often mitigate against obtaining appropriate educational opportunities for the gifted in minority populations or even seeing the potential in children who are perceived as different.

Multiple criteria, including a battery of tests, portfolios, and observations can be used to identify giftedness among minority groups. However, conventional psychometric testing may be culturally biased and may not elicit the cognitive strengths and characteristics of a particular cultural group adequately, if at all. Methods that take into account socio-cultural characteristics, urban acculturation, socio-economic status and family structure and size such as the SOMPA (System of Multi-pluralistic Assessment) suggest factors which should be considered, as do recent and more authentic approaches to assessment in general. Observation of learning potential may be a more productive way of making educational decisions about whether a student would benefit from a gifted program.

There are checklists for different subgroups, which are suggestive for identifying some of the "creative positives" for comparable populations from other cultural and ethnic groups—facets such as language rich in symbolism, imagery, creative ability, figural fluency, flexibility, kinesthetic responsiveness and so forth.

Each subgroup will have different strengths and deficits which may need special nurturing and building upon. Other promising techniques are use of dynamic assessments that look at what students can do with what they learn, particularly through observations, case studies, and portfolios. Using inclusive (rather than exclusionary) screening approaches and staff development for teachers assists in identification of able minority students.

Family Environment

Among certain ethnic groups, the gregarious nature of the extended family and frequent contact between family and friends may militate against individual task commitment, given more pressing social obligations and expectations. In some cultures the upbringing of the child reinforces the lack of inner directedness. Individual initiative and autonomy, generally goals for gifted programs, may be contrary to the emphasis on unquestioning respect for the authority of the father, teacher or other elders. This external locus of control (control by others outside the individual) often leads to a passivity in learning in the school environment. Some cultures also discourage creativity, emphasizing instead skills in mastering traditional patterns.

Students may rebel against the strictures or the ethnicity of their backgrounds. This may manifest itself in behavioral problems, or determination not to succeed, often as an expression of anger. A burden of high expectations to go on to a university may be placed on the shoulders of a young person, sometimes a charge too heavy to bear. Some cultures demand achievement to honor the parents. This may be perceived as an intolerable onus, particularly if the young person feels compelled to pursue a particular direction that provides standing in the community but might not be his or her choice of career. In addition, the language barrier may send the artistically inclined child into math or the sciences and deny the humanities side of education.

Cultural values and beliefs may present coping problems to the child. The gifted child movement is posited on liberal values, embracing openness to discovery and those things valued in a liberal, democratic society. Yet certain religions or cultures may disavow these values, placing a strain on young people in the inevitable compromises they may be forced to make in the wider society. It is all very well to believe in a "critical autonomy" to be able to clearly make the choice to embrace, accommodate or reject one's parents" culture as an end of education, but it is not so easy to maintain that modern western liberal values don't in fact challenge and ultimately deny some of the beliefs and values of specific cultures which a liberal society purports to accommodate. For example, stress may be placed on the Muslim girl in some Islamic cultures not to proceed to higher education in spite of brilliance in schoolwork. Many cultures place great emotional commitment to working and marrying within that community. The costs can be great if one chooses to opt out.

Self-concept

The children of parents who have little education may lack an environment where education or learning is valued, even though their parents may have high aspirations for their offspring. There may be an absence of role models as well as a lack of books and educational toys. Indiscriminate background noise—an unsupervised TV blaring for instance—can deny the possibility of concentration, focus or introspection. Success may be attributed to external forces rather than the result of individual efforts. A lack of self-motivation and low academic self-esteem will likely lead to opting for the utilitarian and familiar rather than believing that higher goals may be attainable.

Racism is an obvious problem that may affect the child's self-concept. Much of the multi-cultural literature seeks to address this through advocacy of curriculum relevant to multi-cultural concerns. In this poem by Phoebe McGuiness-Thomas, age 15, coping with racism is the focus. She says, "I got the idea to write this poem while reading Cynthia Voigt's novel *Come a Stranger*. It is about a young black girl growing up and how she copes, which is by making a joke of herself and by acting "white.""

Twice a Minority

"Ya f.....nigger!"
She closes her eyes,
She doesn't want to hear.
She's heard it every day
Of her brief life.
She is twice a minority,
Black
And will one day grow to be a woman.
How will she cope?
She's been beaten because of it,
Her aunt raped because of it.
How will she cope?
Build barriers,
Act the clown,
Act white.
She has learned this,
And she is only twelve.
This is how she copes.

School Effect

Schools in low socio-economic environments may discourage achievement. Low aspirations of the students and low expectations by teachers may pressure the potentially gifted to conform to the dynamics of the group. Yet teachers have a very powerful influence on students, particularly on children of color, even by second grade. They may set students up for failure by praising work that took minimal effort, perceiving that a child has reached his or her potential because of unexamined beliefs or prejudices. Likewise, there may be stereotyping of certain groups, in which only certain talents are encouraged, such as sports for African Americans or math and science for Asians. This is also true for gender, in which girls are supported to become ballet dancers, but not boys, or boys are encouraged to become physicists, but not girls. On the other hand, the student may be caught between trying to please parents or teachers by achieving and trying to please peers by not achieving and fitting in. The tendency of teachers to rely on textbooks rather than active inquiry can reinforce passivity and stultify the enthusiasm for learning. Concern for the gifted may be viewed as non-egalitarian. Parents may be kept at arm's length, the rare evening meetings being occasions to inform parents of their child's progress, or lack thereof, usually with little attempt made to communicate in languages other than English. Some minority groups place great faith in the responsibility of the school to educate their children and may not question its efficacy to adequately do so.

Social class may play an even more important role than ethnic or cultural group in gifted students" school adjustments. Sub-populations of gifted students, particularly those of disadvantaged environments, were found to be at risk for diminished self-esteem and perceived themselves as less competent socially and academically than advantaged peers. They also expressed feelings that they received less social support from classmates, friends, parents or teachers. Female students were particularly vulnerable to perceived lack of social support. Disadvantaged students may benefit from social support networks that offer the emotional and material support needed to overcome these difficulties.

Teaching Strategies

Often multi-ethnic schools focus on remediation rather than language development and enhancement. This thrust can lead to teaching strategies that do not stretch students but severely constrain them, such as focusing on the student's limited expertise with the English language. Certainly there are real problems to be faced in this area—not only do different languages have different grammatical structures leading to great confusion with English, but some cultures and their languages create different thought processes and perceptions of reality.

If students have been taught basic concepts in their mother tongue in the formative years, they will not be disadvantaged in the acquisition and training of their cognitive skills. In fact, the bilingual student actually may be cognitively advantaged, yet often not recognized for considerable competence in his or her own language. When English is taught, it is often through a basic skills approach, boring the bright child by slow, step-by-step language acquisition, rather than a whole language approach that keeps alive the possibility of intellectual discovery within the classroom.

Correct modeling represents an aspect of good teaching, as is breaking down a task into smaller components that can be readily grasped. Different cultures have different expectations as to how something should be written as opposed to the linear-argumentative style of the English essay. Teachers can try to read the written products by students from different language groups so that they recognize and give credit to the effective transmission of ideas rather than concentrating on the inaccuracies of usage.

Some cultures utilize rote learning or an educational model based on students as recipients of not-to-be-questioned ideas and knowledge. For students from these cultures, confusion may result in environments that stress process, the raising of questions, and individual response. Even the idea of plagiarism, an anathema to us, may be acceptable to some cultures, where original thought is devalued in favor of reproducing an expert's ideas verbatim, if need be. The cooperative learning strategy may be beneficial in developing language skills, but considered peripheral to some cultures that emphasize achieving high grades by the individual.

The multi-ethnic classroom is composed of a profusion of learning styles, as well as values. Different groups will benefit from different teaching styles and may find themselves disadvantaged in quite different ways. Identification of the various characteristics and values integral to optimizing performance in any particular environment is necessary, but beset with problems involving training teachers and changing schools. Without identifying the needs and abilities of specific groups, we deny the very justice for these students we claim to espouse.

Clearly, coping with being culturally or racially different and gifted presents certain problems. For some students, very strong family values toward education and school achievement lead to accelerated progress, recognition by teachers and ability to overcome many obstacles (see the story of Matthew, "Kids" Section'). For others, even being recognized as capable is a dilemma. Teacher expectations may lead to gate keeping, wherein African American and other minority students are overlooked even when they meet the criteria for giftedness in their district. These young people may have greater difficulty negotiating an environment different and perhaps sometimes hostile to their own ways. Added to these problems, gifted students may find that in their peer groups, it isn't smart to be smart. Although the culture certainly has an influence on a given person, that individual's particular strengths and vulnerabilities need to also be taken into account.

The bottom line is that teachers start with the twin notions of respect for the individual from whatever diverse group, and optimizing the development of each child they teach. In addition, learning about different cultures, exploring and reflecting on one's own biases and values, and celebrating diversity in the classroom benefits all students, particularly minorities.

The Disabled Gifted

Identification

If the difficulty of identification of giftedness among normal or culturally diverse young people is complicated by classic problems like underachievement, cultural or personality factors, then how much more problematic is the circumstance of the child with specific physical disabilities such as a visual or hearing impairment, cerebral palsy or orthopedic problems? Or the child with specific learning difficulties or emotional disturbances? Frustration and counterproductive behavior might not only be the outcome of coping with the disability but could be a result of limitations imposed on the intellectual capacity by inappropriate instruction. The focus may be so heavily on remediation of the disability, that intellectual or creative potential is ignored or even denied. There is too often a tacit equating of physical disability with the inability to perform intellectually. This reinforces the disparity between potential and achievement, lowering a self-concept that matches itself against the achievement and social and affective adeptness of the normal gifted.

It might be that those qualities that we associate with giftedness are in some way observable in many of the disabled gifted: superior oral abilities, humor, analytical acuteness, creative problem solving, exceptional memory, motivation to succeed, and so on; but the disability too often consigns disabled children to focus on their problems which must attract immediate and undivided attention (see the story of Andrew, "Kids" Section').

Achievement and Motivation

One of the concomitant difficulties in performing to potential is a tendency to passivity when too much reliance is placed on dependency (relying on assistance from others instead of doing what one can for oneself), or when it is easier to retreat into one's private and comforting imaginative world. While it is easy to imagine how self-esteem will suffer because of the difficulties the disabled face, it is no less a problem when a tendency to self-centeredness is reinforced by a misplaced but understandable sympathy and praise for what may actually be undistinguished performance. A world where time and space are different realities can promote timidity, a disinclination to task commitment and an unwillingness to take initiatives when so many choices may have to be made for the disabled individual.

Developmental delays can be quite considerable. In the deaf, for example, reading ability has been estimated to be between three and five years behind the norm. The problem of language acquisition has been seen to lie in the limitations of sign language to express complex, abstract ideas, and when only 30 percent-40 percent of sounds in the language can be associated with visible lip movements when lip reading. Recent research, however, has argued for the primacy of sign (not signed English)—much as any mother tongue—as essential for early cognitive development.

Obviously those with specific learning disabilities (SLD) will manifest characteristics which seemingly contradict characteristics of giftedness: difficulty in completing work, failure to carry out instructions, poor performance on specific tasks, as well as mediocre grades. Classroom teachers might have difficulty seeing the gifts when asked to look for performance typified by considerable variability across tasks, impaired long and short term memory, low motivation and low task completion, difficulty with visual or auditory processing, poor self-concept, considerable self-criticism, withdrawal or aggression, difficulty following directions, short attention span, and poor relationship with peers. In addition, the child with both gifted abilities and specific learning disabilities may "mask" both the gifts and the disabilities. They may be able to "get by" through compensating for the disability, but not excel in any school subject due to the disability. Because they are sensitive and aware, self-esteem suffers. They cannot understand why everyone else reads so easily and they often blame themselves. Such children are really doubly handicapped and may often become underachievers. Yet when procedures for selection are modified, more learning-disabled gifted children have been identified. Focusing on strengths, such as creative thinking, as well as assistance in developing metacognitive strategies also appear beneficial.

Identification is difficult enough because of the cognitive developmental lag but with inclusion in the normal school setting (placement of a disabled child in the regular classroom) it can be difficult to gauge ability. There is the inevitable comparison with the non-disabled gifted, but there is no obvious norm within the child's own disability group with which comparison should be made to assist in finding any superior capabilities.

Giftedness in the disabled is often not recognized until adulthood. Disabled children are seen to be so obviously lagging in development, so much slower in achieving results, that they are prey to attitudes and environments that militate against independence or understanding of capabilities and strengths. Stereotypical expectations; invidious comparisons with the physically able; and simply not perceiving their intellectual and affective needs and how to accommodate them are the inevitable consequences of being so different from the normal, capable student. Our knowledge of the needs of disabled gifted young people is built around case studies of adults who have succeeded, most often against the odds. But their stories have demonstrated important strategies for coping with their respective disabilities, their home, social and school environments.

Strategies for Home and School

The dilemma of the balance between assistance and encouraging independence can be seen when the possibilities of researching an assignment is considered. Access to the range of materials available to the normal student is circumscribed by speed of accessing material, reliance on others to assist in selection and, if necessary, transference to an accessible media (sound, braille, etc.) or transcription (transcribing from dictation, for example)—all time consuming and, in some measure, denying independence of performance and the possibility of high level achievement. A blind or severely dyslexic child is totally reliant on someone to make the selection, to read the material (and/or braille it, in the case of the blind child). That child is denied the access to research and, in particular, the freedom to explore at will. This problem is exacerbated if the disability is accompanied by disadvantaged circumstances—a school that has inadequate support for inclusion of children with special needs within general classrooms, or a home environment where education is not valued for example.

The ability and energy of the respective families to provide appropriate support impacts on and is affected by the capacity of the disabled individual to cope. To bring out or accommodate such a child's giftedness may place additional stresses on a family. There is often guilt that a parent suffers and this can be transferred to the child. When parents overcompensate and fail to act against dependency, a disabled child can learn to be helpless.

Problems of Inclusion

If inclusion poses challenges in the normal classroom setting, it nevertheless eliminates restrictions of outlook that may impede potential. The world must be met on its own terms. The pace and perspective will not be the same as that which is available to normal gifted young people, but the challenge may lie in possibilities that might be denied the disabled in more restricted settings. Tasks may need to be sensibly moderated to accommodate the particular strengths and weaknesses of the child so as not to produce low self-esteem from a sense of failure or frustration. The young person may need assistance to understand that he or she might not work to potential among gifted peers. One way of assisting the student is to modify the curriculum—less homework to accommodate the sheer time and effort it can take to perform tasks, or the burden which can be placed on those assisting the child, for example. Some understanding of metacognitive skills (awareness of one's thinking processes) could promote self-understanding as well as an appreciation of strengths or weaknesses that need addressing.

A good inclusion program may involve the student being assisted by visiting teachers and aides and will have regular meetings with school staff, specialist teachers and parents to monitor problems and progress. If a child is becoming too dependent on others for help, for example, then alternative strategies might be proposed. This is a way to guard against the tendency of teachers who may attempt to impose a basic skills regimen on a child with superior intellectual gifts in order to make up for some deficiency or other. Any deficits certainly need to be addressed, but not at the cost of frustration and impeding actualization of the child's intellectual, creative and affective capabilities.

Incentives to Performance

To encourage motivation and bring to the fore the strengths and talents of the child, helping to widen his or her world is important. This should be not only in the school setting, but should encompass participating, where possible, in the out-of-school activities with other children. Thus, Scouts, 4-H, or Camp Fire offer a range of outdoor activities. Sports are also a healthy outlet and both have identifiable goals and a sense of purpose. The necessity to encourage hobbies and interests which can be shared is obvious as one would expect with any gifted child. There are activities promoted by the various disability organizations—camps where living skills and independence are promoted, for instance. Indeed, the possible activities and clubs are limited only by the imagination and time.

Outlets for performances and productions, much as with an able child, are available and students should be encouraged, both within various subject disciplines and outside the immediate school environment. For example, most states broadcast radio programs for the blind. Some may allow young writers to share their works. Check with your local school district and look in your telephone book for resources (usually there are listings in the White and Yellow Pages under a specific disability or under "disabilities" for resources in your community or state). The same competitions available to any child, such as Future Problem Solving or Odyssey of the Mind, can also be intriguing for a student with disabilities.

Role models become especially important for the disabled. Teachers and parents could search for examples of individuals with their child's particular disability who have succeeded. Who could fail to be inspired by the Special Olympics, or by the individual accomplishments of people who have defied the odds to be productive members of society? Autobiographies, biographies and films are all useful in this regard. Above all, stereotypical limitations on life possibilities, or occupations, will be seen for what they are: just that. Who could have conceived in their wildest imaginings that a profoundly deaf girl, Evelyn Glennie, would have become one of the world's great percussionists performing and recording with the world's greatest orchestras?

Technology

One of the boons of the technological age is the potential for assistance modern technology promises—computers that can talk and take dictation, that can assist in musical composition, machines that can read aloud from books and print or emboss into Braille, CD ROMs that store whole encyclopedias, television stations that assist the deaf with signing and subtitles, radio stations for the print handicapped, and so on. But these things may come at considerable cost and may more than stretch the average family's pocket. Still, they are innovations that enable greater independence and with a properly funded inclusion program at least some of these things may become available to children. Such assistance will vary enormously from state to state, school to school. Certain community initiatives may provide assistance, such as service clubs, to help with equipment or scholarships. Much depends on the political clout the organization associated with a particular disability might have to create awareness of need and to fight for funds. An organization like that of the parents of autistic children may not be as successful, say, as highly organized groups with long track records devoted to the vision or learning disabled.

Emotional Constraints

An interesting reflection on the relationship of the physically able to the disabled is the question of the visibility of the disability. While any disabled child can be prone to being teased and will have to learn to cope with a certain amount of thoughtless behavior towards him or her, it becomes more of a burden when the disability cannot be seen. To the average child, young people with specific learning disabilities, emotional disorders or autism may be perceived as simply being stupid or weird, reinforcing the vulnerability of the disabled child with feelings of inadequacy, not only intellectually, but socially as well.

The literature is sparse on psychological or emotional disorders among the gifted, but case studies indicate certain patterns related to the negative aspects of the three "emotional tributaries" of the gifted: terrible pain associated with extraordinary sensitivity, unrealistic expectations and paralysis associated with perfectionism, and depression associated with intensity. Gifted young people with emotional disorders suffer extreme negative feelings about themselves and perceptions that they are failures, both socially and academically. They become distraught, depressed, withdrawn, overly-anxious and paralyzed. They may also feel anger, rage and frustration as well as shame, guilt, alienation and hopelessness and they turn these emotions on themselves. Especially if these children have been abused, they need someone to whom they can turn for protection and validation. Clearly, the need to deal with emotional stresses must be addressed before growth in learning can occur. Intervention by counselors, psychologists or psychiatrists is generally advised (see section on depression and suicide).

A case can be made for some autistic young people to be considered as potentially gifted. There are highly talented individuals within this group, and schools can serve an important function in the socialization and affective needs in these children's lives. Equally, though, the problems of autism are such that the special dedication of a mentor may be required to help the autistic child to realize his or her potential as a full human being.

A teacher might take inspiration from the work of Reuven Feuerstein with his mediated learning, assessing learning potential rather than IQ as indicative of a child's capacities. If nothing else, the success which he has demonstrated with children that others have virtually given up on challenges the idea of the fixed IQ. But that example, as well as the successes that others have found with disabled and gifted young people, can assist teachers to trust intuitions, look for glimmers or sparks of ability, focus on those possibilities and be wary of notions of giftedness as something immutable.

Perfectionism

Characteristics of the Perfectionist

Meticulous, careful, fussy, nit-picking, hyper-critical, precise, over-refining, being a stickler, being a hard task master.

> **Making an effort is not enough. It's the standard of the work that counts for these children.**
> —*Pringle, 1970*

Of the characteristics linked with the onset of social/emotional problems in gifted students, perfectionism is the most significant cause of stress. Perfectionism is the inner drive for flawlessness that makes the gifted child discontented with any performance short of what is perceived as perfect. This drive for perfection is not necessarily unhealthy. The major advances in science and creative arts have been achieved by gifted individuals who strove for perfection and were satisfied with nothing less—a drive for excellence. Perfectionism can be self-oriented, when one sets high personal standards and evaluates one's performance against these; or it can be other-oriented, when one sets unrealistic standards for significant others. But the problem occurs when perfectionists may also try to live up to his or her perceptions of standards held by others. The label "perfectionist" carries negative connotations, which would be viewed positively if described as *persevering* or *high-achieving*. However, gifted young people are especially vulnerable to feelings of inadequacy and inferiority, tying their success at school to their worth as a person. The drive for perfection may lead the young person to experience an acute sense of failure when anything other than "A" grades are achieved. Such a student may withdraw from a course rather than risk a lower grade, or may not complete or even attempt a project. Perfectionism is a sign that students are having trouble coping.

Severe cases of perfectionism can prevent the gifted from achieving anything at school. Perfectionism can immobilize the imagination, motivation and risk taking that quality learning demands. For the perfectionist, the learning activity ceases to be fun. Worst of all, perfectionism is generally accepted as being a warning sign in teenage suicide research. "Perfectionistic teenagers begin to equate personal *worth* with personal *success* so that any defeat is seen as a devastating loss of pride ... Adolescents may give up entirely—on schoolwork, on sports, on themselves ... Suicide may then become a viable alternative."

Who Sets the Standards?

Gifted perfectionists cannot use the comparison of their classmates" work to set serious standards of excellence. They learn not to trust the praise of their teacher, whose standards must be too low. Thus, these children are usually most responsive to their internally-held reference values. Their strong perceptions of how things should be overrides the opinions of others. The perfectionism displayed by the gifted young child often re-emerges in adolescence. However, in adolescence the stakes can be more costly to the young person's self-image and self-esteem. Gifted young people set unrealistic goals for themselves and are very harsh critics of their own performance.

At times their high expectations are fueled by well-meaning adults. There is a danger that teachers and parents will set unrealistic goals and have unrealistic expectations for these young people. Teachers and parents are proud of the achievements of the child. Even if they do not set unrealistic goals, the young person may feel that more and more is expected and become caught up in a vicious cycle of feeling the need to prove superior abilities again and again. As one goal is reached, the young person feels pressed to achieve even more. Gifted children who are perfectionists or whose self-concept is weak, hear negatives over the positives. The child is praised for a report card of A's and B's, but the child may hear the message as a warning to do better. Teachers and parents must be aware of the dangers of these pressures and reassure the young person that leisure time spent in non-intellectual pursuits is not only desirable, but essential.

All gifted children can be plagued by perfectionist tendencies. However, the problem for gifted boys can be especially acute. Boys may be raised in an environment stressing competition, achievement and success. Parental pressure can turn gifted boys into "paralyzed perfectionists." Boys may be especially at risk if they are emotionally disconnected from their fathers. They are often not encouraged to develop the same capacity to give or receive emotion as girls. Their sense of self-worth may be inextricably tied to their accomplishments. This can reach tragic proportions—the gifted boy may become anxious and depressed, feeling helpless and inferior. He will avoid challenge because the risk of failure is too great. The issue may be one of competition: excessive competition and parental pressure can be detrimental to a gifted boy's self-concept and ego development. His ego feeds on external rewards such as the marks he receives. The perfectionist boy restricts his behavior to that which is tried and safe, for he fears failure in any new venture.

Staying in Control

Perfectionism is not just a side issue or example of gifted young people's difficulties. It is a part of a *major* issue in gifted education—that of *control*. It is difficult to cope with life unless we have some measure of control over it. Most gifted students have a natural tendency to organize, or bring structure to people or situations. In an effort to control they often dominate any activity in which they're involved. Perfectionism seems to be a symptom of young people struggling to take responsibility for and gain control of their existence. Their ability to discern the difference between the mediocre and the superior becomes a way of controlling success and failure. They are determined to control a given process from beginning to end and achieve a perfect result. The paradox is that sometimes by letting go, rather than losing control, we gain it.

In a *physical* sense, the gifted can be frustrated by a lack of control over their own bodies. They may try to meet the demands of complex tasks without having the physical prerequisites needed to succeed. Sadly, some students fail to take into account the years of practice, maturation and facing hardship such achievements require. They simply feel they cannot cope with the tasks they want to perfect. They also may not have had the experience of having to apply effort to something, especially since school tasks may be so easy. Learning about individuals such as Jackie Robinson, the first black big league baseball player, Evonne Goolagong, brilliant Aboriginal tennis player, Lucciano Pavarotti, world-famous opera singer, or any Olympic gold medalist or other athlete, famous musician, artist, or scientist can be a great resource for such young people in helping them understand the role of effort in accomplishment. Other gifted young people work at having perfect, slim bodies through strenuous diet and exercise, sometimes resulting in anorexia (see pp. **119-123**).

Ironically, their perceptive *sensory* awareness can actually work against them in their struggle for perfection. Their ability to perceive problems in their work can be greater than their ability to solve them. Gifted imaginations can dream up the most wonderful visions of what the finished products ought to be. Bitter disappointment follows for perfectionists whose work can't help but fall short of their expectations.

The perfectionist whose *intellectual* capabilities far exceed those of classmates will generally find routine schoolwork very boring. Yet the gifted student usually has no control over the type of work assigned. By giving a 100% commitment to completing each task perfectly, every time, these children are seeking a challenge worthy of their ability. They are controlling at least one aspect of their learning. This compulsive behavior helps them cope with the wasteland of too many school experiences.

While other children tend not to dwell on unsolved dilemmas, the gifted child can feel a *moral* responsibility to create a perfect world. Anxiety about their inability to control social or family problems may result in a need for perfection in an area they can control: schoolwork.

Intervention Strategies
for Overcoming Perfectionism

Before their mental health is put at risk, gifted perfectionists need appropriate home and educational settings, with support from parents, teachers and counselors who understand their needs. Paralyzed perfectionists need to learn to make mistakes, to fail, without becoming unduly distressed. They need help to understand that they do not have to be perfect at every activity.

Perfectionism is best "headed off" when the child is very young. Parents can play an active part before the problem becomes serious. If a preschool child begins to fuss excessively about her "just so" appearance or refuses to try something because "I'm not good at it," intervention should begin immediately. Mom's mistakes, like wearing two different shoes or putting salt in the sugar bowl accompanied by lots of laughing at herself models self-acceptance. Deliberately requesting a "great goof" of the child before he leaves for school with accompanying mirth can also help. "Oops, the milk spilled. Hooray, we've had a goof for the day!" And most important is acknowledging the young child's feelings, not denying them when the conception exceeds the capacity. For example, a child is close to tears with frustration because he cannot make his pencil write letters correctly. He needs to have his feelings acknowledged as well as finding an alternative. "You are really angry because you want to write to Grandma but your hand hasn't caught up to your words. Would you like to try to write it on the computer or would you like me to make dotted letters for you to

connect?" To say, "Well I think it's a very nice letter to Grandma" tells him his judgment isn't valid as well as marking you as a poor judge.

Parents can help preadolescents and adolescents by ensuring time for fun and relaxation without overloading on lessons, practices or the filling of every free minute with social activities. Comparisons with other peers or siblings or offering rewards for grades should also be avoided. Offering unconditional love, rather than only validating young people for accomplishments is another way of helping perfectionists. You accept them the way they are just for being themselves. Try a hug or even a note on the bathroom mirror with "I'm so lucky to be your Mom (or Dad)", not as a reward for a good report, but perhaps when a young person seems a bit down. Admitting you were wrong gives the message that it's okay not to be perfect. "I'm sorry I yelled at you yesterday when you asked if you could have two friends sleep over. It wasn't your fault. I was stressed about my job and took it out on you."

Some of the anxiety experienced by the gifted adolescent could be lessened by the use of humor in our educational programs (and at home). Unless encouraged, this characteristic is often absent in the gifted adolescent. In contrast, one of the marks of a young gifted child is a well-developed sense of humor. If gifted children are encouraged to use humor in class, if teachers model laughing at themselves, tensions can be released and good will created. The sense of humor of gifted children is integral to their personality and when developed can increase their understanding and commitment to fellow students—and to the world. Perfectionists will find it hard to survive!

Discoveries, inventions and artistic creations are often the result of playing with ideas, experimenting freely with possibilities. A rigid classroom environment is best avoided—gifted children have strong curiosity and a sense of wonder and intrigue which need a caring, warm educational setting. We need creative, resourceful graduates, not paralyzed perfectionists, if we are to solve the problems of our modern age.

Gifted students need to evaluate their personal aspirations and expectations. This can be facilitated by trusted adults who understand the vulnerability of the gifted adolescent. Surprisingly, perfectionistic young people were found to gain relief when they were provided special academic programs that placed demands upon them commensurate with their abilities. The ability level in these classes was sufficiently high that no student could expect to consistently achieve the top grades or the perfect project. Thus the students experienced a reduction in pressure to some degree. They could relax and rely upon the class system to establish appropriate goals, rather than constantly striving towards ever-higher standards of perfection.

A pattern was found between disabling perfectionistic behaviors of adolescents and discrepancies between actual and idealized self-perceptions by Reva Friedman, a researcher in the field. She developed a three-phase model to empower gifted teenagers to understand and use their potential. The first phase is knowledge about giftedness. School staff and family members meet together to gain necessary knowledge. The second phase is self-awareness—school and family share their perceptions. The third phase is empowerment—constructive strategies are planned and school staff and family members meet to share feedback. She demonstrates this model by means of a case study, Carol.

Carol was taking longer and longer to complete assignments as none of her work was ever quite up to her exacting standards. Her perfectionistic behavior was leading to acute distress, and Carol was falling behind her less able classmates. To change the situation, Carol, her teacher and her parents agreed that she could work for only 15 minutes each day on any independent assignment. Time for recreation, not for high-quality work, was emphasized. After initially completing no work, Carol began to enjoy "racing the homework clock," and as she progressed the 15-minute limit was relaxed. Carol was empowered to use her potential and break out of her paralyzing perfectionism.

Perfectionism, then, should not be seen as merely a negative trait which should be modified or eliminated. Educators, parents and counselors should not try to "cure" the qualities of the gifted child which constitute the potential for higher achievement. However, intensity and perfectionism can lead to frustration and depression, so capable young people need help to understand the forces that drive them. Perfectionists need to be allowed to take control of their education (and their lives) and alleviate their sense of helplessness. In this way the pursuit of excellence can propel gifted students forward, rather than hold them back.

What Teachers Can Do
for Perfectionist Students

☞ Encourage the process of making or producing something, rather than the result. Ask students to plan their projects in small steps. Don't always correct the finished product. Accept rough notes, sketches or outlines and discuss the quality of the **ideas** behind them.

☞ Set some challenges in which the perfectionist has no experience. Encourage them to enjoy something new, just for the fun of it. Make effort the basis for reward.

☞ Use class discussion, private diaries or role playing to teach students that:

> ☞ There are various levels of accomplishment.
> ☞ Mistakes and risk taking are part of learning.
> ☞ We simply don't live in a perfect world.
> ☞ We can all improve with practice—but we'll never be perfect!

☞ Make an effort to identify and encourage the students" interests—focus on their personality and their effort rather than their achievements.

What Teachers Should NOT Do for Perfectionist Students

☞ DON'T be too lavish with praise—if they show dissatisfaction with a quality project don't contradict them!

☞ Take them seriously and ask:

 ☞ What particular part don't you like?
 ☞ How can we improve this area next time?
 ☞ What parts are you proud of?

☞ DON'T put extra pressure on them, and make them feel "different," by using their work as an example to others of perfection.

☞ DON'T use "healthy competition" as a way of motivating students.

☞ DON'T set up open-ended research projects for the individual and then forget about them! Constant support, and a limit on how much work is expected will work a lot better.

☞ DON'T label them as being the best in the class, or introduce them by referring to their abilities. Even flattering nicknames can be hurtful.

☞ DON'T be perfectionist yourself, or constantly tell other class members their work doesn't measure up.

Helping the Perfectionist
• For Parents and Teachers •

☞ Don't single out the bright child for special attention.

☞ Don't ignore a persistent teasing problem and hope it will *go* away.

☞ Don't discipline teasing by drawing more attention to the bright child's situation.

☞ Don't give them the same repetitious work—have something they're interested in for early finishers.

☞ Don't use bright children as teacher's aides, without asking them.

☞ Don't punish kids for misbehaving when there is nothing interesting to do.

☞ Don't teach them topics over and over.

☞ Don't encourage perfectionists to spend hours on headings or perfect handwriting.

☞ Do encourage them to explore their own passions.

☞ Do allow them to work ahead of their grade level—but be there as a support.

☞ Do recognize that teasing is painful. "Sticks and stones may break my bones, and names hurt me inside ..."

☞ Do discuss strategies with the child, like answering back or ignoring them.

☞ Do differentiate between an offhand remark that wasn't meant to be cruel, and persistent teasing.

☞ Do recognize the gifts of all children so they don't feel or appear to be very "different."

☞ Do reward creativity, the alternative ways of doing things—not just perfect right answers.

☞ Do ask them what type of things they would rather do, and set realistic goals.

☞ Do let children fail.

Helping the Perfectionist Grow
• For Parents and Teachers •

☞ Don't treat academic and non-academic activities as two unrelated extremes! Recognize achievement in all areas.

☞ Don't criticize anyone's "passion," or special area of interest—try to get others to share in it instead.

☞ Don't force children to participate in things they hate!

☞ Don't let study interfere with eating and sleeping.

☞ Don't assume bright children always have great study skills.

☞ Don't value your subject as being THE most important.

☞ Don't approach school staff without discussing things with your child.

☞ Don't demand A+ grades all the time.

☞ Don't expect children to do everything—study, family outings, sports, helping at home.

☞ Do recognize that all gifts are valuable, and point out the gifts of others.

☞ Do encourage the joining of popular clubs or activities such as computers, sport and drama.

☞ Do select sports teams or work groups yourself sometimes.

☞ Do encourage individual differences and unique approaches.

☞ Do list priorities and make a plan for the week.

☞ Do give enough time for projects.

☞ Do ask students about their workload and confer with other staff.

☞ Do teach time management and study skills.

☞ Do value quality rather than quantity.

Boredom

What is Boredom?

Weariness with tedium; finding things devoid of interest because of repetitiveness, lack of novelty, already attained mastery, slowness of pace, busy work.

Some Facts

♦ A gifted young person may be absorbing information at several times the rate of the "average" students—those to whom the teacher is addressing the lesson. The gifted, particularly those who are exceptionally able, cannot concentrate on unstimulating schoolwork. "Their minds take off on journeys beyond their control." Research shows the teacher will not normally move onto the next stage until 80% of the class has coped with the previous stage. Hence, gifted children are spending a large proportion of their time dealing with information already familiar to them.

♦ Much of the work in class is already known to them before the class starts.

♦ Many exercises which suit the majority of the students are seen as "busy" work by gifted students—coloring in pictures, doing more problems of a type which they have already mastered, and so on.

♦ Gifted students spend much of their time in many classes totally bored!

Responses to Boredom

♦ Every young person responds differently to different situations. Every gifted child responds differently to boredom in the classroom. Some common responses have been noted; all students have to deal with the frustration in some way.

◆ Bored students may become disruptive. To entertain themselves they become the class clown or nuisance. This behavior is more commonly recorded with boys. It is this behavior which can lead to the identification of a gifted child, and may then force action to be taken. Alternatively it may just lead to the labeling of the child as an "arrogant pest.'

◆ Bored students may become withdrawn. They daydream in class, lose concentration and may then underachieve at school.

◆ Bored students may learn to slow down their work rate to ensure they don't finish quickly and have to suffer boredom. Over time, this becomes their work habit and they will then underachieve. This is more often noticed with gifted girls.

◆ Gifted young people may not like to attract attention to their abilities due to the often negative social reaction to their intelligence. They may prefer boredom and trying to perform as their friends do, in preference to such labeling.

◆ Bright students may drop out of school altogether as a way of avoiding boredom. Many cases of students with high IQs and early high achievement have been found in school drop-out populations.

What Can You Do?

◆ Listen to the student. Respond according to the individual. Give extra, different and interesting work—quietly, if this is appropriate. By talking to the young person alone, you can work out what is appropriate for that individual.

◆ Don't give the child more of the same! Many students complain that in math they are usually given more problems at the same level of difficulty to keep them occupied. These are the very students who don't need repetitive, simplistic work. The same goes for other subjects.

♦ Allow for individuality and creativity. Many bright and creative students will approach the task in a different way from their peers. Try to avoid stipulating a single approach or standardized product and rigidly enforcing them.

♦ Try to free the progress through a topic from a lock-step, task-completion model. Given freedom to move at their own rates and cover different work, produce products of their choice or work to a different depth, gifted students often may be happily and gainfully involved in a mixed abilities classroom.

♦ Extend assignments with an open ended question at the end, which can be taken to greater depth. Assessment criteria need not be the driving force. Use this section to extend the student into the higher levels of thinking—analysis, synthesis and evaluation-type activities.

♦ Relate the topic to other disciplines to broaden the scope. For example, in science, add a question dealing with the social relevance or the ethical aspects. In English, ask about how someone from a difference socio-economic background might respond to the same question. Have the student role play such a person, and respond accordingly.

♦ Use the traits considered to be common to gifted children—a heightened sense of morality, a heightened sense of justice, a sense of humor, a desire to follow issues to greater depth, a desire for knowledge, a desire to create and hypothesize, and so on, to draw new aspects out of the given material.

♦ Help students understand that we learn in layers. Each time we learn something, our experiences to that point make us learn it a little differently. If the same novel is read more than once, a character or the plot may be perceived on surprisingly different levels. If reading about an historical event, the information may be assimilated to another topic. For example, if reading about the Russian Revolution of 1917 for the second or third time, recent events in the former Soviet Block may make that information meaningful in a different way. Suggest that students try to see what new things they can get out of studying something more than once, especially if there is a considerable time interval between the earlier introduction of the topic.

♦ Accept the intelligence of young people as a gift—and enjoy teaching them. You will learn from them, too!

For Class Discussion

☞ Are you ever bored?
   When? Why?

☞ Have you found ways to cope with boredom?
   How? Where?

☞ What does your mind do when it's bored?
   ☞ Puts you to sleep?
   ☞ Makes you misbehave?

☞ Do other kids get more bored than you?
   Who? Why? What do they do about it?

☞ Are some classes worse than others?
   Which ones? Why?

☞ How could you ask your teacher politely to modify your assignments?

☞ What can you do about boredom?
   ☞ Can you find ways to extend yourself beyond the required work?
   ☞ Can you use time to think productively about a topic or project that interests you?
   ☞ Can you read in class when finished with an assignment?

☞ Can you learn something new about a familiar topic by listening or reading very carefully and tying the information to more recent experiences?

☞ Are you bored at home? What are the causes? Is there some other dissatisfaction in your life that you label "boredom" instead of facing a painful emotion or a difficult situation?

☞ What else can YOU do to relieve boredom?

Underachievement

What is Underachievement?

Underachievement is a performance which is significantly below the child's potential for academic achievement.

A large proportion of highly intelligent students do not perform to their potential. Such underachievement is often determined by discrepancies such as high scores on standardized tests of academic achievement or intellectual ability (typically the top 5 percent) but low grade point average (under 2.25), but underachievement may also be less visible. A leading expert on this topic, Joanne Whitmore, estimates that approximately 70 percent of gifted students underachieve. Why is this so, and who are these underachieving students?

There is No Such Child as a Typical Underachiever

Often, however, especially with discrepancies between performance and ability, underachievers are male, not necessarily of poverty or at-risk backgrounds, and not usually antagonistic toward school.

Consider the following cases:

1. Jenna is a model seventh grade student. She is the most able student in her humanities and math classes. She is

quiet, courteous and always attentive. She is the "ideal" student. However, Jenna is gifted academically. She has the ability to work at a much higher level—indeed she would enjoy the challenge of working with other students in grades 9 or 10, especially in mathematics, which fascinates her. Jenna's underachievement is *hidden*. Her teachers regard her as an excellent student, and this is the heart of the problem. *Any gifted student who is achieving at the top of her classes in the normal curriculum for her age is almost certainly underachieving—perhaps by three years or more.*

2. Jeremy is in the same classes as Jenna. However, he is far from being an ideal student. He is rowdy and impolite. His work is messy, and he rarely finishes a written task. His teachers suspect he may have learning problems, but at times he reveals a surprising knowledge when he is interested in a topic. Jeremy is also gifted.

He has the ability to work at a much higher level. He has responded to the frustration he has experienced since entering school in kindergarten by unruly behavior and the production of limited, poor quality work.

Both Jenna and Jeremy entered school eagerly. They were both accomplished readers, with a wide general knowledge and a wide range of interests.

Underachievement for some gifted children is a pattern begun on their first day of school when faced with typical beginning reader material.

What are the Causes of Underachievement?

School factors

♦ When the school environment does not encourage or highly value academic success, the atmosphere may actually be anti-intellectual. Young people who do well at sports and perhaps artistic pursuits (art, music) may be applauded. The academically advanced student or the creative thinker may feel devalued and may not bother to achieve. This may lead to contempt for school and for teachers.

- The curriculum may be inadequate for bright students. Highly intelligent young people lose interest. They become bored and refuse to complete work which is irrelevant to them.
- The classroom environment is rigid or authoritarian. Gifted students want some control of their learning experiences.
- Allowance is not made for individual differences. All students must progress through the curriculum at the same rate. Young people who finish work early are given "more of the same" or left to help others.
- Students may downplay their abilities rather than appear different from age peers in class.
- Student learning styles and teaching styles may be mismatched.
- Students may be overlooked by educators because they don't demonstrate behavior and attitude problems. They simply don't get noticed, particularly girls.

Home factors
- Learning is not valued or encouraged and achievement is not rewarded.
- Parents lack positive attitudes towards their own careers; for example, the father may be an accountant, but denigrates his work.
- Learning is encouraged, but parents dominate. The young

person does not develop internal discipline. Parents may also control management of time. The young person's time is over-committed and he or she may not have time to make friends or pursue personal interests. The parents expect too much.

♦ Student's achievements are a threat to parents" need for superiority.

♦ Power struggles within a family, particularly when one parent is liberal and the other strict, set up winning and losing and the child is torn between the parents or forced to choose sides. Underachievement may result.

♦ Low socio-economic status, especially if accompanied by limited parental education and low educational or career aspirations for the children may lead to underachievement. However, some financially impoverished families value education and support their able children, and some affluent families lack interest.

♦ The family is dysfunctional for any of a number of reasons, including alcohol or drug dependency; lack of parenting skills; divorce; job loss; family histories of abuse; or illness. Sometimes this dysfunction is a temporary problem, as when a parent has to be hospitalized for an injury. Other times, it is chronic. In a dysfunctional family of this type, members distrust each other, physical health may be neglected, communication is vague, problems are blamed on others and left unresolved. Values are inconsistent, frequently there is abuse (physical, sexual, and/or emotional), privacy is denied, and secrecy to hide the difficulties are an unwritten rule.

♦ Cultural differences (See section on "Ethnic Gifted').

Other Factors

♦ Being differently-abled, that is, having a learning disability, a disabling condition or a modality preference incompatible with the teaching style (See section on "Disabilities," pp. 104-110) can lead to underachievement, as can emotional disorders.

♦ Personality factors such as perfectionism, hypersensitivity, deficiency in social skills or tendencies to overextend into too many activities may lead to coping difficulties and underachievement.

- ◆ Troublemakers—these students may be overlooked for gifted programs because of focus on misbehavior.
- ◆ Shame—feelings of self-perceived defects, not being good enough, anticipating rejection brought about through training in the home or at school that it is a personal responsibility "not to disappoint." The shame must be hidden, leading to depression, perfectionism, self-hate, or sometimes violence, and often to underachievement.

Reversal of Underachievement

Depending on the cause, underachievement can be difficult to reverse. The main task for schools is to create an environment which fosters creative learning. The earlier the problem is detected, the easier it is to deal with the problem.

- ◆ Students suspected of underachievement need to be assessed by the school counselor or psychologist to determine potential learning ability.
- ◆ Students who have been underachieving for some time will have gaps in their knowledge and understanding of basic curriculum areas. They need to be helped to overcome any deficiencies.
- ◆ Students need instruction appropriate to their individual needs. Schools generally provide for children who are "average" or "slow" learners; they must also provide for the "fast" learning child. Children should be encouraged to do their best work, but without pressure, stretching without stressing. They should be encouraged to move ahead quickly in basic skill areas. Boring repetition of facts already known should be avoided.
- ◆ Underachieving students need to be given back control of their lives. This usually requires teachers, parents, and sometimes counselors or psychologists working together to help the young person gain self-esteem and control, avoiding blame.
- ◆ Remember that **underachievement is a learned behavior in response to a variety of stresses. Focus on seeking solutions rather than blaming others for the problem**.

Drug and Alcohol Abuse

Some General Information

Drug and alcohol use continues to occur in epidemic proportions among adolescents, despite the increasing awareness of physical and social consequences. In one major study, susceptibility to peer pressure and peer alcohol use were the best predictors of individual substance use. There are over 10 million alcoholics in the United States and approximately 2.3 percent of the US population of child bearing age is probably in need of treatment for use of drugs other than alcohol. An estimated 20 to 25 percent of children in any given classroom are children of alcoholics (COAs). Such children are disproportionally living in poverty. The family situation of alcoholics is "The most widespread cause of severe stress for school-age children in the United States today." Such young people are statistically at greater risk for developing alcoholism. There is a 50 percent risk if one parent is alcoholic and 80 percent risk if both parents are alcoholic. There is also an increased risk to abuse other drugs as well. Genetic predisposition is a factor, wherein the genetic propensity is passed from parent to child. Another risk is related to use of drugs or alcohol during pregnancy which predisposes the child to physical problems and cognitive impairment. Other risks result from dysfunction of chemically dependent families, where abuse, neglect, distortion and denial of reality, family conflict, high rates of divorce and separation, isolation, unpredictable and inconsistent discipline, and emotional stress makes young people more vulnerable. In a study of chemically dependent adolescents, the overwhelming majority of clients were either children of alcoholics or children of non-drinking alcoholics.

In intrapersonal arenas, aggression (even in primary grades), depression and impulsivity were the best predictors of drug use. Self-reported grades were a predictor for females (i.e. the better they did at school the less likely they were to take drugs). Generally others have reported a robust association between school achievement, school behavior and drug use. Chemically dependent young people as a group seem to be frustrated by a lack of control over their learning environments and experiences. They have not had insulative factors or developed the coping mechanisms needed to lead productive lives.

Parental monitoring impact has not been shown as directly relevant, as succumbing to use of drugs or alcohol may be mediated by peer and other interpersonal variables. Motivation to use drugs in the school environment include peer influence, tension-reduction coping strategies, and the drug effects. For example, Eric's story in the Kids" section, describes his concerns about not giving in to peer pressure and using drugs.

In light of most glaring adversities, it is unusual for more than half the young people to succumb. It is rare for single stress factors to occur in isolation — divorce, plus discord, plus difficulties at school often occur together and compound difficulties. Yet resilience is built up through encountering and successfully coping with stresses, in which competence increases through mastery of the situation. The qualities of resilience are not constitutional or unmodifiable. Children can be helped to develop adaptive qualities. Teachers may provide a mediating effect, as well as other adults who serve as substitute primary caregivers. Thus, a close and caring relationship with a teacher or other adult is important for developing resilience.

Some ten percent of COAs do survive their alcoholic families and grow up to be well-adjusted and healthy. There are five protective factors that appear to assist such young people: 1). Leaving the alcoholic environment, 2) leaving the co-dependent parent, 3) developing competence at appropriate tasks, 4) experiencing and internalizing healthy relationships, and 5) developing functional coping strategies. The most useful coping strategies were found to be focused on solving the problem rather than emotional coping to reduce stress.

Substance Abuse and the Gifted

Very little research has been done on gifted young people and alcohol or drug abuse. In one of the few studies, the self-report of substance use patterns was, with a few exceptions, similar to the general population. However, fewer able young people used alcohol or drugs. The gifted and talented students valued how decisions to use substances might affect themselves, their friends, or their families. Earlier substance abuse education in the elementary grades had a positive effect on 6th to 12th grade gifted students" decisions not to drink, smoke, or use drugs. In addition, gifted non-users were highly involved in academic, physical and extracurricular activities.

In contrast to this study, some 35 percent of the clients at Project Independence, a post-detoxification academic and treatment center for chemically dependent youth, identified themselves as having been selected for gifted programs. This study focused on using principles extracted from educating of gifted children to provide appropriate educational programs for chemically dependent young people. Findings indicated that academic gains were substantially higher for students provided this educational approach.

Gifted children whose parents were alcoholics were more often found to have lower self-esteem than children of non alcoholic families. They also had a lower tolerance for failure. Children with lower self-esteem were found to score lower on achievement test scores and grades, but parental alcoholism did not correlate with low test scores. Some children from alcoholic families did have high self-esteem and high test scores. It appears that some young people are more resilient and have more coping resources in dealing with alcoholism in the family.

How to Spot the Warning Signs for Chemical Use
School

It is usually a combination of these warning signs, rather than a single one, that indicates problems, particularly if observed over time.
- Frequent and unexplained absences;
- Poor performance;
- Discipline problems;
- Poor concentration;
- Boredom; and
- Low Energy.

Home
- Changes in eating, sleeping habits;
- Sudden mood changes;
- Irresponsible behavior;
- Repeated health complaints;
- Repeated dull eyes and a steady cough;

- Depression and a general lack of interest;
- Becomes argumentative;
- Breaks rules;
- Withdraws from the family;
- Has new friends who are less interested in home or school activities;
- Gets into scrapes with the law; and
- Unconventional style in dress or music.

What to do:
- Talking is the key.
- Do not raise your voice.
- Do not give ultimatums.
- Listen—Young people complain that they are not listened to.
- Use humor.

Prevention:
- Find ways to help young people to gain control and responsibility over their environments in school and at home. Offer choices and avoid rigid, competitive classrooms. Help students self-assess their work, determine their own schedules, find resources (See section on Power Relationships, "Teaching for Coping").
- Focus on prevention efforts that help in controlling circumstances surrounding drug use that lead to immediate risk, such as driving under the influence. Simplistic ways of handling peer pressure ("Just say no"), are not sufficient.
- Help young people consider the consequences and learn to be assertive about their real preferences. Gifted students tend to be principle-oriented. They use their mental abilities to grasp the "rules of the game" or "principles of the thing," particularly when assisted. Drug education and role-playing help.
- Consider other options/coping strategies for dealing with stresses.
- Seek support from counselors or clergy when there are big problems and help is needed.
- Help young people to develop resilience by allowing them to fail safely and learn from their own mistakes.

- Talk about making friends with others who do not use alcohol or drugs, and avoiding those who do.
- Seek assistance in the telephone book (see section on Suicide for help here).

Anorexia and Bulimia

Anorexia and bulimia are both eating disorders. They are often linked together.

What is Anorexia?

Anorexia is an eating disorder leading to a loss of at least 25 percent body weight resulting from refusal to consume sufficient food, despite extreme hunger.

What is Bulimia?

Bulimia is an eating disorder that involves fasting followed by eating binges followed by self-induced vomiting and/or abuse of laxatives to avoid weight gain.

Some Facts:

♦ Anorexia nervosa occurs in about 1-2 out of 100 preadolescent and young teenage girls. Children as young as the age of 7 are being admitted to hospitals suffering from anorexia. Some young people with anorexia have blood pressure so low that their feet have become gangrenous.

♦ Anorexics are very good at keeping their plight a secret—they hide their bodies in loose clothing so parents and others may not notice their extreme weight loss for some time.

♦ Bulimics are mostly female. The prevalence of bulimia in reported studies of high school females ranges from 2 percent to 29 percent.

- Binge eating is common among adolescents with 43 percent reporting doing it twice monthly.
- Bulimia is more common where mothers had less than 8-11 years of education.
- Bulimic symptoms are a fear of fat, anxiety, and depression. There is low self-esteem and concern about control.

YOU STOP SEEING YOURSELF AS YOU REALLY ARE... AND YOU GET SICK.

Profile of an Anorexic

- The sufferer is probably female—95 percent of all sufferers are female.
- Sufferers come from all backgrounds and many different styles (and sizes) of families.
- The sufferer is typically of above average intelligence, although there have been cases of mental retardation as well. More intelligent girls are particularly vulnerable to the development of anorexia. They have greater perseverance, achievement orientation and a predominantly cognitive control. These girls are especially successful at con-

trolling their weight with dieting. However, in the course of the weight loss, the illness develops a dynamic of its own. Thus gifted anorexic girls are admitted to the hospital in a more emaciated state than patients of normal intelligence.

♦ The sufferer is often described by parents and teachers as "an ideal child without any problems.'

♦ Anorexics tend to set unreasonably high goals and to aim for perfection in all they do. The degree of external expectation perceived by the individual is high.

♦ The anorexic suffers from low self-esteem; she finds it difficult to cope with the pressures of everyday living.

♦ The sufferer's perception of body image becomes disturbed. The anorexic may regard herself as fat, overestimating body size the thinner she becomes. She has an intense fear of becoming "obese" and of losing control of eating.

♦ The sufferer exercises obsessively. Anorexics often use exercise as well as diet to ensure weight loss.

♦ The sufferer is often preoccupied with the preparation of food—for others to eat. The anorexic may collect recipe books, slimming magazines and acquire a knowledge of "sensible eating" facts.

♦ The sufferer cannot think clearly or concentrate. She may undergo a complete personality change. Anorexia places a tremendous emotional strain on sufferers. Malnourishment causes a reduction in mental capacity when anorexia is at an advanced stage.

♦ About 40 percent of anorexics develop bulimia later.

Family Patterns, Anorexia and Bulimia

There is no certain familial patterns associated with eating disorders, nor is there a single pathway or mechanism of influence in families of anorexics. However, certain genetic factors may predispose an individual to greater sensitivity and vulnerability to family experiences that adversely impact self-esteem and self-efficacy. Families that are overprotective, rigid, avoid conflict and resolve conflict unsatisfactorily make individuals more vulnerable to develop pathological disorders such as anorexia or bulimia. The binge cycle provides an apt metaphor for the family's recurring excesses and deficits. Just as the bulimic craves food during the "binge" phase, and purges subsequently, so the family craves nurturance and soothing which, as part of the cycle, is then followed by aggression or frustration towards each other. In some studies, bulimics have seen their families as less cohesive, less expressive, and active in recreation. Bulimic women have described their families as less involved and less supportive, more conflicted and less structured, and generally felt more isolated. Other studies have found that families of bulimics are more "belittling, walled off, and neglectful." Often there is an increased family prevalence of eating disorders.

Generally, it can be argued that such deficits in family functioning can result in behavioral deficits in coping and being overwhelmed by "painful and disruptive affective states." Eating disorders are often accompanied by depression being experienced by the individual or within the family. Although the predisposition to eating disorders may originate from genetic and personality dispositions, their ultimate expression requires the presence of disturbance in the family and/or pressures from the surrounding culture.

Side Effects of Anorexia

- ♦ Severe sensitivity to cold.
- ♦ Loss of menstruation.
- ♦ Growth of down-like body hair.
- ♦ Possibility of kidney dysfunction, imbalance in bodily chemicals and damage to the colon or urinary tracts.
- ♦ High incidence of bone density loss.

**Untreated, anorexia (and/or bulimia)
can lead to death.**

What Causes Anorexia?

♦ There is no single answer. It is an over-simplification to blame the mass media with its portrayal of the slim "ideal" female figure. However, society's increased emphasis on the slender, fit body places pressure on many girls.

♦ Some sufferers are reluctant to mature physically (sexually) and find it difficult to mature emotionally.

♦ Issues of personal control between parent and child could contribute to some cases of anorexia.

♦ Some sufferers may be sexually abused and attempt to regain control of their bodies and their lives through rigorous dieting.

♦ Specific performance areas may induce anorexia or bulimia, such as gymnastics or ballet. Ballet requires that female dancers be 15 percent below their ideal body weight. Dancers who are not naturally thin have the greatest stress, particularly those with family histories of obesity. Public weigh ins, advice by instructors and coaches not to eat, coupled with unrealistic expectations and perfectionism lead to these disorders.

♦ Severe manifestations of Anorexia Nervosa are quite complex in their origins. Anorexics are often perfectionistic, aiming for the "perfect" body shape. In addition to the dissatisfaction with one's body image (which is in turn associated with poor self-image), anorexia is generally associated with a struggle for control; not only of one's eating, but assertiveness and control in the family context.

♦ Some sufferers come from families where high achievement is expected and anything less than excellence is seen as failure. In some of these cases, parents do not expect excellence, but the young highly intelligent teenager feels she must achieve excellence.

♦ Low self-esteem and a sense of inadequacy—the need to receive others" approval may be contributing factors. The young teenager may find it difficult to express her own needs and feelings, including anger.

How Can You Help a Child
Who Appears to Be Anorexic?

♦ Anorexics will usually deny having a problem. The first step is to bring the problem into the open, but great care and sensitivity must be used. The teenager may be willing to speak with one particular teacher or school counselor if she cannot discuss her plight with a parent.

♦ If anorexia is advanced, expert advice should be sought as soon as possible, therefore parents must be informed. Hospitalization will probably be necessary—sometimes for prolonged periods. Usually, the family doctor refers such cases to a specialist familiar with treating anorexic patients.

♦ The sufferer needs reassurance that teachers, friends and family members will not blame her, and will be patient with her.

♦ Once professional help has been obtained, the young person must be responsible for her own recovery. Parents cannot take charge. However it is vital that she be offered continued love and support from family and friends, as well as expressions of concern from caring teachers. Communication is very important.

♦ Join a support group, and become informed about anorexia and its treatment. Children's hospitals in large cities will assist here.

♦ Write to the National Association of Anorexia Nervosa (ANAD), P.O. Box 7, Highland Park, IL, 60035 to receive a packet of information and referral to a therapist in your community. Enclose a self-addressed, stamped (78 cents) business envelope. Or call the hotline at (708) 831-3438.

Depression and Suicide

There is a distinction between depression and sadness. Sadness is a universal emotion expressed by all of us at some time. It is a conflict-free emotion where we are aware of what sometimes feels like inescapable pain at a sense of loss or disappointment which can usually be explained by the circumstance.

Depression is a state of being pressed down upon. The very word has a core idea of "pressing down." There is a notion of conflict which is absent from sadness. Along with the conflict goes  aggression which is not always turned against someone else but can be turned inwards. Aggression that individuals turn on themselves is frequently labeled *self-destructive behavior*. This is often expressed through eating and drinking disorders. One of these extreme eating disorders is anorexia (refer to previous section), where the lack of will to eat eventually becomes an inability to eat and in severe cases results in death.

Depression is considered to be a cognitive-affective disorder. That is, it is related to the thoughts and feelings that individuals have about themselves and their circumstances. The cognitive-affective changes result in lowered self-esteem, distortions of perception about what is going on (things look gloomier than to everyone else) and there is a devaluation of the self. This is often accompanied by feelings of helplessness and hopelessness. Some 11 percent of men and 25 percent of women wrestle with depression at some point in their lives, but young people are not immune.

There is a continuum of severity which can be considered as moving from sadness to depression to the most severe outcome, suicide, conceptualized as a failure to cope. Individuals who commit suicide are characterized by a total sense of despair, a feeling of extreme futility. Adolescent suicide is on the increase in our communities. The overall incidence has tripled between 1970 and 1990, and even more so for white males. It is not only associated with poverty but occurs in affluent suburbs as well. The incidence is higher in the exceptionally able than in the regular community, with better students making more severe attempts at killing themselves. Suicide is the third most frequent cause of death for young people (following accidental injury and homicide), accounting for about 19 percent of all deaths between 15 and 24 years of age. In the United States, some 5,000 to 7,000 young people take their own lives each year and an estimated 400,000 attempt suicide. Further evidence suggests that even young children are attempting suicide.

Attempts at suicide are a cry for help. Sometimes there are warnings but family and friends may fail to see any such signs. Talking about suicide or previously attempting suicide should be taken very seriously, as over 50 percent of attempted or actual suicide victims either threatened or attempted to kill themselves earlier. Teen suicide is often associated with drinking or drug use prior to attempts at ending life. Feelings of alienation, issues of intimacy, and gender identity confusion are often related aspects. Major stresses particularly involving losses or seriously humiliating experiences may make a young person vulnerable. The greater the number of risk factors, the greater the risk of suicide.

In one study of suicide attempts, nearly 19 percent involved students of high ability. Gifted students may be particularly at risk due to heightened sensitivity and awareness, particularly when there is instability, trauma and lack of control. Perfectionism and suicidal ideation also are related to giftedness. Factors for suicide potential among the gifted include distorted perceptions of failure (belief that perfection is the only acceptable level of performance, thereby setting oneself up for failure); socially prescribed perfectionism (concern about living up to perceived standards of others, or external pressures); developmental dysplasias (gaps between social, emotional, or physical and cognitive abilities); success depression (stress of maintaining continual success); conflict between trying to please parents by doing well and fitting in with peers by not doing well, wherein one's talents are considered an embarrassment; feeling powerless to affect outcomes about world problems; inappropriate educational settings; and loneliness. Fear of making mistakes, self-doubt, alienation from others, and worry about measuring up are indicators. In a study of three suicides in a special school for academically gifted, the victims were intrigued with the dark side of music and literature, two of the three kept journals in which they discussed suicidal thoughts at considerable length, they were profoundly critical of themselves and the world, and they were reinforced by peers in thinking about suicide as an honorable option. In addition, suicide of a media idol and friends appeared to trigger the final act.

One 16-year-old girl said despairingly, *"I think that the world sucks. We won't reach 2000, no way. The world is going to be destroyed."* Where there is a general sense of extreme hopelessness, suicide is a high risk.

Signs Related to Suicide Risk

Margaret Appleby and Margaret Condonis, in their book *Hearing the Cry*, identify the following signs that generally relate to suicide risk behavior:

♦ Threats by writing or hinting. They should be taken seriously.

♦ Previous attempt(s) which can be in the form of any self-inflicted injury.

♦ Depression which can be manifested in listlessness and withdrawal. Sometimes there are signs of sadness and at other times there are signs of agitation and aggression. Changes in eating or sleeping patterns and loss of concentration are also signals for concern.

♦ Feelings of guilt, hopelessness and helplessness which is a feeling of being stuck without the power to influence one's life. There is an inability to see options and alternatives.

♦ Withdrawal from family and friends. Individuals who attempt suicide often believe that they are a burden on others.

♦ Giving things away. The gesture of parting with things can signify an abandonment of the present, and wanting something to be taken care of for the future. It can also be a cry for help.

Some gifted children display characteristics that can make them vulnerable to suicide. These include non-productive coping strategies, deficit social skills or social isolation, and unrealistic expectations. But warning signs may be ignored, particularly as the gifted may be better at hiding the depths of their pain.

A poem by Stuart Pritchard, grade 10, captures the feelings of a young person who may be vulnerable to suicide:

The Scream
She's lost,
An outcast
From her family,
An outcast
From her friends.
In their world she's not wanted,
In her world she's confused.
That's why she stands on the bridge,
Wondering why there isn't a reason
Why she should live any more.

What Can You Do?

♦ **Listen**. Be available to listen. If that is not possible right there and then you may need to negotiate a specific time and place when you are both available. The setting should be one that is peaceful and where privacy is possible. If self-disclosure occurs or sensitive issues are raised, confidentiality can be maintained. Listen for both the feeling and the content.

♦ **Offer Acceptance**. Convey unconditional acceptance by being non-judgmental or critical about what is being said. The concerns that individuals have are legitimate worries to them. Don't give advice unless asked and even then do so cautiously.

♦ **Evaluate**. If the individual is seriously depressed, assess the severity of the depression and the need for help. Ask yourself: Is this person at risk of making an attempt on his or her life?

♦ **Be Direct**. If you think that suicide is an option the young person is considering, ask directly. Sometimes the person is relieved that someone has noticed the extent of despair and offers of help may be readily accepted.

♦ **Use Bibliotherapy**. Use of reading material can help through modeling how others cope with difficulties. Useful books can be found by talking with the children's librarian in the public library, using the most recent edition of *The Bookfinder: When Kids Need Books* (by Spredemann-Dreyer), or using materials specific to gifted young people (see end notes).

♦ **Use Positive Self-talk**. Point out the link between the student's inner thoughts and covert behaviors, such as needing to be in control, or always feeling victimized. Help the student come to grips with and modify the self-defeating inner dialog that predisposes him or her to behave according to irrational beliefs.

♦ **Offer Support**. Offer support in terms of your time, interest and availability. Offer any concrete assistance that you can.

♦ **Find Something to Live For**. Sometimes, doing something positive for others provides something to live for and raises self-esteem; for example, helping a first grader learn to read and write or assisting an elderly person.

♦ **Seek Assistance**. When clinical depression is suspected, rather than sadness, *seek help from a professional counselor or adviser, especially if the young person is thinking about suicide.* You can start by contacting:

Covenant House Nine Line: 1-(800) 999-9999 (this charity organization helps young people consider options for a variety of problems in addition to depression and suicide).

Telephone Directory: In large cities there is frequently a hotline telephone number that can be called to help a young person who is extremely depressed, experiencing a crisis, or considering suicide. It may be listed under a special page on community resources, perhaps under the heading "Crisis Hotlines". Be prepared to call a few numbers to find the right resource. Also look in the Yellow Pages and in the White Pages under such headings as "Mental Health", Crisis Counseling," "Alcoholism", "Drug Abuse", or "Crisis Intervention". Because phone books vary, it might be useful to write that number in a prominent place in your phone book or on a bulletin board. Other social agencies that serve youth and families can assist young people in crisis as well. Do **NOT** give up if you get a busy signal, particularly on a hotline.

Call the Police emergency number: Usually **911**.

Please be sure not to abuse any hotline numbers with crank calls, as individuals in crisis may not get help when they need it.

School Counselor, Doctor, Clergy person: These people are trained to find assistance for young people in crisis, as well as to listen to problems. They will treat matters confidentially.

Go to a Hospital Emergency Room

In doing research for this section in America, we were surprised that phone numbers published within the last five years as suicide crisis lines are no longer in existence, and that there is no 800 number provided by the US Department of Health and Human Services or other federal program to help young people in distress, although their are state and local numbers available to help adolescents in serious stress find appropriate resources. A useful project for able young people would be to gather and publish a list of local resources for youth in crisis that could be made available to students in schools.

In this chapter we have looked at some of the problems typical of gifted youth and suggested some of the ways teachers and parents can help young people cope with these difficulties. In the next chapter are other strategies for teachers to use to help young people cope.

IT'S NOT
SO HARD
IF YOU USE
THE PHONE
IN PRIVATE.

TEACHING FOR COPING

What Do You Do When An Able Child...

1. Is depressed (running out of time and energy; puts head down; no eye contact; listless; usually tired or restless).
2. Has the weight of the world on his or her shoulders.
3. Never says anything—is very passive or shy.
4. Rarely/never completes a project.
5. Does a minimal job, way below potential.
6. Refuses to do any work.
7. Is bored with classwork.
8. Doesn't pay attention: is in "lala land."
9. Is over-extended with too many activities/responsibilities.
10. Is a worrier—wants constant feedback on every little thing. "Is this right?" "I can't do this!"
11. Is overly perfectionistic. "It's never good enough!"
12. Is getting too thin—you suspect anorexia or bulimia (or is getting too heavy).
13. Is teased or ostracized by others.
14. Is a loner but doesn't want to be.
15. Bullies other children: threatens or is physically abusive.
16. Takes over in class.
17. Is smart-mouthed: "This is a stupid assignment." "You can't tell me what to do."
18. Is the class clown; disruptive in class.
19. Leads others into negative behaviors (smoking, drugs, alcohol, stealing, cheating, etc.).
20. Demonstrates very cynical or negative behavior—"We can't do anything about that problem" or "I hate school" or "Everyone in this class hates me."
21. Is involved in illegal or unacceptable behaviors: smoking, alcohol, drugs, cheating, stealing, prostitution, etc.
22. Has too many responsibilities at home.

23. Doesn't have the financial means to deal with school needs or compete with others at school who have expensive clothes or travel extensively on vacations.
24. Is in a special program for bright children but gets teased by peers at home; gets little or no support at home.
25. May have to work to help support the family.
26. Comes to school unclean.
27. Comes to school hungry or doesn't get proper nutrition (buys potato chips and soda for breakfast or lunch).
28. May be being abused.

Usually disruptive, passive or aberrant behavior indicates a problem. The young person is trying to cope and is sending out distress signals.

♦ **What personality characteristics, environmental factors or emotional difficulties do these behaviors indicate?**
♦ **How can YOU and other school staff help young people cope so they do not need to demonstrate these behaviors?**

Teaching for coping is like teaching everything needed to learn for life. By taking a genuine interest in and showing respect for young people, the trust needed to help adolescents find coping strategies that work better for them can be developed. For this book, we have chosen to deal with those aspects that have emerged as most critical that have not been dealt with readily elsewhere. In addition, we suggest that capable kids can use their creative thinking and metacognitive strategies to help them develop their coping repertoire.

In this chapter, several suggestions are offered related to teaching for coping. Using preventative guidance to develop coping skills and distinguishing between affective education and counseling are discussed first and include discussion of five key problem areas. Suggestions for use of creative thinking strategies and metacognition to expand coping options follows. Kids" discoveries about school and a teacher's discovery about learning from students are the next topics. The chapter closes with use of humor to help students cope.

Developing Coping Skills

According to Khatena, a psychologist who has studied creativity and giftedness for many years, what is needed is preventive guidance to help young people learn to cope and master stress. He says that many of the problems faced by gifted and creative young people result from attempts to express their uniqueness which are too often misunderstood by society. The young person's creative character may become deformed, stifled, or denied. The counselor (or caring adult) anticipates stress-inducing conditions and provides opportunities to develop coping skills before the stress becomes intolerable. In the interpersonal area, the gifted young person may need support in coping with pressure to conform. He or she must learn how to continue to be unique without antagonizing others. Khatena suggests that one way to do this is to help the student recognize how his or her talents can be used for the benefit of the group. Another problem area is the prevention of isolation or estrangement, so that the gifted young person's intense need to communicate is not thwarted. Learning to tolerate separateness and help in finding compatible peers are part of the preventive guidance. Khatena suggests using the intellect for constructive behavior to overcome the perceived mismatch between information coming in to the individual's and his or her processing of it. Khatena also suggests developing five coping mechanisms:

1. Risking or avoiding: Help a student understand why he or she is hesitating, offer reassurance, suggest making tentative decisions and "trying them on" before making a final commitment, or allowing students to take their own time on making decisions are ways to help gifted young people take risks in coping.

2. Mastering or failing: Fear of the unknown may inhibit making changes. Offering wide choices, helping the student understand the situation, having trial experiences, or role playing can all make a new situation more familiar.

For example, trying out a variety of career possibilities helps a student to consider interests, concerns, or even failures.

3. Overloading or unloading: Help the student to release feelings caused by accumulations of stress. Talking about the stresses often is useful. Sometimes, help in structuring a situation is needed, such as managing time for final exams.

4. Denying need or making peace: Bad judgments may be made when the demands of a situation interfere with effective thinking. The threat of the situation needs to be counteracted to encourage enduring, not surrendering. Sometimes the energy to be expended is not worth a fight, so the individual needs to learn to make peace with a situation by gathering objective information and assessing whether withdrawal is a better route.

5. Encouraging the continued fight: Use of support groups and better use of personal resources can help a young person persevere and not give up a fight.

What Silverman describes as affective (related to feelings) education we would describe as teaching for coping. While the topics listed by Silverman below are suggested as suitable for the affective development of gifted students, most are useful discussion starters for all students as well. Others have called these topics the "hidden curriculum" since they are not always an explicit part of schooling.

Topics for Affective Development

Understanding giftedness	Introversion	Sensitivity
Self-expectations	Peer pressure	Tolerance
Fear of failure	Competitiveness	Family dynamics
Expectations of others	Guilt	Study habits
Feeling different	Social skills	Leadership skills
Uneven development	Dealing with stress	Career exploration
	Responsibility for others	

Curriculum must be responsive to the needs of the group; therefore the presentation of the above topics and the amount of time spent on them is determined by the problems and concerns that are pertinent to the particular student(s). Teachers are often reluctant to start such a program because they feel that they have not had enough training or developed any skills in counseling. While training in counseling may be helpful, it is not essential. Teachers can set up classroom programs to deal with a range of real life issues and simply focus open discussion on them. Such programs may be very important both in terms of helping young people learn to cope with their stresses and in skill development for a lifetime.

It is not within the scope of this book to be able to deal with most of the above topics. Only five)including three not on Silverman's list)—goal setting, coping with change, dealing with power relationships, feeling different, and developing social skills— will be addressed here. Programs or courses relating to meeting the social and emotional needs of young people can be taken by classroom teachers at a university or through in-service programs. Books and other resources are also useful (see Resources for Teachers). However, the teacher should be aware of the differences between affective education and counseling and be able to refer students to the counselor when no longer able to meet the young person's emotional needs. Cooperative learning strategies can be useful, particularly with groups of gifted students, to focus on social and emotional development. Social problems appear to diminish, students become more responsible, and self-esteem and a sense of belonging increases, along with academic performance.

The following list, also by Silverman, shows the main differences between affective education and counseling.

Affective Education	**Counseling**
♦ Oriented towards groups	♦ Oriented towards individuals
♦ Usually directed by the teacher	♦ Directed by a trained counselor
♦ Involves self-awareness and sharing of feelings with others	♦ Involves problem solving, making choices, conflict resolution, and deeper understanding of self
♦ Consists of planned exercises and activities	♦ Private or group sessions in which content is determined by students
♦ Unrelated to therapy	♦ Closely related to therapy
♦ Students helped to clarify their own values or beliefs	♦ Students helped to change their perceptions or methods of coping
♦ Personalizes the curriculum	

Some models for educating the gifted encourage students to explore their personal, social and emotional development as well as nurturing cognitive growth. Betts" *Autonomous Learner Model*, particularly the *Orientation and Individual Development Dimensions* is recommended in this regard. The affective and intuitive aspects of Clark's brain-based *Integrative Education Model* are also valuable. Tannenbaum's *Enrichment Matrix (Starfish) Model*, particularly aspects dealing with self-concept, social development and ethics; VanTassel-Baska's "Comprehensive Curriculum," including the affective and leadership aspects; and the Williams *Model for Developing Thinking and Feeling Processes* can also be considered. Two models particularly applicable to whole-school improvement in a gifted education perspective are Renzulli's *Schools for Talent Development* and Treffinger and Sortore's three-volume series, *Programming for Giftedness*. This latter series focuses on several affective areas, including independence and self direction, personal growth and social development, and career perspectives and future orientation.

Teachers can provide opportunities to study topics that deal with abstract, complex concepts that enable students to examine social, ethical or moral issues and problems. Focus on such topics also encourages understanding and awareness of their own and others" values. Concepts appropriate for study include:

prejudice	sharing	jealousy
peace	caring	power
sensitivity	persistence	pride
inhibition/repression	alcohol/drug abuse	current events
politics	civil rights	crime
death/dying	divorce	famous people
nuclear power	war	disabled people
minority groups	philosophy	occult
the elderly	women's issues	religions
population problems	social problems	marriage

On the next pages are five topics related to teaching for coping that are particularly germaine to capable kids.

Goal Setting

Many highly able people fail to turn potential into purposeful and productive work. Career failure can be caused by difficulties beginning early in the school career of an individual who finds it difficult to make decisions and plan for short-term and long-term goals.

Three types of young people with high potential are particularly at risk: females who are overlooked due to social pressures and low expectations; those with multipotentiality who are highly capable in many areas but often make decisions for the wrong reasons, such as peer conformity or parental expectations rather than their own needs, interests and values; and early emergers who have a highly focused interest area from an early age. The interest may remain unnoticed, be ignored, or even belittled.

Responses of These Children at Risk

1. *Females* are socialized to hide their intelligence. They frequently opt out of mathematics and science subjects and are not encouraged to be risk takers.
2. *Multipotential* students have difficulty making a choice when given the opportunity. They may have many hobbies and experience short bursts of interest before giving up the hobby. They achieve well in most if not all school subjects.
3. *Early emergers* show a keen interest in one subject area. They have uneven profiles across subjects. They make successful careers in an area of interest.

What Can the Teacher Do?

Help female students in the following ways:

♦ Discourage stereotyping. Set up situations where girls try options they might not otherwise select.
♦ Teach math and science from their interests; for example, instead of teaching about gears in physics through bicycle or car gears, consider using an old-fashioned egg beater.

- ◆ Make parents aware of social bias and give them strategies; for example, the mixed message that young adolescent girls get to both achieve and be popular can be discussed openly in the family.
- ◆ Show benign disinterest when they adopt social attitudes in relationship to gender concurrent with stereotypical behavior.

Help multipotential students as follows:

- ◆ Encourage activities that require goal setting, such as working towards scout badges or class projects.
- ◆ Make available biographies of people who are eminent in areas of interest or of renaissance people who made contributions across fields.
- ◆ Encourage volunteer work and opportunities for work experiences.
- ◆ Help students to identify their own values and deep-seated interests.

Help the early emergers as follows:

- ◆ Help students to plan long-term goals.
- ◆ Provide opportunities to meet people working in an area of interest, consider mentors, explore university options and participate in work experiences.
- ◆ Provide encouragement and support in areas of interest.

Coping with Change

Do I turn to cafes, company, chocolate cake or candy?
Or do l like a chameleon seek out camouflage?
Do I conform, compromise, conceal, seek consolation?
Or do I concentrate on concoction and condemnation?
Do I confide, confront, cajole and conquer?
Or am I captive, confused and full of castigation?

—Christine Durham

What is Change?

According to the Oxford dictionary, change is making or becoming different, a variation or a substitution of one for another. We may believe that people resist change. But do they? Do they resist an allowance increase? Do they resist replacing the broken computer? The degree of resistance to change depends on the type of challenge involved and how well it's understood. What people resist is not change but loss or the possibility of loss.

Change and Loss and Capable Young People

All people have to learn to cope with this loss side of change. Change is most likely to be resisted for the following reasons: The first is loss of the known or tried. It's scary to contemplate the unknown. The second is concern over personal loss of something one already has. Change threatens the "investment" that has been made in the status quo. A third reason change is resisted is "overload" of sensory information. The person is weighed down with decisions to be made, seeing the complexities of the issues, worrying about the future. A fourth reason is that significant change has the potential to disrupt the present balance of power, leading to uncertainty and ambiguity. A young person may be silently wrestling with a myriad of changes, from a disappointment in the difference between expectation and performance; changes of friends or schools; changes in parental expectations; separation of parents; serious illnesses in the family; changes in financial situations and so forth.

According to Buescher, "Young adolescents, those between the age of 11 and 15, seem to be particularly vulnerable to the confusion and misinterpretation precipitated by their outstanding abilities." The adolescent's changes in body and its image and changes in relationships, as well as tension between performance and expectation, the push and pull of competing expectations, low tolerance for ambiguity and the quest for immediate identity all affect how change is not only perceived but coped with.

Coping and Acting or "Shell Building'

With the heightened sensitivity of capable young people comes a vivid awareness that things are not as they have been. They quickly discover that other people cannot cope with "change" and so they may "act" to pretend that massive changes have not taken place. Only then do those around them feel comfortable. For example, a child caught between parents in a bitter divorce may pretend that nothing is happening in order to protect the mother or father. This protection of parents is true for many children, not just the gifted. Others, the "grown ups" or the "experts," have difficulty coming to grips with the change and its repercussions, and so the charade continues. The inference is that life goes on in just the same way. The young person continues to reinforce the notion that those about them reinforce, so the change gets buried deeper and deeper. Puzzlement as to what is really wrong grows and the young person becomes further confused, sometimes unable to cope with the fact that life is no longer the same. The self-concept becomes diminished and underachievement may be induced, perpetuating the problem.

How Can You Help Young People to Cope with Change?
Acknowledging change through ritual

Robbins speaks of the value of rituals, ceremony, story and symbolism dealing with transitions. These elements can be used with capable young people to assist them to come to terms with change. For example, among certain tribal groups in many parts of the world, as well as in some religions, ceremonies that mark the beginning of adolescence help the young person to make the transition between childhood and adulthood. Birthday celebrations, debutante balls or graduations also mark such rites of passage. Likewise, ceremonies are held to mark the birth of a child, marriage or a death. Parents and teachers can plan activities that acknowledge such changes. Judith Duerk in her book, *A Circle of Stones*, offers the following:

How might it have been different for you if, on your first menstrual day, your mother had given you a bouquet of flowers and taken you to lunch, and then the two of you had gone to meet your father at the jeweler, where your ears were pierced, and your father bought you your first pair of earrings, and then you went with a few of your friends and your mother's friends to get your first lip coloring;
and then you went, for the very first time,
to the Women's Lodge,
to learn
the wisdom of the women?
How might your life be different?

Activities such as camps, that ask young people to test themselves in difficult, but controlled conditions; use of myths, legends or biographies of individuals that deal with transitions; or studying ceremonies of change in various religions or cultural groups could be useful in helping young adolescents cope with the physical, emotional, cognitive and social changes they are all experiencing. Asking the young person or group of young people how they might like to mark a passage could also be an option.

Changing perceptions

To a given person, something that seems small to others can loom quite large. One 16-year-old had moved to another city recently. On her first day of school she had carefully selected a red print shirt and red gym shoes to go with her jeans. She came home in tears because her shoes had been noticed ("Nice shoes, Amanda!") and everyone else was wearing joggers or boots. She felt that she had failed her "acceptance test." To help her put the event into proportion, she might be helped to see the humor in the situation once the feelings are acknowledged ("What will you tell your grandchildren about your red shoes?"). However, it is important that the young person not feel that humor is being used at his or her expense. Talking about it with a caring teacher and small group of peers who share an embarrassment they experienced where small seemed enormous could also be useful.

Part of the problem with change is perceiving a loss of control. Sometimes rehearsing what is going to happen during a change can make a gifted young person feel more in control. For example, if a student is very stressed about going to a new school, perhaps a visit to that school ahead of time, making friends with a student at that school before classes begin, or talking through what it might be like can help.

Changing Belief Systems

We see people as we expect them to be. Perception of others is very much an active, constructive process, in which the perceiver's knowledge and past experiences are sometimes more important than the actual characteristics of the person to be judged. Others may judge the same person quite differently. In other words, beauty (or any other characteristic) is in the eye of the beholder and self-fulfilling prophesies may become a reality.

An example of this has to do with expectations. In an experiment, teachers were told that a group of randomly selected children were very bright. They had high expectations for these students and anticipated that they would do well. At the end of the year, these students showed a real gain of over 10 points in IQ testing. This is proof of the power of the attitude of the teacher on the outcome and development of students. Likewise, if students are perceived negatively, if they are judged for their overexcite-abilities, their intensity, perfectionism or sensitivity, their difficulties may be compounded.

When gifted students violate behavioral or academic expectations and are graded lower, they may begin the self-fulfilling prophecy of underachievement. If criticism, real or implied, is directed at the young girl who becomes anorexic or the boy who misbehaves out of boredom, such perceptions may make the situation worse.

If a student believes that a teacher doesn't like him, or that she is being picked on, the likelihood is that this may happen. Believing that a change will be a problem is also likely to lead to difficulties. For example, feeling like others won't like you before entering a new school or believing that you are hopeless at math can lead to fulfillment of those expectations. Helping teachers and parents to develop realistic expectations as well as assisting a student to change perceptions could be very useful. One particularly useful strategy is using DeBono's Six Hats or lateral thinking strategies to consider the situation (see pp. 176-178).

Dealing with Power Relationships

Gifted young people are often powerful young people (as are many of their average peers), wanting to be in control of themselves and their worlds, as we learned in "Giftedness." One area that provokes difficulty is when they are given little control over their learning experiences or their personal forms of expression. What happens when an extremely creative and intelligent young person must conform to what he or she considers to be stupid assignments or ridiculous rules? For example, consider the student who is graded lower on a writing assignment because she took an unusual point of view (although she addressed the requirements) or the student who is not admitted to class because he is wearing a cap, not permitted in the school policy. All of the personality characteristics of bright young people come to the fore. Feelings of pain, shame and anger can lead to withdrawal or passivity, or they can lead to explosive outbursts in self-defense that compound the problem, particularly if students believe they have been humiliated in front of peers. Incidents like these may lead to self-doubt and the lowering of self-esteem as they try find ways to cope with their stress.

Young people need to feel that they have some say in their own education (and their lives) and that they are not being judged. When adolescents are given little or no choice in school and are treated with what they consider to be a disregard of their personhood, they may rebel or do worse, and become depressed. At least in rebellion, students empower themselves with their anger. In depression, their feelings of self-blame and shame are turned inward with sometimes tragic results. What can teachers do to avoid power and control conflicts with capable young people?

What You Can Do to Help

Several strategies are available to teachers. The simplest is to recognize the young person's need to exert some control and permit him or her to do so. Choices of assignments, instruction at the appropriate level and rate, helping students to become independent learners, listening to students and respecting them are obvious ways to empower students.

Expand choices rather than limit options

A young person may feel his or her needs are not being considered and there is no freedom of choice; for example, a grade 7 student given no decisions about school courses after considerable opportunity to select topics in elementary school may feel that the school is oppressive. If at all possible, some choices of courses can make for less difficulty. A choice between two or three languages, or a choice of drama, music or fine arts are possibilities. If choice of subjects is not a possibility, then teachers can give some options for assignments within a course or can accept creative interpretations of an assignment.

Teach them to be autonomous learners

Students do not necessarily know how to function as independent learners although they may wish to do so. Some young people may even be reluctant to start a project because they do not know how to go about it. They think that somehow they're already supposed to know it before they have had instruction. Programs are needed to encourage autonomy in which students learn how to establish their own goals, select a topic, conduct appropriate research, organize time and materials, and so forth. An excellent model for helping students to become autonomous learners is that of George Betts, which focuses on a series of specific activities to help students become independent learners.

Level the playing field

Teachers, by virtue of their position, are automatically in a power relationship with students because they assess student work. The threat of poor grades for a student who does not comply is sometimes enough to force a disinterested student to meet requirements, especially if the consequences are perceived as considerable and important by the student. On the other hand, if a student does poorly, it may really be an evaluation of ourselves as teachers. If the purpose is to have students learn the information in our course, we fail if a student does not do so.

We can begin by asking ourselves the reasons for lack of success. If we suspect that a student does poorly because of boredom or disinterest, how can we engage him or her? What options can we offer in terms of accepting different types of products that demonstrate mastery of material and at the same time, relate to student interests? Perhaps the student has other serious problems with which she is trying to cope, such as jobless parents or a serious illness in the family. A private discussion with offers of support and the opportunity to redo weak or missing assignments may be in order.

Students can also assess their own work using scoring guides or rubrics (these should be explicit at the beginning of a unit), or on their own criteria. Effort and how much the information has been integrated and related to other knowledge are useful standards. If the student's self-grade is more than one grade different from the mark the teacher considers appropriate, could the student have the opportunity to redo assignments and improve the mark?

Some gifted young people avoid taking classes designed for brighter students because they fear that their grades will be adversely affected. If students who are accustomed to earning A's are marked on a curve, they may be wise to do so. What would happen if you were to say, "I expect everyone to earn an "A" in this class"? The likelihood is that you would get what you expected. What would happen if you tried this idea with a general group of students? (See the section "Changing Belief Systems," p. 159-160).

Who does the adapting?

Adaptation should be a two-way street. Parents and students often feel that schools expect young people to do all the adapting. They are expected to change themselves and conform to a myriad of requirements and policies, sometimes confusing and sometimes downright arbitrary or even wrong for them from the students" viewpoint. Can the school also do some adapting to meet the needs of the student? For example, if a very gifted student is doing 11th grade work in a graphic arts, perhaps he could use his great passion for and knowledge of computers to do computer graphics, rather than work with a pen like most of his classmates. Can the eighth grade girl who is making a puppet have her unusual puppet design accepted, although it is not from the pattern the teacher provided?

> *"The reasonable man adapts to the world around him. The unreasonable man expects the world to adapt itself to him. Therefore, all progress is made by unreasonable men."*
> —George Bernard Shaw

Could you accept and even encourage students to discuss with you ways of better addressing their needs? Could students politely request that you turn to face the class before talking when writing on the board, for example, to meet an auditory learning style? Could they suggest an alternative assignment if they have already learned the material? Could students be placed in classes in which student learning style and the style of teaching are matched? For example, some students may have a linear sequential style and prefer teachers who are very explicit about exactly what is expected and in what order. Others who are big picture thinkers may prefer a teacher who allows considerable freedom in selecting topics and choosing the form in which it is to be expressed.

Pick your battles

All of us need to pick our battles or our efforts are dissipated and our energies go to trying to control too many unimportant things. In school, some policies and requirements are non-negotiables, such as school starting time, consideration of others, school discipline policies, or state test dates. Others are more flexible. If a student acknowledges a deadline for an assignment, showing you the 14 pages already completed and requests one additional day to finish copying the rough draft, can you give her the extension, knowing that most other projects will be only five or six pages maximum? Likewise, is it so important that a student attend every physics class if she has the opportunity to "shadow" a famous judge every Friday, a career she is seriously considering?

Help in owning problems

Many of us have difficulty admitting we have a problem or we made a mistake. Owning up to our problems may be particularly hard for highly sensitive perfectionists. Often, there is an attack on someone else or putting the blame outside ourselves, sometimes with vehemence, in order to protect the fragile, sensitive person on the inside. Surprisingly, sometimes the most sensitive may appear to be brusque, insensitive to others or downright vulgar, a shell put on to protect the self from pain anticipated or inflicted by others. Owning responsibility is a sign of maturity. If a student neglects homework to watch TV, can she feel safe enough to admit it and to live with the consequences? Class discussion about owning responsibility can be a starter. Sometimes it's easier to write about a particular incident than say it. Learning to say "I'm sorry" or "I made a mistake" is a step to be applauded.

Sometimes this is an issue of winners or losers. There is a belief that if someone is to be right, the other person must be wrong. Helping students find ways to solve problems so that both sides win is a useful strategy. Several self-help books on the topic may be helpful, both for the teacher and the student.

Address concerns and reward the positives

A group of very able students at a large high school were asked what could be done to make school a better place for them. They came up with several very sound suggestions for the administration to consider:

1. Allow us to use the computer room and library at lunch and after school. We want to do our best.
2. Give each subject a testing day, for example, math on Monday, Science on Tuesday, and so forth. Because we are here from early morning for band, theater and orchestra practice until late at night for sport, we need to plan our study time. We feel so stressed when everything gets piled on us at once.
3. Recognize our accomplishments. Honor our achievements in assemblies or over the loud speaker like you honor the athletes or musicians.
4. Let us earn privileges, like an open lunch once a month if we have earned all As and Bs and have no unexcused absences or latenesses.
5. Above all, show that you respect us and care about us as individuals. A hello in the corridors is appreciated, as is interest in our concerns or willingness to discuss our problems.

Help them to understand the rules of the game

Parents and teachers may typically overestimate the degree of cooperation they will get from capable young people in managing their lives. "I don't understand why our son isn't happy. We've sent him to the best school, but he doesn't seem to want to do the work. He says he hates it, but he did so well at his other school." This problem may arise because of confusion: Young people may not know what is required of them and may feel helpless, a "lesser being," with nothing in their experience that assists them to know what to do. They simply do not know "the rules of the game." Their family and friends are perhaps equally bewildered.

Other young people who perhaps are better at sizing up these rules from the context of their environment may not have such difficulties. For example, Adrianne, a new student at a large middle school, was not particularly good at academics, but she knew the names of all the teachers, their room numbers and their reputations within the first week of school. She remembered all her classmates" names almost immediately, knew who has been absent in class, for how many days and whether they had brought an absence note. She also knew who liked whom, where the important "hang-outs" were, what she had to do in each teacher's room to get by. She picked up a great deal of information from the environment that many others simply do not.

Dealing with the "game" very explicitly may help. For example, the school might have older students assigned as peer support for younger students to answer questions about the "unwritten school rules." Classes on personal development and coping could be offered as a setting where such issues can be discussed. Class meetings, advocated by several authorities on classroom management, would be excellent forums for such discussion, as would student advisory periods. Asking students to try to observe the unstated rules of the game at school and share these with each other could be a tactic. Implicit rules, such as not humiliating a teacher in front of the class when the teacher is wrong, not saying things in anger that may come back to haunt you or recognizing that certain styles of dress influence those around you could be topics. Techniques, like how to politely disagree, how to tell when humor hurts instead of being funny, or how you say it is as important as what you say can be suggested. Perhaps making a scroll, an "unwritten constitution" might be a fun way for a group of young people to try to work out the hidden agendas and implicit rules.

Use the "language of caring"

The words we use profoundly influence the tone of our classrooms. When we use "Please walk" (a preference statement) instead of "Don't run!" or (in private) "My purpose in talking with you today is to let you know that I expect you to be on time from now on," (a purpose statement) rather than "You're late! Next time it's a detention." we show respect for the other person and diffuse hostility. Students, likewise, can learn to use preference statements, purpose statements and impact previews or reviews. These are processes of planning and practicing for experiences. For example, if a student is to have a job or university interview, we might ask, "How might you be effective in getting your strengths noticed?" Or, if a student wants to initiate a talent show at school, we might role play how she could discuss the idea with a school administrator.

Discuss outer conformity, inner control

Students can be helped to realize that "external conformity, inner control" is a possibility through an understanding of consequences and making conscious choices. For example, if an eighth grade student wants to get a skinhead haircut and brings this up in class, it might be helpful to consider the possible reactions, both at school and in the general community. On the other hand, if he conforms on the outside through a conscious decision to do so, he can have inner control. Talking with the young person, either individually or with peers, and asking him to think about consequences is a benefit, as long as value judgments are not made for or about him.

"If you have a skinhead haircut, how will your classmates react? What do you think your teachers might do? Is there a difference in the way a store owner treats skinheads and other kids? Are you prepared to live with it for at least two months until it grows out enough to have a change?" Values can also be explained. What does being a skinhead say about your beliefs? Do you want to be associated with people who share beliefs that denigrate certain groups of people?

Rather than getting into a power struggle, the young person can be given the opportunity to consider repercussions and make the choice to exercise inner control. If he still decides to go ahead with the haircut, he will have to live with the consequences.

Parental intrusion and the use of power and authority over schoolwork, grades and assignments should be avoided. Handing over responsibility and control of success and failure in this arena enables students to make choices providing there is a clear understanding of consequences, such as not getting into a university of their choice. Such an autonomous approach allows the student to deal with external expectations by the use of inner control.

Dealing with Feeling Different

Many people, especially in early adolescence, do not want to be perceived as being different. For bright young people who equate intelligent behaviors as making them different, this is a particular difficulty. The problems are compounded when there are perceivable differences, such as physical disabilities or cultural differences. Yet differences do exist and acknowledging that everyone is different and has different needs frees students from the tyranny of trying to be the same.

What You Can Do to Help

♦ Set a climate of caring and acceptance for everyone.
♦ Be sensitive to and aware of singling out a student. Academically gifted students often become teachers" favorites and they pay a price for it with their peers. The other students may become jealous or the singled out student may be picked on.
♦ Recognize different learning needs and offer instruction appropriate to each student. For example, a boy who masters a second language very rapidly and is bored to distraction with the slow pace of the class might be offered an opportunity to use his skills in writing a letter to a pen pal in another country rather than repeating phrases with his classmates that he mastered long ago.
♦ Allow students to tell you their needs and to suggest alternative assignments that meet them. For example, if a student has already mastered linear equations, instead of

doing the pages assigned to the class, she might ask to do a research project that involves use of linear equations in her analysis.

♦ Have a unit in English or Social Studies that focuses on the positive aspects of differences, perhaps even as a theme. Use biographies of famous or popular individuals who overcame difficulties to contribute to society.

♦ Help the student to develop an awareness of what is required for both keeping their creative personalities intact and for getting along with others. This may be accomplished through discussions with other able students and through observing what works for popular peers and "trying on" some of the tactics. One bright 13 year old asked her classmates, "What do I have to do to be less of a nerd?" She followed through on some of their suggestions (dressed like they did, smiled more, changed her hairstyle) and was amazed at the change in receptiveness to her. It is important here to remember "outer conformity, inner control".

♦ Discuss vulnerabilities in a climate of trust and safety: "Sticks and stones can break my bones, but names really hurt me."

Developing Social Skills

As we described in "Teaching for Coping," the area of self-concept where gifted young people have the greatest difficulty is in relationship to peers. Although they may cope quite successfully with peers in settings other than the regular classroom, such as with neighbors or in a youth group, as well as in special programs for gifted students, they may have difficulty in dealing with their normal peers in the school setting. Feeling like a "dork" or an outcast is a common problem. In fact, in one study, "nearly every young adolescent … identified the peer group as the major source of stress in life." In Judy Gailbraith's "Eight Great Gripes of Gifted Kids," four of the eight gripes have to do with social relationship problems. Here are some ideas that teachers can use to help these young people feel better about their abilities to relate to age peers.

What You Can Do to Help

♦ Help students to find compatible peers by grouping by interest or ability at least part of the time. If students have opportunities to work with others who share interests or skills, they can develop relationships with others more likely to become friends. Groupings should be flexible and change with activities and learning tasks.

♦ Use co-operative learning activities to teach students how to work together. Learning to listen attentively and paraphrase, be a leader and a follower, support others" ideas, take different roles or look for strengths in others are all important skills, but too often neglected in the assumption that students already have them. Model such interactions, discuss roles and mediate until a group can function successfully independently. Co-operative learning really means learning through working with others. It does not mean rigidly grouping students (one bright, two average, one slow). Be careful of assigning marks based on the work of the whole group, as the brighter student too often ends up doing all the work and feeling angry and helpless.

♦ Vary groupings. Do not always allow students to select their groups, as the more reticent or the less socially competent can be made to feel even more unwanted. Mix and match students occasionally.

♦ Notice the young people who are not usually included. Consider possible friendships and seat such students near friendly, socially-adept students or put them together in work groups, being careful to avoid grouping isolates with each other.

♦ Have discussions about being friends. Include moral issues, such as what to do when a friend does something dangerous (taking drugs, threatening suicide), wants you to do things you do not believe are right (underage drinking, smoking, stealing), or maintaining old friendships when your social circle changes. Have students write about having or being a good friend.

♦ Use sociodramas, role-playing, or simulations to deal with social situations wherein students can think about solutions to social difficulties without having the real problem pressing on them. They can observe how another person resolves a situation, as well as learn to "step into someone else's shoes" through switching roles.

♦ Discuss the notion of giving and finding grace—the idea that we are all vulnerable and all want to feel good about ourselves. How can we learn to accept ourselves and others? Model and lead by example.

♦ Ask students to notice qualities in others they would like to have for themselves. Suggest telling the person what you admire about them: "I really like your enthusiasm in P.E. It keeps me wanting to help the team." Ask them to try to notice things about people you think they would like to have noticed and say it. "Is that a new shirt? It's a great color."

♦ Ask students to examine qualities they dislike in others and search themselves for those same qualities. Have students ask why they dislike those qualities so much in themselves and think about how that affects their viewpoint of others. If a student dislikes people who are shy, for example, maybe she hides her own shyness.

Using Creative Thinking Strategies

Teachers can use creative and critical thinking skills for dealing with social and emotional issues, rather than limiting these skills to academic content. Such techniques and heuristics can help young people develop a broader range of coping strategies. Having such a "bag of tricks" to apply as needed allows the student to consider options in systematic ways. The following tables show some of the creative and critical thinking skills that can be used to tackle solving personal problems as well as the more typical cognitive ones.

Creative Thinking Skills	**Critical Thinking Skills**
♦ Fluency	♦ Classification
♦ Flexibility	♦ Comparison
♦ Originality	♦ Patterning
♦ Elaboration	♦ Sequencing

- ♦ Brainstorming
- ♦ Modification
- ♦ Imagery
- ♦ Associative thinking
- ♦ Creative problem solving
- ♦ Attribute listing
- ♦ Synectics
- ♦ Forced relationships
- ♦ Lateral thinking

- ♦ Cause and effect
- ♦ Labeling
- ♦ Observation
- ♦ Webbing
- ♦ Logical thinking
- ♦ Bloom's Taxonomy
- ♦ Planning
- ♦ Hypothesizing
- ♦ CoRT (PMI and CAF)
- ♦ Inferences
- ♦ Predicting
- ♦ Decision making
- ♦ Inductive reasoning
- ♦ Deductive reasoning
- ♦ Dilemmas
- ♦ Thinking errors

A few of these strategies will be described as applied to dealing with social or emotional difficulties and finding alternative coping strategies. An excellent source book for a variety of thinking strategies is *Developing Minds*, by Art Costa (1992). Other useful materials are described in "References.'

What is Synectics?

Synectics (from the Greek word synecticos) means the "joining together of apparently unrelated elements." The synectics process was developed by William J. J. Gordon, who identified the thinking strategies that creative people use unconsciously, and put these strategies into a form that could be used by all people. Synectics is a creative problem solving process that uses analogies and metaphors.

The two main principles involved are:

making the strange familiar
making the familiar strange

Students can use analogy and metaphor to solve familiar problems in new ways and to create new and unusual uses for familiar ideas and materials, or they can use synectics to make new or unfamiliar ideas and materials and problems meaningful.

Synectics gives students the opportunity to work cooperatively, gain empathy and to see problems in different ways. A stated problem is solved in a round-about way, through a process that takes the students further and further away from the original problem and finally leads them back to it, having gained more understanding of the problem as well as ways of solving it.

Provide opportunities for students to become confident in using *metaphors, forced relationships, direct analogies, personal analogies* and *compressed conflict* (see activities that follow). When they are feeling comfortable in using all of the above processes then you can finally attempt the complete synectics process.

The Synectics Process: A Step-by-Step Guide to Using Synectics in the Classroom

Step 1: Warm-up

Teacher poses warm-up questions to start students thinking.
For example: *Why is a table like the sky?*
Which is faster, jealousy or an ant? Why?
How is crying like an apple?

Step 2: Presentation of the problem

Student states a problem.
"Nobody will hang out with me at lunch-time."
"I can't get my parents off my case."

Step 3: Students identify with the problem

Students discuss their own experiences related to the problem.
"I'm always the last one picked for a team."
"Kids won't talk to me outside of class."
"My parents won't let me go anywhere by myself and I'm 13 years old!"

Step 4: Students create a direct analogy

Teacher asks the students to compare the problem to something else. If it is an abstract problem compare it with something concrete; if it is organic compare it with something inorganic.

"What animal is this problem like?"
"What piece of furniture is this problem like?"
"What machine is this problem like?"
List students" answers on the board. Gradually erase the original suggestions until you are left with one analogy. When students start getting excited go on to the next step.

Step 5: Students create a personal analogy

Teacher asks the students to choose a direct analogy and to make it personal. Ask them to be the thing. Then they can describe or act out how they feel, look and behave as the thing.

"You thought that the problem is like an apple with a worm in it. Imagine you are that apple. How do you feel? What do you do?"

Step 6: Students create a compressed conflict

The teacher identifies key words from students" personal analogies and writes them up on the board so that there are two columns of opposites, for example positive feelings and negative feelings.

As an apple you felt:

unwanted	*necessary*
frustrated	*excited*
tired	*alert*

Step 7: Students create a new direct analogy

The teacher asks the students to use compressed conflicts as the basis for a new direct analogy.

"Let's choose from these pairs and discover a new direct analogy. What is an example of an unwanted necessity?"

Step 8: Students return to the original problem

The teacher directs the students back to the original problem and they apply the new direct analogy to finding solutions.

"An example of unwanted necessity is having an injection. When you are having your injection you think of all of the benefits that the injection will provide you with, you distract yourself by thinking of something else or by talking to the nurse, and that it will only hurt for a short time. Maybe when no-one will hang out with you, you can think of the benefits of being by yourself—no-one can argue with you, you can invent interesting games in your head, you can prac-

tice shooting baskets. Or you can engage yourself by reading a book, going to the library or computer room, or talking to a teacher."

Forced Relationships

The method of forcing relationships "is an associative thinking activity which helps develop the ability to see unusual uses for things and the combination of things from different viewpoints". There are four main approaches:

Listing Techniques
1. A problem is presented to the students.
2. A list of unrelated objects is suggested by the students or the teacher (this can be done before Step 1).
3. The students take each object on the list in turn and associate it with the problem.
4. After all relationships have been suggested, the students go back through the list and mark the ideas as plus or minus and suggest whether the ideas should be changed, developed or implemented.

Following is an example of a Forced Relationship technique using the above method: Problem—*'Bored in class.'*

List	Freely Associated Responses	Evaluation
magazine	Take magazines to class for diversion	+
grass	Think about lying under a tree on a grassy hillside and watching clouds float by.	+
oil	Give the teacher castor oil and watch him gag.	-
ice	Have an ice-cream after school to reward yourself for putting up with it.	+

Catalogue Techniques
1. The problem is stated.
2. The objects to be used in association with the problem solution are picked randomly from a catalogue. The student can use any object seen in the catalogue as a solution to the problem. Continue as for "Listing Techniques".

Focused Relationships
1. Problem is stated.
2. A list of objects is presented that has some relevance to the problem.

3. The relationship of the objects to the problem is freely associated, one object at a time.
4. Evaluation of the solutions occurs as above.

Arbitrary Forced Relationships
1. There is no problem presented.
2. A list of words, objects or ideas is presented.
3. Two or more objects are selected at random and forced together. Ideas can be created and developed using this technique.

Below are types of arbitrary forced relationships exercises:

The Fishbowl Game

Fill a fishbowl with slips of paper. On the paper write the names of randomly chosen objects. The student pulls out 2 slips of paper, reads the names of the objects and forces them together to create a new idea or object. (This can also be done using 3 slips of paper.)

Dictionary Game

Student closes eyes, opens dictionary and points to a word. The word is written on the board. The procedure is repeated. The two words are forced together to create something new.

Random Choice

Teacher presents students with a list of objects. Students close their eyes and check two items on the list. Students create a new idea or product from the items (This can be done with 3 items after practice.).

*DeBono's Six Hats

Another type of creative thinking strategy useful for application to social and emotional difficulties is DeBono's Six Hats. This strategy is especially useful because it allows the student to step out of adversarial, argumentative or analytic cause-effect thinking to parallel thinking, by developing multiple perspectives on the topic. Too often, analysis is an excellent but inadequate tool to solve the problem, as it is not always possible to find the causes and eliminate them. By dealing with the different ways of thinking separately and then bringing them together to focus on the problem, active perception is involved, allowing the seeing of patterns. Not only is the strategy faster (2 minutes per hat to generate many ideas), but it unlocks multiple perspectives and opens up various possibilities for coping. The hats are applied to the problem as follows:

"I feel like an idiot because I never seem to say the right thing."

Feelings

Permission to put forward feelings, intuitions, hunches, emotions with no justifications.
Example: I feel that whatever I say never comes out how I want it.

RED HAT

Weaknesses; Critical Judgment

What is wrong with this? Judges whether something fits or not to facts, experiences, systems, policies, ethics, values.

Danger: Overuse. Be cautious.
Example: It inhibits me from doing many things that I would like to do.

BLACK HAT

Data and Information: What Are the Facts?

Look at what information is available, the nature of that information, availability, what is missing, how to collect it.
Example: People don't tell me that I say the wrong things. I criticize myself. I don't talk much at school.

WHITE HAT

Logical Positive: The Strengths

Benefits, values, feasibility—the reasons why. (Harder than black hat. Much effort needed.)
Example: I don't say a lot of stupid things, so people can't use my words against me.

YELLOW HAT

Creative Effort

GREEN HAT

New ideas, further alternatives, possibilities; playing around with provocations, hypotheses, speculations, changes.

Example: Speak with people I don't see frequently to get into the habit of talking to people.

Process Control

BLUE HAT

Thinking, metacognition, managing the process

Example: The first thing I'm going to try is to make an effort to be friendly and not block people out because of my worries.

By applying these different thinking strategies to personal difficulties or to problems they face in the world, capable young people can find other options to help them cope. Another technique is to use metacognition as a tool to help in thinking about how one solves one's problems. This is the topic of the next section.

Using Metacognition

Metacognition: What is It?

The Greek term, *meta*, means "beyond or transcendent" and the Latin, *cognition*, means "knowing." Thus, metacognition means "transcending knowing," or "awareness of knowing." Metacognition, then, refers to the awareness of one's thinking processes. It includes the ability to discern what one knows and doesn't know, and to deal with the knowledge about one's cognitive processes and products. In short, metacognition is the state where a person is conscious of his or her thinking and problem solving while thinking. Although not everyone develops this type of awareness, students are helped to do so by reflecting on their processing. Metacognition is also a developmental phenomenon more associated with adolescent thought.

Metacognition has two aspects: the control of both knowledge and procedures as well as the monitoring and interpreting of ongoing experience. Control involves thinking about what one knows and how to plan or manage it. This entails "our ability to plan a strategy for producing what information is needed, to be conscious of our own steps and strategies during the act of problem solving, and to reflect on and evaluate the productivity of our own thinking." The control aspect of metacognition includes understanding and selecting strategies among a repertoire of tactics, which are carried out in the service of some cognitive objective or goal. The monitoring and interpreting of ongoing experience includes self-questioning, predicting the consequences of actions or events, checking on time and space, and reality testing which involves comparing subjective impressions to more objective criteria.

Metacognitive processes enable individuals to better control their thinking and thereby become more efficient and flexible learners. The more knowledge students have about their abilities and learning strategies, the more able they are in acquiring knowledge and skill. Metacognitive knowledge is crucial in the selection and implementation of problem solving strategies. The more accurately young people understand their own processes, the more likely they will be to use this knowledge in understanding the value of newly acquired strategies, thus incorporating their representations into their long-term memory. Students who have advanced metacognitive knowledge are more likely to deal with instructional gaps, developing appropriate strategies to achieve a goal. Therefore, as metacognition increases and the awareness of processing strategies improves, so should performance in a greater variety of situations.

Metacognition as a Social Coping Device

Metacognition can be a useful tool to help students become aware of their coping strategies related to their social and emotional processing. Flavell, a developmental psychologist working in the area of learning, made the suggestion that metacognition is not only related to school learning but is also linked to social cognition. He interprets social cognitive enterprises as consisting of

"all intellectual endeavors in which the aim is to think or learn about social or psychological processes in the self, individual others, or human groups of all sizes and kinds (including social organizations, nations and "people in general") ... It could also be

the social interactions and relationships that occur among individuals, groups, nations and other social entities."

To be able to regulate aspects of social cognition, a degree of objectivity is required. Thus the metacognitive component of monitoring social cognition keeps track of how the cognitive enterprise fares as well as taking the correct intervention measures needed to deal with the social aspects. There are four classes of phenomena for monitoring social-cognitive enterprises. These are: *metacognitive knowledge, metacognitive* experiences (these occur when one is required to do a good deal of deliberate conscious social thinking, occurring before, during or after a social cognitive enterprise), *goals* (or tasks) and *actions* (strategies).

The term *metaesthesis* perhaps better characterizes this idea of metacognition as applied to the affect because aesthesis means "feeling" or "sensing" in Greek. A term that transcends both of these notions and deals with the grasping of consciousness, that awareness behind both cognition and affect, is *metapignosis.* Tom Harvey, a high school sophomore, thinks about his feelings. He is clearly aware of his processing:

Feelings are the waves inside my head,
Swelling, tickling.
As thoughts pass,
The ripples turn to waves
And a violent storm arises.
Thoughts are tossed to and fro
Through the anarchy,
But seldom will you see
The white-capped emotion
Appear on the surface.
The sea can be very deceiving.
I look up at the surface
Searching for an opening,
For a dim ray of light.
The water clears, sparkles silver.
I swim upwards,
Figures appear.
I break the surface gasping,
The loneliness ceases,
Confidence returns.
The sea lies acquiescent.

Several strategies are suggested that can help students become aware of their internal processing related to coping. Some involve helping them to use *inner dialogue*, a sort of talking to oneself inside one's head. Others involve use of other languages of thought, including imagery, spatial learning strategies and kinesthetic processing. In terms of coping, asking students to reflect on their processing of how they deal with difficulties can help them to consider other alternatives.

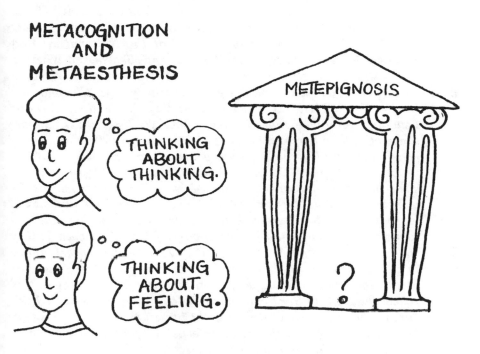

Suggested Strategies for Inner Dialogue

Below are several strategies that can assist in helping the student become aware of his or her inner dialogue. Direct teaching about metacognition (or metapignosis) may actually inhibit productive thought in young people. The techniques suggested elicit metacognition indirectly, with the exception of "images of wide scope." These strategies are arranged developmentally by categories. Some deal with thinking about thinking. Others focus on thinking about feeling.

Modeling

Modeling is a highly recommended technique to encourage inner dialogue. Sitting at a computer with a group of students around her, a teacher might model inner dialogue in the writing of a letter to a teacher in another state about setting up pen pal exchange. It might go like this: *"Let's see. I met Sue Brody at the National Teachers of Writing Convention last year. When I suggested that our classes become pen pals she seemed eager to do so. Since I haven't written to her before, I guess I should remind her of our meeting at the convention. It was in Chicago, wasn't it ? Here's her address. I'll put the heading on now* (puts on heading). *Dear Sue, Last October we met in Chicago at the National Writing Teachers Convention. No that's the National Teachers of Writing Convention* (changes it). *I should make it more friendly. Maybe it should say, "I had the pleasure of meeting you in Chicago last October at the National Teachers of Writing Convention." Perhaps I should remind her what we talked about. We discussed the importance of kids understanding what life is like in different parts of America as well as getting into a heavy conversation about the problems kids have to cope with nowadays. I should write that so she remembers me.* (writes similar). *Now, what was my purpose in wanting to set up this exchange? I know I want my students to learn about life in a big city. It would also be great for my students to make new friends and get perspectives from others on how they solve problems. Hmm, instead of waiting for her response, I'll have my class write pen pal letters about themselves and their interests. Maybe they could pose some of the difficulties we're having in this school that kids in Sue's class could help solve to get us started. It's sure to get greater commitment to the project than just sending my letter. Hmm, I wonder if she's on Internet. I'll give her our electronic address, so she can answer back electronically."*

The students can see how we think and write in a recursive fashion, modifying our written product through inner dialogue as well as planning both the letter and strategies to get the pen pal exchange started.

Explaining Problem Solving Steps

Having students explain their problem solving steps is another idea. Math problems are a good starting point. A student might stand at the blackboard and explain how she solved an algebra

MISTAKES ARE THE BEST WAY TO LEARN.

problem, talking through the steps while doing it. Other students could be invited to share different ways they found solutions, in order to encourage flexible thinking. Alternatively, the teacher can also circulate and listen to individual students while the class is doing seat work. Or, pair students and have them explain their steps to each other. When used as a technique for coping with problems, this pairing strategy might be a first step. What might you do first, second, and third to deal with peer pressure, for example? Group sharing can follow. The climate in the classroom should be supportive to let a student comfortably expose his or her thoughts. To take the risk, the student must know that it is safe to make mistakes and that we learn from errors rather than being penalized for them. Fear of failure inhibits good thinking.

Related to this idea, ask young people to describe where they are in a problem solving sequence, what steps they have covered, what pathways and dead ends they have encountered on their way to solution. This could be done in pairs or small groups, using images as well as words to describe the paths to a solution. A fun activity to accompany a research report might be a "mind map" that documents this experience. By sharing with others, students realize that there are many possible pathways to an end point as well as verbalizing their inner dialogue.

Questioning Techniques

Teach students self-questioning skills, particularly for reading comprehension. Model this self-questioning, having students follow in a text. Use questioning templates such as Who is? What is? When is? Where is? and encourage students to formulate questions for themselves prior to and during reading. In addition to its application to reading, posing questions is a form of inner dialogue requisite for inquiry and for creative thought. It can also be very useful in developing alternatives for coping with a problem. For example, if the problem is feeling depressed, asking oneself when it arose, how often it happens, who is involved, what alternatives there are might be productive in getting to the root of the problem.

Encouraging the class to listen to each others" questions, "piggyback" (associate ideas to those put forth) on them, and have their own self-questions even though someone else may have the floor, encourages inner dialogue. Simply providing three to five seconds of wait time after we ask a question allows students to create dialogue in their heads before answering. And of course, asking questions when we don't know the answer will be much more likely to engender real thinking and inner dialog than "guess my rule, I have the answers" questions. For example, "How do you remember things?" would likely spark lively discussion as well as provide multiple strategies to consider.

Pair Problem Solving
Another effective strategy is "pair problem solving." One student is designated the listener, while the other solves the problem aloud. The listener's job is to promote dialogue, asking for the next step, paraphrasing for understanding, requesting clarification, suggesting another direction and continually checking for accuracy, but not giving the answer. Then the roles switch. Eventually, the external dialogue becomes interiorized. Students have a dialogue with themselves as they listen to a discussion or read to themselves without the need for the external listener to be prompting dialogue. This technique could be beneficial in dealing with stresses, especially after practice with more academic problems that have known solutions. For example, students could try pair-problem solving to work out a difficulty about dealing with peers, or a morality issue.

Witness to Invention
A fifth technique is to use Perkins" "witness to invention" strategy. Perkins, a professor at Harvard, believes that we can eavesdrop on the inner dialogue used in the process of thinking or creating. Students can do this in pairs, the listener sitting beside the creator and prompting on principles 2, 3 and 5, but especially 2 (below), saying "What are you thinking now?" if the creator does not talk. There are six principles for a complete record:
1. 'Say whatever's on your mind. Don't hold back hunches, wild ideas, images, intentions.

2. Speak as continuously as possible. Say something at least once every five seconds, even if only, "I'm drawing a blank."

3. Speak audibly. Watch out for your voice dropping as you become involved.

To discourage over-explanation:

4. Speak as telegraphically as you please. Don't worry about complete sentences and eloquence.

5. Don't over-explain or justify. Analyze no more than you would normally.

6. Don't elaborate past events. Get into the pattern of saying what you're thinking now, not of thinking for awhile and then describing your thoughts.

Art activities may be easiest to start with, but this can also be used with any problem solving or creative activity. A tape or video recorder helps, especially as taking notes rapidly may be difficult. Its value is both in capturing another's thought processing and in helping students become aware of the varied strategies employed, especially if the teacher engages the group in a discussion about this aspect. Consider applying the technique to a student working out ways to solve a difficulty.

Journal Writing

Interactive journalizing is still another way to focus on the inner dialogue. At the end of a social studies class, for example, the students might answer the following questions in the last five minutes:

1. What did I learn today?
2. What puzzles me?
3. What did I enjoy, hate, accomplish in class today?
4. How was my performance in class?
5. What connections did I make to other areas, ideas, subjects?
6. What do I expect to work on in the next session?

The responses are reflective inner dialogue captured on paper. The teacher responds with his own reflections as he reads—no "put-downs" or criticisms, but interactions with the dialogue. A side benefit is that the teacher gets to know the students in a more profound way as well as gaining deeper understandings of their difficulties and anticipations through reflecting on the students" responses. Starting the next class reading a few puzzlements or feelings from class members both refreshes the class on the previous topics of discussion and opens doors for relating to feelings. Initially, do not name students in this sharing. Once safety has been established, it becomes possible to name students, read their comments verbatim and seek ideas or suggestions. *"Peter said, "I feel like I'm going to lose it and I'm not sure it's worth it. There are so many things coming at once. It's hard to concentrate on any one thing and do it well." Do any of you have similar feelings? Is there anything we can do to help?"*

Other forms of journal keeping or diaries are also effective, as long as the teacher helps students to see the difference between simply describing what events occurred and their thoughts, new ideas and feelings about those events. Older students might keep a journal about the process of learning something new—skiing, Japanese, how to repair a motor—or they might keep a journal about how they resolve a particular difficulty. The aim is to see how we make connections, relate new to old, understand how we advance in levels—in short, a dialogue with ourselves about our mental (or emotional) processing.

Note-taking

Teaching students to take notes and listen to their inner dialogue at the same time is useful. The notebook paper can be divided with a broad left hand margin about a third of the page. Notes from text or class discussions are taken on the right side of the line. On the left are reflections, questions, connections, feelings— one's inner dialogue—related to the material. Another technique is to use index note cards with three colors of ink. Notes from text or class discussions are taken in blue or; connections, reflections, feelings or questions are written in red; and green is used in reviewing the notes to highlight important relationships in further dialogue with oneself. The computer might be similarly used, varying print type for reflections (e.g.. italics for reflections and inner dialogue) and perhaps bold face for important relationships and emphasis.

Deep Processing

Marzano's "deep processing" strategy may be used for any learning activity. In this strategy, not only the inner voice, but other modes of thought are noted and are necessary for thought development. This can be done as a note-taking activity by dividing the notebook page into quadrants. Label sections "words," "images," "senses" and "emotions," and put notes in each section as appropriate. The page margin might be used for what is called "bracketing." In this category, ideas extraneous to the topic at hand that get in the way of thought are noted, such as, "I wish my boyfriend would call. Maybe he's going out with someone else."

Spatial Strategies

Webbing, mind mapping or concept mapping are all spatial strategies that help the young person engage in metacognition by considering the relationships among ideas. In spatial strategies, both the content and the relationships are specified. In webbing, a topic to be explored is placed in a center circle and subtopics enclosed in circles branch off from it, extending outward in a series of circles or ellipses connected with lines. Concept maps add the aspect of specifying the relationship through use of verbs or prepositions on the connecting lines or branches. Pictures may also be used. After placing the word "Amphibians" in a circle in the center of his page, the grade 8 student might say to himself as he makes a web for his independent research report, *"Let's see, types of amphibians—that's one category. I'll put that down first. Then I'll split it into three branches: frogs, toads and salamanders. I know about leopard frogs, tree frogs and bull frogs. I'll make new circles linked to the frog category. I'll have to find out about other specific animals. Another big category is habitat."* And so forth. Webbing can also be a useful way to think about a problem and figure out options. What might a web look like if "My stepmother is so mean to me" were in the center?

Mode Switching Strategies

Cohen developed a strategy called "mode switching." It evolved from findings that highly creative people use different languages of thought, frequently images, as metaphors to generate new understandings. Students create a metaphoric representation in a different modality (say from images to words, or from words to physical actions) to synthesize readings and/or class discussions on a particular topic. It could be expressed through any one or a combination or figures, symbols, words, musical interpretations, feelings, or even actions. This transformation process requires very active thinking and integrates the information into the mind's structures.

Along with the representation, students keep a written log of how they created the mode switch, what the various symbols represent, how it ties in with their current interests. These images are shared with fellow students at the beginning of each class, promoting multiple perspectives and stimulating active discussion about aspects of the information as well as the process employed in its construction.

What Are You Thinking Right Now?

Finally, one extremely simple and effective technique for any age group is to stop in the middle of a story or discussion and ask the students, "What are you thinking about right now?" or *"What is your inner voice saying to you as you are listening (reading, etc.)?"* By eliciting their answers, dignifying the importance of their connection-making, and valuing and respecting the varied responses, young people become aware of how others make meaning by connecting new ideas to their own previous experiences and feelings. They also become more aware of their own metacognitive processing.

What the Kids Discovered about School

➤ *I've discovered that I wish we had a three day weekend.*
—Stan, 13

➤ *I've discovered that school is pretty boring, but I'd die if I was at home alone.*
—Julian, 14

➤ *I've discovered that I feel I am too old for the discipline, regimenting, being told what to do, etc. I feel that the social and sometimes academic activities of school are very immature, and yet it seems that others in my grade level can only talk about the narrow world of school.*
—Steve, 17

➤ *I've discovered that I am really happy at school if I have kept up with my work and had a good social day.*
—Megan, 15

➤ *I've discovered that I haven't really learned much this year. I don't know what it is this year but we're sort of re-doing everything I know.*
—Liz, 11

➤ *I've discovered that I think of a good teacher as someone who'll go over the basics with you. He'll come back for you even if you're behind. He'll try new things, not just do the same old things.*
—Ken, 15

➤ *I've discovered that homework is often busy work.*
—Larry, 14

➤ *I've discovered that I don't like the subjects that my dad picked for me and I'm stuck with them.*
—Alex, 16

➤ *I've discovered that I love to learn and I do well, but I hate it when teachers get used to me doing well and stop patting*

me on the back or look at me like I'm stupid when I mess up.
__Robbin, 13

➤ *I've discovered that I like challenges—I like to succeed, I don't like having something that I can't complete.*
—Neil, 15

➤ *I've discovered that the best thing about school is that teachers care—they want to help you learn and to succeed.*
—Jessica, 11

➤ *I've discovered that in school I feel safe being around people that care about you.*
—LaTonya, 12

➤ *I've discovered that the kids have a system of social levels which are strictly adhered to but nobody is put into them. You kind of put yourself into them based on who your friends are and how you feel about yourself.*
—Jamie, 14

➤ *I've discovered that I love doing math, but it's too easy, so when I have finished I help the other kids at my table. Sometimes the other kids in my grade level tease me, so I often keep it a secret that the work is so easy, but the others know.*
—Sandra, 10

➤ *I've discovered that I am happy now but it was hard at first. The girls were in cliques—they had known each other since sixth grade and I was the only new girl in eighth grade.*
—Jenna, 15

➤ *I've discovered that I wish the teacher would give me one really hard problem instead of all those easy ones that are so boring!*
—Ben, 11

➤ *I've discovered that I hate it when students take advantage of the teacher's soft spot. If students only focused on learning they'd glean more benefits. They must stop being selfish.*
—Jason, 13

➤ *I've discovered that I would like teachers to make learning more exciting.*
—Rashad, 12

➤ *I've discovered that teachers sometimes come into class in a bad mood and take it out on students—I'll try never to do that.*
—Dan, 12

➤ *I've discovered I like all the new books in the school library the most.*
—Tyler, 10

➤ *I've discovered that I wish teachers would just listen to what kids have to say.*
—Bill, 13

➤ *I've discovered that I can't work to a "B." I want perfection.*
—Louise, 17

➤ *I've discovered that I hate myself for giving in and pretending to be dumb.*
—Beth, 16

➤ *I've discovered that when I get bored in class I stare out the window and when the teacher asks a question I answer still staring out the window—it really bugs them!*
—Peter, 13

➤ *I've discovered that I want respect from everyone and to be acknowledged and congratulated for good work.*
—Michelle, 14

➤ *I've discovered that the teachers who are mean, cold and have a slim understanding of adolescents get picked on and not listened to by students.*
—Rebecca, 15

➤ *I've discovered that the teachers at my school automatically place a lot of trust in each student, without a student having to earn it. I don't like that.*
—Juan, 15

➤ *I've discovered that when I'm backed against the wall and the teacher doesn't give me room for a way out, I sometimes say things I wish I hadn't.*
—Lisa, 14

➤ *I've discovered that I am very intolerant of others" slowness or messiness because I am meticulous.*
—Sean, 15

➤ *I've discovered that I hate it at school if I can't understand something because then I feel dumber than usual.*
—Helen, 16

➤ *I've discovered that teachers get stuff wrong all the time in the tests but they're convinced that they're right.*
—Miranda, 15

➤ *I've discovered that I love learning stuff that is mentally stimulating.*
—Orquidea, 16

➤ *I've discovered that one of the things that frustrates me is the difference in marking and preparing for exams and assignments between teachers and the process of standardization. Although I realize that standardization is used to help students pass, the only effect it seems to have on the more academically able students is to lower their grades, and it seems that this too occurs at different levels according to different teachers.*
—Peter, 17

➤ *I've discovered that provoking teachers gives me great satisfaction.*
—Brett, 15

➤ *I've discovered that the thing I like least about school is the amount of paperwork we have to do before we learn anything.*
—Helen, 16

➤ *I've discovered that gray buildings and drab, cold classrooms in winter are depressing.*
—Haley, 16

➤ *I've discovered that if I am finding a particular lesson boring (this does not happen often), I make myself contribute and learn something. Occasionally I challenge myself with a problem harder than the one given.*
—Jonathan, 16

➤ *I've discovered that some schoolwork has no point to it yet you have to go over and over it.*
—Eric, 15

➤ *I've discovered that teachers should admit they're wrong instead of sidetracking and changing the subject.*
—Don, 15

➤ *I've discovered that I wish teachers would explain more fully: they don't like insatiable appetites!*
—Margaret, 16

➤ *I've discovered that when a teacher gives you a fair amount of freedom, not too harsh discipline, and not boring work, the teacher will gain the respect of the students.*
—Emmy, 14

Could any of these things have been said about you?
What do kids say about you and your classes?
Ask them!

Here is what one teacher learned:

"I set up questionnaires and did interviews with small groups of capable students to find out what problems they were facing at school. I gained so much from the insights and observations of these young people. I realized that we in schools tend to make decisions for our young people based on what we think they should be doing. It has taken me too long to realize that our best source of information is the students themselves."
Helen Weir, Teacher, Grade 7

What could YOU learn from your students?

Knowing the Kids

A Teacher's Story:
"One of my 11th grade girls came up to tell me she didn't think she could do physics next year. She is one of the highest achievers in the school—and yet is sure she is not capable of doing well in her final exams. After ten minutes of talking about self-concept she rolled up her sleeve and showed me a patch of eczema, which she says is related to her continual state of stress. She eventually talked about how much she hates her father, who left her when she was young, and has since left his next family. She was almost crying when she told me of how he yelled at her step-brother when he was having trouble with his reading, and how

this was when the eczema started. When I asked if he had been as tough on her when she was little, she said she can't remember anything except how much they "hung around together."

She talked this afternoon with some senior girls whom I suggested had felt similarly inadequate as juniors and were fine now. She said it helped knowing she was not the only person who knows one thing and believes another. She knows she always does well at school—she believes she can't. What has done this, and what can change it? After all my deep and meaningful attempts, we were walking out of the lab, when I told her I was surprised by this admission. She has only joined my class this term, and I mentioned my only knowledge of her ability beforehand was because of the number of people in the staff room who have named her as being particularly bright. She stopped me, and made me tell her again. "Really?" She was delighted!

Maybe we should just tell them!"

—Lynne Kelly, Physics/Math Teacher

Using Humor to Help Cope

Laughter has been considered "the best medicine" and "an uncensored wit the best therapy." It has been said that life with all of its problems, difficulties and tragedies can be born with stoicism and forbearance but transcended only with humor. It is therefore a form of expression and a means of communication and self-reflection highly recommended for all. In fact, it may be just the ticket for bright kids in helping them deal with stress. In a study on humor as a coping mechanism, gifted adolescents were very receptive to use of humor, particularly when opportunities and methods for using humor were provided. They were better able to cope with stresses in their lives, and continued to employ humor as a coping strategy.

Humor is not just jokes or anecdotes, but the making of laughter out of the immediate situation. It may be a slip of the tongue or pen or the juxtaposition of contrary ideas not ordinarily related. It may be based on situations taken to the extreme of absurdity or perhaps the opposite: a very serious reference absurdly trivialized. Humor of this kind is dependent on the spontaneity of the teacher or students. The common element in all types of humor is that fun is usually made of the pathos of the human condition.

Humor can be a mode of release of fear or other emotions, e.g. Woody Allen's statement, *"I'm not afraid to die. I just don't want to be there when it happens."* It can be a way of concisely encapsulating a range of ideas about the world or oneself. For example, by lampooning, satirizing and drawing attention to what is happening in the world, cartoonists allow us to laugh and gain perspective at the same time. Ultimately, humor is both a mechanism for communication and release ... and it works!

Creatively gifted people have both the capacity to produce and enjoy humor. Among other qualities such as enhanced sensitivity, lack of rigidity, playfulness, heightened independence and less of a preoccupation with what others think, creative young people are often characterized by their humor. They are more divergent thinkers, that is, they can think of problems and situations as having more than one answer and therefore can both generate and appreciate multiple solutions to different problems.

Humor has a place in both the school and the family setting. With few exceptions, it is difficult to imagine a 45-minute class period passing without some comic relief to punctuate the attention and tension that a unit of work requires. Humor is the flux that eases the mind through the roughs of doubt and confusion. When frustration gridlocks the interplay of thoughts or social relationships and is treated to a light-hearted interlude, a solution often readily lends itself. A good laugh can be healthy and productive.

Adults can model these modes of communication and they can encourage environments for them to develop. There is no single or right way of folding humor into a recipe for teaching, given that teachers will vary in their own capacity for employing and indeed enjoying it. Use of humor requires sensitivity and should be constructive. One should be able to laugh at oneself as well as the antics of others, but should be wary about being sarcastic. Humor needs to feel good to all parties. It can be encouraged as a valued form of literary and artistic expression which is to be prized and credited along with other school-related activities. Above all, share a joke and enjoy a laugh.

♦ **Discuss Types of Humor**

Discuss the different types of humor: lampoon, wit, slap-stick, satire, and so forth.

♦ **Make Cartoons**

Have students study cartoonists and make cartoons about topics of study, news stories and about the problems of coping with daily living. Share and pin on bulletin boards. Or erase the captions in cartoons and have students fill out their own witticisms.

♦ **Make the Most Ludicrous Faces**

To break the tension before or after an exam, for example, even older adolescents might enjoy parading in small groups in front of the class, making their most ludicrous faces for their classmates. Try funny walks too. If the teacher does it, all the more fun. Of course, you have to know the group and whether such an activity will become too unruly.

♦ **Write Humorous Poems, Limericks, Plays, Stories**

Even subjects like math, social studies or science can be lightened and learned better through use of humor. Can they see what's funny about paramecium, quadratic equations or medieval life?

♦ **Share Your Foibles**

Talk about your foibles, mistakes, embarrassments, particularly when it is germane to what is going on in class. If you are working with a physical education class you can tell them about the time you got lost during an orienteering race. Or share the embarrassment on a first date when you tripped on your coat and fell out of the car instead of climbing out smoothly.

♦ **Joke of the Day**

Encourage jokes in class from both male and female students. Discuss what is appropriate for school settings with students ahead of time.

♦ **Laugh at Yourself**

If they catch you making a mistake, laugh at yourself. "I really must be in lalaland. You're right. I misspelled "principle." Guess my meeting with the principal just wiped out my brain." Or, what happens when you get really embarrassed? One teacher was digging in her purse for chalk, absentmindedly pulled out a tampon, and begin "writing" on the board. She cracked up laughing with her ninth grade students! This ability to laugh at yourself especially helps perfectionists.

♦ **Teach Positive Uses of Humor to Cope with Stress**

Teach positive use of humor to help students cope with difficulties. Take a difficult situation and have the class consider humorous perspectives, for example, when kids pick on someone who seems different.

♦ **Use Humor instead of Punishment**

Frank had put his feet up on a desk one time too often in his eighth grade class. The teacher walked over to the desk where the feet were offending. He gently lifted a corner of Frank's pants leg to reveal a hairy leg above the sock and remarked, "Nice angora socks you've got there, Frank." This humorous statement met its objective and Frank sheepishly removed his feet. How much more effective it was than giving Frank a detention or punishing him by making him write "I will not put my feet on other people's desks" one hundred times.

I DIFFUSE BAD SITUATIONS BY MAKING A JOKE.

FAMILY FUNCTIONING AND COPING

The family is one of the important, if not the most important, settings in which we develop. It is the place where the individual is nurtured to grow and flourish. It is also the setting where there are role models for young people to follow so habits and practices are acquired.

As parents we might sometimes wish that children came into the world with a list of specific instructions attached to help them become capable, happy people. No matter how much they were wanted, no matter how carefully we prepared for becoming parents by reading or studying about child development, there are times when we may feel that we have failed parenthood. While parenting may sometimes be difficult, it can also be wonderful and rewarding.

There are no formulas to help young people cope more successfully. Each person is unique and reacts somewhat differently to the environment. Our intuitions and our caring within the context of a loving relationship will generally enable young people to blossom.

The association between family life and coping can be investigated from a number of perspectives. A brief summary of what research has found regarding family functioning and child coping abilities will first be discussed. These findings summarize data across a great many families and indicate general patterns. While no family is ideal, these are the emphases we should aspire to. This does not mean that if your child is experiencing difficulties your family is not healthy or you are to blame. However, stepping back and examining your family patterns of functioning and thinking about whether you want to make any changes might be beneficial. Also, just about everyone has difficulties coping for short periods at one time or another. One question to ask yourself is whether this is a particular developmental phase or whether the child is having more serious or chronic problems.

The next section offers some suggestions that parents discovered worked for their children. You may find that some of their ideas might apply to your situation. Following is a section describing coping strategies we learned from mothers and fathers in working on this project. Again, some ideas might apply to your circumstances. A series of questions parents might ask themselves comes next. Note that there are no answers to these questions. Solutions come through careful reflection on the specific child and the difficulties encountered. A few areas of particular concern follow with some possible ideas to consider and resources that may be of assistance. Finally, a memo from children to parents helps with perspective.

Research on Family Functioning and Coping

The family has been found to be the context where young people spend a great deal of their time. Secondary school students in the United States were asked at random times where they were, what they were doing and what they were thinking and feeling. This study found that schooling, classwork and studying occupied 25 percent of their time, 27 percent was spent in public settings and 41 percent of their time was spent at home, with the remainder in other locations. Therefore, young people were found to spend more time in the family setting than in any other environment.

In families, parents operate much as did the families in which they grew up or sometimes as a reaction, they establish family life that is in direct contrast to what their families had been like. The family is the microcosm where coping strategies are modeled, taught, tested and modified. It needs to be a safe, openly communicative environment where that can happen. There is no template as to what is the ideal family. However, attempts to describe such a family characterize it as one in which:

♦ Communication is positive and effective.
♦ The adolescent receives strong support from parents.
♦ The adolescent feels free to express feelings and opinions.
♦ There is discussion on issues and there is a climate where conflicts may be raised.
♦ Members negotiate plans when it is appropriate.
♦ There is co-operation and trust between parents and adolescents.
♦ Parents can express concerns about likely consequences.

Researchers have found that in general, adolescents are better adjusted when they perceive family members as: committed and connected with each other, expressive of ideas and feelings, orga-

nized and encouraging of each individual's independence. In general there is agreement that families should provide members with moderate levels of cohesion (connectedness) as well as moderate levels of flexibility about roles and rules. Independence should be encouraged and communication should be clear and direct. These are the qualities that are to be fostered in family life. Not all families achieve these goals, but there is enough evidence that it is these features that work best.

The association between healthy family climate and functional coping is confirmed by studies of adolescents conducted over several years in Melbourne using the Adolescent Coping Scale. When young people were asked to describe how they perceived life in their family and then to record which of the eighty coping actions they used, a close association was found between the ways adolescents perceive aspects of their family and the ways in which they report that they cope with everyday life.

In families where members show commitment, help, provide support to each other and are encouraged to act openly and to express their feelings directly, young people report making less use of non-productive and emotionally charged strategies. They do not declare that they cannot cope, nor do they indulge in wishful thinking or seeking relaxation as a means of escape. In these families young people become involved in social action, seek the help of professionals and make use of friends and some form of religious or spiritual activity. This all adds up to a picture of positive coping.

Generally, in families that encourage personal growth, young people display industry and hard work and are resourceful in using the social support of others. In families that are high on moral and religious functioning young people use spiritual support and use relaxing diversions. Parenting styles that reflect democratic decision making within the family are associated with dealing directly with problems and working hard. In contrast, parental control in an authoritarian sense appears to be counterproductive to hard work and industry. That is the opposite to what controlling parents want to achieve.

In families where there is conflict there is a predictable usage of non-productive strategies. In functional families where there is intimacy and high level of personal growth, young people seek social and spiritual support, work hard and focus on the positive in attempting to solve their problems.

Where adolescents perceive families in terms that can be described as healthy, the adolescents use coping strategies that enable them to deal with problems more directly and more productively while not worrying excessively or needing to draw on emotion charged strategies to alleviate their stresses.

In research by others, girls are usually found to communicate more with parents than do boys and communication with mothers is generally viewed more favorably by adolescents than is communication with fathers. Mothers are seen as more understanding, accepting and able to negotiate while fathers are seen as more judgmental and less willing to discuss feelings.

In a study of American families which has been replicated in Australia, families videotaped their meal time interactions. It was found that female family members took a more active role in positive and negative aspects of domestic negotiation and the role of the mother was central in these interactions.

The main issues which have been sources of conflict in families have remained continuous conflict areas from the 1920's to the 1990's. The issues are part of everyday living and include such things personal hygiene, disobedience, school/social activities, friendships, helping at home and conflict with siblings.

There are cultural differences in the sources of conflict within the family and how these conflicts are resolved. For example, issues that provoked significantly more disagreement in both Italian- and Greek-Australian homes than in Anglo-Australian households related to adolescents were:

♦ Going out with friends of the same and opposite sex;
♦ Choice of future career;
♦ Use of spare time away from home;
♦ Choice of friends; and
♦ Drinking and/or smoking.

Most of these issues revolve around the level of autonomy granted to the adolescents. The researcher speculated that: "In Anglo-Australian families more individuality is tolerated, with greater stress on personal freedom. In Greek and Italian families, adolescents experience more authoritarian parent-centered control, with greater expectation that they will fit in and conform to family demands." The same kinds of issues occur in American families as well. However, in general, adolescents report that they want to maintain good relationships with their parents and they want:

- ◆ Close relationships with parents;
- ◆ More equality—more consultation and negotiation; and
- ◆ More independence and autonomy in the context of a supportive relationship.

There is a relationship between reasoning level and a family's habitual negotiating style. It is expected that in families where there are capable young people there will be vigorous discussions. Rather than creating conflict, these discussions are likely to promote cognitive growth. Where families engage in discussions about positive and negative matters, it was found that the adolescents scored higher on measures of self-esteem than in those who avoided conflict.

There is an association between level and frequency of criticism experienced by the young person and self-esteem. Generally, the less criticism from parents the higher the self-esteem. In addition, it has been found that parents have the most significant impact on future-directed decisions of young people. Both parents and children have a great deal of investment in contributing to the health and well-being of the family.

Helpful Things for Parents to Do: Advice from Parents

Maureen

Maureen is the single parent of a gifted 11 year-old boy who has perfectionist tendencies and was becoming an underachiever. She tried the following to help her son. For a university class, she applied Betts" "Autonomous Learner Model" to her own child. In assisting her son through the Orientation Dimension of the model, she did a research project along with him. She also read to him from books on the gifted. One that had particular impact was Krueger's *On Being Gifted*, particularly the sections on "Inner Pressures" and "How to Cope".

Reading about Gifted People, Their Problems and Triumphs

"As I read aloud, David acknowledged that he could relate very strongly to points particular students were sharing. He was constantly stopping me and requesting me to reread the paragraph or sentence and finally responding with, "Yeah, that's me, that's me." In the "How to Cope" section, one student wrote of his times of feeling depressed and suicidal. David expressed that he sometimes felt this way and so we went on to discuss his feelings quite freely. He expressed that he felt that he was the only one who felt this way and that it was really good to hear that others had similar problems and thoughts."

Sharing Feelings

"It was easy for me to assume that as a gifted child, David would be raring to go with his choice of research study. I naturally presumed that he is confident in areas of his interests because he appears to be such a self-assured and self-motivated child. When he eventually confided in me that he was scared when he first began things because he didn't quite know where to start or where to go first, I remembered I had read of this behavior being a characteristic of one type of gifted child ... I have located some material on perfectionism and wonder if this might be behind David's reluctance to start ... Doing nothing is a preference to failing. Striving for perfection may require dependence on others for confidence and self-esteem. David was relieved that I would be there to guide him through the research process."

Using Temperature Readings

"I found that using "temperature readings," a technique used to help the individual learn more about themselves and others, was very helpful. Each person has a certain "emotional temperature" which describes how the person is feeling at the time. The scale for the temperature is from 1 to 10. I ask David for his rating and an opportunity to communicate why he has chosen that rating. Then I *share mine. We respond differently to a person if they are a "1" (low) rather than a "10" (high).*

I see the temperature readings as being terrific for making David aware of how much, how often and how quickly his "temperature" can and actually does change throughout a given activity or day. If David can create a habit of consciously and independently allocating himself a rating from 1-10 at frequent times throughout a day, his fluctuations in "temperature" may help him to remember that when he does feel down, he probably won't be feeling that way for a very long time."

Developing Autonomy

"I telephoned the public library and learned of a resource area devoted entirely to the performing arts. I was so excited I could hardly wait to tell David. When I did he wasn't as excited as I expected.

I realized then that I had missed an opportunity to allow David to be the one to make the discovery. I should have been patient and let David call. I also missed an opportunity for David to develop telephone skills and confidence to call and seek information. I must stop taking ownership of David's research and become a facilitator. He is the decision maker. Any ideas I get I must save until I can share them with him."

Jill

Jill is the mother of three adolescent boys. The oldest, Jeff, a very bright 20-year-old, is completing a double major in law and science at the university. He has become compliant and "boring" as Jill says her other sons describe him, essentially giving up his creative spark to be accepted by his peers. He just wants to get by. The brilliance seen in his earlier school work is conspicuously absent. The middle boy, Peter, aged 17, is a highly gifted and creative person in his last year of high school. He is struggling through what he considers to be often boring and trivial exams and assignments. He is already being paid well for his outstanding work in computer graphics. He is very sensitive but is alienated and experiences periods of depression. He has difficulty with social relationships. The youngest, Ben, is undersized for his age of 13, looking more like an 8-or 9-year-old, and has been taking growth hormones with little apparent gain. He has great enthusiasm and energy, loves music and acting, and is socially very astute. These are some of the things Jill learned, particularly about Peter.

The Message They Give out
is Not What's Really the Message

"Peter appears to be testy, sharp and acidic, but he's usually funny. When Pete teases someone and that person attacks back, he can't take what he dished out. Although under that hard exterior is a very sensitive, creative, shy person; he cannot not put himself in the place of the person he is undermining. It's sort of a "kick the dog" syndrome. He turns off other people from liking him because he is aggressive with his words. For example, when the boys were small and we would put the three of them in the car for a trip, he would insist on the seat one of the others wanted, instead of working out which one he really wanted. I think his reaction is really based on "I don't like me, so how can I trust that anyone else could like me?" What he really wants is acceptance but the message does not get across and he expects (and often gets) the opposite. Because of his humor, kids seem to want to get close, but he doesn't really let them. He is writing to a girl in another city he has never met. He sends her reams of letters and leaves them lying about. He seems to pour out his heart to her. It's been a great comfort to him. I'm almost afraid of their meeting because he might be disappointed."

Things Could Be Worse

"In spite of the fact that Peter is a rebel and "does his own thing," he has not tried drugs, alcohol, smoking or other dangerous activities. I guess we're fortunate in that regard. Underneath the wild hair and non-conformity is a pretty sensible kid."

Taking Another's Perspective

"Pete thinks he's the least cared for of our boys, while from my perspective, I think he gets the most time and energy. Also, he can't say to someone they did something well. You'd think that such a bright child would be able to do so, but he can't. I guess it's how you look at things."

I Can't Impose My Values

"Pete and I used to have head on clashes until I realized I couldn't impose my values. We discussed this openly, including

potential results of his actions. He now has his way but has to accept the consequences. It's cut down a lot of tension. He makes his own decisions. Because I'm cold, for example, doesn't mean he's cold. Because I like short hair doesn't mean he can't look like Beethoven."

Ellen

Ellen is the mother of two adolescent girls. She learned the following about helping her daughters cope.

Self-regulation

"I visited a dear friend in another city for a few days. It was a pleasant experience to watch her interact with her 14-year-old daughter. What struck me was how capable and independent this young person was. There was no nagging about bedtime, cleaning up or schoolwork. I realized with dismay that I was still telling my girls when to go to bed, awakening them and calling them to do chores. Upon my return, we immediately instituted their own regulation of bed time and getting up for school, as well as marking chore days on the calendar. Life is easier at our house now that they control these aspects. I can't believe I was controlling so much."

Being in Charge of Achievement

"I was constantly nagging my 16-year-old daughter, Melanie, about her marks, homework and long term assignments, as she usually started each year needing some prodding. After one such nag, she put her hands on my shoulders and said, "Mom, whose education is this? Please let me be in charge of it myself. I know what I have to do to get into a university. I don't want you to ask me one more question about homework or grades. I'll tell you what I want you to know." I backed off, she took charge and has been doing beautifully."

Everything We Needed to Know About Coping We Learned from Our Mothers ... and Fathers (or almost everything)

Coping with Loss

Mom had lost her mother when she was 3, and at age 5, witnessed her father drown when he hit his head on a rock while diving in a river. She was adopted by an aunt who took her to America shortly thereafter, claiming her as her own daughter. Because my mother was taller than her own son of the same age, she was declared to be two years older. This was not a problem as there were no birth certificates at the time, although she wondered why she reached puberty so much later than the other girls in her class. At the age of 9, the aunt died, and Mom, with her three step sisters and step brother, was put in an orphanage. At 18, her fiance died of meningitis. I used to ask her what gave her the strength to cope with so much grief and loss. She replied that the strength came from remembering the love her father had for her, taking her for walks in the woods, reading her stories. It's the little things we do with our children when they are young, the unconditional love that provides the strong base. This remarkable woman was loved by all who knew her. Her suffering had given her great strength and great compassion.

Learning about Things Reduces Fear

When I was about 9 years of age, I developed a terrible fear that shooting stars were going to land on my head and kill me. We had a very basic little vacation cabin and I remember well the terror of taking the walk down the path to the outhouse at night, my arms folded over my head to protect myself against the dangers of falling stardust. I confided my fear to my mother. A few days later, she gave me a book about the stars. She said, *"Read about what frightens you. When you understand it, you won't be afraid any more. Knowledge is power."* After some four years of passionate interest in astronomy, I learned she was right.

Big Feet Mean Big Hearts: Accepting Yourself

For my twelfth birthday, I got a ballet costume complete with pink tutu and pink toe shoes, size 7. For this aspiring ballerina, it was the present of my dreams. I could hardly wait to get up on point. But I started to grow, first out, then up. My feet grew from size 7 to size 10 in less than six months. The largest toe shoes were size 9. Clearly, my aspirations of being a ballerina had to be modified. To compound this problem, women's shoes were not even available in that size. I had to wear men's shoes. One recess, Carl, the best looking boy in seventh grade, put his arm around my shoulder. I was deeply moved until he called all the other kids over to show them my feet were even bigger than his.

Wrapped in my Mother's comforting arms while I poured out my heartache, she said *"Sweetheart, you are the way you are. You cannot change some things about yourself. But maybe big feet mean big hearts. Change the parts of you that are changeable if you don't like them and try not to focus on things you cannot change. Let others know you for your loving nature."* Just about everyone feels that something is wrong with them—their ears stick out too far, they are too short or too tall, they reach puberty to soon or too slowly, they don't like their body image, their eyes are too close together—in short, they have a secret or not-so-secret problem that nobody else has. Added to these are the young people with obvious differences: skin color, language or disabling conditions. Learning to accept yourself by being reflected as valued from loving parental mirrors helps. Knowing that everyone has a vulnerability and feels inadequate sometimes also lets us know we are not alone. Perhaps the most important message, though, is that we can improve aspects of ourselves that are modifiable, like the ability to laugh at ourselves, and focus on our positive attributes.

Choices We Make

Learning to make responsible decisions was a hallmark of Mom's philosophy in raising us. She did not hesitate to discuss possible consequences of our actions, but it was our choice to go ahead with them or not. When I was 13, I was invited to go to the movies with a group of older teenagers. Mom questioned whether I would feel ready for this, but I was delighted to be considered mature enough and dressed myself in black shorts, a black T-Shirt, bobby socks, and penny loafers, the costume of the day. When the older girls wanted me to put on lipstick, I began to worry. When they asked me to smoke with them, I was terrified. I recognized I had made a choice and had to bear with it, but would apply this lesson in making future decisions.

Better Homicide than Suicide

Dad used to say, *"It's better to get your anger out than turning it against yourself. Better homicide than suicide."* By this metaphor, he clearly did not mean that we should consider killing someone else. He was telling us that to cope with angry feelings, we should express them so that they would not be turned against ourselves in self-blame, hopelessness, helplessness and depression.

Distinguish between What's Important and What Is Urgent

When we would get worried about too many stresses on our plate at once, Dad used to tell us to distinguish between what was important and what was urgent. The urgents are all those things we consider as shoulds, musts and got tos that get thrown our way. Sometimes urgent things are important and we must learn to distinguish what is important from what is only immediate. The important things are those that really make a difference in the long run. Towards the end of my junior year in high school, I was cramming furiously for exams, preparing for a concert and getting my art portfolio ready for evaluation—all the urgents of the moment. In my whirl of self-preoccupation, I received a phone call from my best friend, telling me his father had just died of a heart attack. Dad helped me to see the difference between the important and the urgent right then. He helped me to realize that what was important was that Dan needed my support. Schoolwork was only urgent.

Our Own Burdens are the Lightest

Mom was a nurse in a poor inner city school. One day shortly before Christmas, the single mother of a young boy at the school had an epileptic seizure in the schoolyard. After helping the woman through her difficulty, Mom escorted her home. That night, Mom told us what she had seen and we resolved to take Christmas to the Cruz family. On Christmas Eve, Mom and I, then aged 16, bearing a warm blanket and a toy car, took the train to deliver our gifts. We entered the filthy block of flats that crawled with cockroaches and climbed three flights of stairs to Mrs. Cruz" flat. We entered the room, lit with a single dim light and warmed only by the heat of a gas burner on the stove. On the dirty green wall was taped a paper bag with a Christmas tree drawn on it. Under it was a box of cereal, the single present for her son. Mrs. Cruz opened the door to the only other room and there, asleep huddled under a coat on the bare mattress he shared with his mother was the young boy. Her joy at showing us her son and thinking about how happy he would be with his toy made me think of the child being celebrated that night. Our burdens seem very heavy to us, but when compared to others" profound troubles, they are put in perspective.

Murdering Old Witches:
Using Fantasy to Cope with Pain

For the span of two years that my sister and I were in fifth grade, Miss Quinn "lived at our house." She was a cruel teacher who used punishment liberally and humiliation constantly. If we dared to play the wrong note on our flutes, we were promptly bopped on the head with her flute. If we made mistakes in math, we were embarrassed publicly. Mother had tried in vain to remove us from her class or remove her from the school, so we had to cope with this miserable woman we nicknamed "the witch." Each day after school, my sister, our friends and I would commiserate with each other around our kitchen table over an ice-cream or some other treat Mother had left us. When she came home after work and joined us with her cup of coffee, then the misery turned to glee. She would ask us, *"All right, dears, how shall we murder the old witch today?"* We would create fantastic tortures, and by so doing, change from tears to laughter. *"We'll string her up by her three hairs on the electric line and light matches stuck in her toenails."* Only this catharsis allowed us to cope with another day of torture. My mother knew we were good children, that the teacher was wrong and that we felt helpless and powerless. She gave us tools in our fantasy to cope with that teacher's power.

The Hottest Places in Hell: Doing the Right Thing

Mom wasn't much for aphorisms, but the one small poster we had in the kitchen said, "The hottest places in hell are reserved for those who do not take a stand in times of great moral crisis." It wasn't enough to work at being honest, kind and charitable. We had to do the morally right thing. The kids in my eighth grade class were cruel to Warren Klump, a disabled boy. One particular day, they were stomping on his feet and making him cry, calling him "retard" and "Klumpy," and pushing his face in the drinking fountain. I couldn't stand this horrid game, went over to Warren, pulled him back into the safety of the school building and told the kids to leave him alone. That weekend, Warren found his way to my house and asked me to marry him. Naturally, the word got out and I got teased unmercifully, *"Hey, Mrs. Klumpy, Klump, Klump. When ya gonna have a baby?"* *"Hey, Klumpies, when's the wed-*

ding?" Coping with the teasing was very painful, but I had taken the high ground and knew I had done the right thing.

Fly, My Child, Fly

I graduated from high school in January, seven months before classes at the university would begin. My father had a small inheritance in Brazil that could not come out, so my parents decided to send me there to learn about the culture and language. Just before boarding the plane with my best friend, Mom kissed me good-bye and said, *"The most important thing a parent can do is free her child when he or she is ready. Fly my child, fly, with my blessings."* Those words meant total acceptance, total trust, knowing I could always come home. With such wind under my wings, I could cope with anything.

Parents of the Gifted and Talented, Can You Read the Writing on the Wall?

Do these questions lurk in the hidden recesses of your mind only to be examined at times of crisis and then re-buried amongst the cobwebs and dust of life?

Maybe by taking a little time sitting in the sun or in front of the fire with a cup of coffee, with no issue clouding your feelings and judgments you could think about the following questions and maybe even jot down how you think at the moment, so when there is a trauma to be faced you have something to refer to, to compare with, remembering that things change.

- What is important in life?
- In the big picture of my child's life what is going to be most important for him or her?
- Can I, as a loving parent, make the path less rocky for my child?
- What priorities do I emphasize ... consciously or unconsciously, vocally or with my body language?
- What "writing on the wall" does my child read about me and my goals for me and her or him?
- Does my child "catch" my frustration, anxiety, fear and

concern about her or him not getting treated fairly at school?

♦ How important was getting into that gifted program, etc?

♦ Does my desperate desire that my offspring gets due acknowledgment and the "official seal of approval" of being identified as "gifted" cloud my judgment, cloud my days and cloud the present and the horizon for my child?

♦ Am I afraid that I'll be seen as a "pushy parent"?

♦ Am I frightened of possible negative consequences if I advocate on behalf of my child?

♦ Do I have difficulty being believed by the teachers?

♦ Do I have doubts about whether my child is gifted and if so, how gifted? (Wouldn't it be wonderful if you could put a gadget like a fever tester to your child's head and get a reading of "giftedness'? ... and also "normalness'!)

♦ What is "giftedness" anyway? Aren't all children gifted to some extent?

♦ What should be done about "giftedness'?

♦ Is it best ignored?

♦ Should my child be accelerated or enriched at school?

♦ What can and should I be doing at home to help my child find fulfillment?

♦ Do I feel I can't share experiences of my child with friends and neighbors because they may think I'm boasting?

♦ Do I have to help my child cope with peer pressure, maybe to hide his or her giftedness?

♦ What should I do when my child says that school is boring?

♦ Do I have to struggle just keeping up with my child?

♦ Do I secretly feel threatened because my child seems to be "brighter" than me?

♦ Am I afraid I will lose the respect and love when she or he discovers what I am really like?

♦ Does my child or do I suffer from the "impostor" syndrome where we "act naturally" instead of being natural?

♦ Is my child involved in so many things I am worn out from organizing and driving?

♦ Do I find it excruciatingly difficult balancing between perfectionism (mine or his or hers) and what is sensible and attainable?

♦ Is it frustrating living in a society where the tall poppy syndrome and everyone being equal is espoused?

♦ Does the community and school policy of neglecting the gifted because "they can cope" enrage me?

♦ Are we really such a primitive society where people seem to believe deep down that there's only a certain amount of "brains" to go round and be shared so that if my kid has "brains" there is not enough for their kid?

♦ How can I help my child be safe and avoid the pitfalls of drugs, alcohol, gangs and violence? And how can I make the world safer for all our children?

♦ What do I really want for my child for the future?

Capable Kids, Capable Parents

In addition to coping with your own adult stresses, you experience aspects of your own childhood again through the growing pains of your own children. You may very likely see yourself in the

descriptions of able students, their personality patterns and their strengths and difficulties. When you read about these students" problems, they may sound familiar. Try to think back to the problems you had in adolescence—how did you deal with them? Even if you made a mess of things, share your knowledge and experiences with your children. It feels great to know that even parents make mistakes! And you will help them learn to cope.

When your child brings up a problem, try to avoid offering the same old clichéd advice. Instead of saying, *"When you're older, these problems you're facing with other kids now will seem very unimportant,"* remember that child in you. How might your life have been different if your parent had said, *"That must have felt terrible. I remember when I got teased by ..."* Your inner child would have been addressed. Can you do this for your own child?

Information Parents Want

Material for this list was collected from interviews with approximately 80 parents of able young people. Many of the concerns have been dealt with in various sections of this book, as noted in the last section. Others that are included are asterisked. A few are too complex to deal with briefly in this book and require pursuit of more complete references. Look in the reference lists for ideas and suggestions.

Some issues clearly belong in different types of books, for example on teaching able learners, resources for out-of-school activities or on parenting. A good number of these books exist, but some topics, such as community resources, might be projects for parent or community groups to consider writing. Some issues would be a starting point for parent or teacher discussion groups, for example, concerns related to responsive schools or issues related to becoming informed parents. Others suggest action, for example, setting up a kids" support network. You might also wish to add to this list through discussion with others who share your concerns. (See Resources for Parents of the Gifted.)

Responsive Schools

♦ Greater education of teaching staff to allow students greater freedom to excel and not to be threatened by questions.
♦ A sequential school program for gifted children.
♦ More awareness and education for teachers so they can advise parents.
♦ Alternative assignments that encourage kids to stretch, rather than more of the same.
♦ Gifted children not to be held back.
♦ Ways of dealing with boredom and poorer teachers.
♦ Competency-based learning in schools.
♦ Excellence rewarded.
♦ Public acceptance of provisions to develop talent and intelligence.

Learning Activities out of School

♦ Strategies to engage and extend children out of school time.
♦ Provision of opportunities for young people to learn about and get involved in various activities in the community, such as law courts or community service projects.
♦ Outdoor education projects.

Information for Parents

♦ Awareness of available options for gifted children and parents of gifted children.
♦ Lists of resources/information/books.
♦ Information on parent groups.
♦ Parent in-services.
♦ Parent interaction with good professionals.
♦ How to help a child develop good writing skills.
♦ How to approach the school. What is the parents" responsibility and what is the school's responsibility?
♦ How to cope when society demands a certain behavior from gifted children.

♦ What to do when parents first find out their child is different.

Guidance in Helping Kids Deal with Feelings

♦ Workshops to allow these kids to express their feelings without fear of ridicule.
♦ Guidelines on how to handle kids who completely withdraw from help.
♦ Support groups for kids.

Information on Topics Covered in this Book

♦ To understand the temperament of children of high intellectual potential.
♦ Information on the gifted adolescent.
♦ Strategies that would encourage children to produce their best while helping them to see that they won't always achieve their specific goal. In other words, how to cope with competition.
♦ Strategies for children on how to be part of a group and deal with keeping up with their peers. Making their own decisions and coping with peer pressure.
♦ Strategies to instill confidence in children.
♦ How to encourage young people to make the most of their skills.
♦ Information on underachieving gifted children.
♦ How to stand up for themselves. Acceptance of the child as he or she is.
♦ Working through possible responses to difficult situations prior to having to face up to them.
♦ Stress management.
♦ Discussion of common problems.
♦ A list of needs.
♦ Tell children they are bright.
♦ Social skills/peer relationships.
♦ Time management skills.

A Memo from Children to Parents

This section encapsulates a wide range of suggestions from young people spanning childhood to adolescence.

1. Don't spoil me but acknowledge my needs. I'm only testing you.
2. Don't be afraid to be firm with me, it makes me know my boundaries.
3. Don't let me form bad habits. I have to learn to rely on you to detect them in the early stages.
4. Don't make me feel smaller than I am. It only makes me behave stupidly "big.'
5. Don't correct me in front of people if you can help it, especially my friends. I'll take much more notice if you talk quietly to me in private.
6. Don't make me feel my mistakes are sins. It upsets my sense of values.
7. Don't protect me from consequences. I need to learn the painful way sometimes.
8. Don't be too upset when I say "I hate you." Sometimes it isn't you I hate but your power to thwart me.
9. Don't go overboard about my small ailments. Take care of me but don't pamper me.
10. Don't nag. If you do I shall have to protect myself by appearing deaf.
11. Don't forget that I cannot always explain myself as well as I would like. That is why I am not always accurate.
12. Don't put me off when I ask questions. If you do, you will find that I stop asking and seek my information elsewhere.
13. Don't be inconsistent. That completely confuses me and makes me lose faith in you.
14. Don't tell me my fears are silly. They are real and you can do much to reassure me if you try to understand.
15. Don't ever suggest that you are perfect or infallible. I know that you are not and I feel angry when you are dishonest.
16. Don't ever think that it is beneath your dignity to apolo-

gize to me. An honest apology makes me feel surprisingly warm towards you.

17. Don't forget I love experimenting. I couldn't get along without it, so please put up with it.

18. Don't forget how quickly I am growing up. It must be very difficult for you to keep pace with me, but please try.

19. Don't forget that I don't thrive without lots of love and understanding, but I don't need to tell you, do I?

20. Please keep yourself fit and healthy because I need you.

Derived in part from "THINKING" Volume No. 10, Number 2, The Journal for Philosophy for Children, IAPC, Montclair State College.

END NOTES

2. GIFTEDNESS
Definition of Giftedness

Personality

References and Readings

Abraham, S. & Llewellyn-Jones, D. (1987). *Eating disorders – The facts* (2nd ed.). New York: Oxford University Press.

Abroms, K.I. (1983). Affective development. In Karnes, M.B. (Ed.). *The underserved: Our young gifted children* (pp. 118-143). Reston, VA: Eric Clearinghouse.

Abroms, K. I. (1985). Social giftedness and its relatonship with intellectual giftedness. In J. Freeman (Ed.). *The psychology of gifted children* (pp. 201-219). Chichester, GB: J. Wiley & Sons.

Adderholdt-Elliott, M. (1987). *Perfectionism: What's bad about being too good.* Minneapolis, MN: Free Spirit Publishing. (Republished through Hawker Brownlow Education.)

Adkins, K. K. (1994). *Relationship between perfectionism and suicidal ideation for students in a honors college program and students in a regular college program.* Unpublished doctoral dissertation, University of Alabama, Tuscaloosa.

Ahmad, W. Z. (1992). *A comparison of coping mechanisms, coping resources, and levels of self-esteem between gifted and nongifted adolescents.* Unpublished doctoral dissertation, Indiana State University, Terre Haute, IN.

Albert R.S. (1980). Family positions and the attainment of eminence: A study of special family positions and special family experiences. *Gifted Child Quarterly, 24,* 87-94.

Alvino, J. (1991). Social and emotional well-being. An investigation into the needs of gifted boys. *Roeper Review, 13,* 174-180.

Andrews, D. (1994). *Alcohol and drug awareness, attitudes, and use among gifted and talented students.* Unpublished doctoral dissertation, Ohio State University, Columbus.

Appleby, M. & Condonis, M. (1990). *Hearing the cry.* Sydney: Rose Educational Training and Consultancy.

Arnold, K. D. (1993). Undergratuate apirations and career outcomes of academically talented women: A discrimant analyis. *Roeper Review, 15,* 169-175.

Austin, A. B. & Draper, D. C. (1981). Peer relationships of the academically gifted: A review. *Gifted Child Quarterly, 25,* 129-133.

Baldwin, A.Y. (1985). Programs for the gifted and talented: issues concerning minority populations in Horowitz, F.D. O'Brien (Eds.). *The gifted and talented: developmental perspectives* (pp.223-249). Washington, DC: American Psychological Association.

Baum, S. (1984). Meeting the needs of learning disabled gifted students, *Roeper Review, 7,* 16-19.

Baum, S. & Owen, S. (1988). High abilty learning disabled students: How are they different? *Gifted Child Quarterly, 32,* 321-326.

Bennett, C.I. (1990). *Comprehensive multicultural education.* Boston, MA: Allyn and Bacon.

Bennet, M., Spoth, R. & Borgen, F. (1991). Bulimic symptoms in high school females: Prevalence and relationships with multiple measures of psychological health. *Journal of Community Psychology, 19,* 13-28.

Betts, G. (1985). *The autonomous learner model.* Greeley, CO: Autonomous Learning Publications. (Available through Hawker Brownlow Education.)

Betts, G. T. & Neihart, M. (1985). Eight effective activities to enhance the emotional and social development of the gifted and talented. *Roeper Review, 8,* 18-23.

Betts, G. T. & Neihart, M. (1986). Implementing self-directed learning models for the gifted and talented. *Gifted Child Quarterly, 30,* 174-177.

Betts, G. T. & Neihart, M. (1988). Profiles of the gifted and talented. *Gifted Child Quarterly, 32,* 248-253.

Betts G. T. (1991). The autonomous learner model for the gifted and talented. In N. Colangelo & G.A. Davis (Eds.). *Handbook of gifted education* (pp. 142-153). Boston: Allyn & Bacon.

Beyer, B.K. (1986). *Developing a thinking skills program.* Boston: Allyn and Bacon.

Blackburn, A.C. & Erickson, D.B. (1986). Predictable crises of the gifted adolescent. *Journal of Counselling and Development, 64,* 552-555.

Bland, L. C. , Sowa, C. J., & Callahan, C. M. (1994). An overview of resilience in gifted children. *Roeper Review, 17,* 77-80.

Bleedorn, B.B. (1982). Humor as an indicator of giftedness. *Roeper Review, 4,* 33 - 34.

Bloom, B. S. (Ed.). (1985). *Developing talent in young people.* New York: Ballentine.

Borkowski, J. G. & Peck, V. A. (1986). Causes and consequences of metamemory in gifted children. In R. J. Sternberg & J. E. Davidson (Eds.). *Conceptions of giftedness* (pp. 182-200). New York: Cambridge University Press.

Borland, J. H. & Wright, L. (1994). Identifying young, potentially gifted, economically disadvantaged students. *Gifted Child Quarterly, 38,* 164-171.

Bosma, H. & Jackson, S. (Eds.). (1990). *Coping and self-concept in adolescence.* New York: Springer-Verlag.

Bourke, C.J. (1990). Cross-cultural communication and professional education: an aboriginal perspective in C. Hedrich & R. Holton (Eds.). *Cross-cultural communication and professional education* (pp.38-48). Adelaide, S.A.: Flinders University Centre for Multicultural Studies.

Braggett, E. J. (1992). *Pathways for accelerated learners.* Melbourne: Hawker-Brownlow Education.

Breyne, R. P. (1990). *The implementation of a talented and gifted model in the educational program of a youth CIRT.* Unpublished Masters paper, University of Oregon College of Education, Eugene.

Breyne, R. P. (1992). *A promising approach: A talented & gifted model for chemically dependent children.* Unpublished Masters paper, College of Education, University of Oregon, Eugene.

Breyne, R. P. (1993). *Research Report: High risk youth: Considerations for schol integrated AOD prevention and treatment.* Roseburg, OR: Phoenix School of Roseburg.

Brody, L., Fox, L.H. & Tobin, D. (Eds.). (1983). *Learning-disabled/gifted children.* Baltimore, MD: University Park Press.

Bronfenbrenner, V. (1977). Toward an experimental ecology of human development. *American Psychologist, 32,* 513-531.

Brown, A. L. (1978). Knowing when, where and how to remember: A problem of metacognition. In R. Glaser (Ed.). *Advances in instructional psychology, Vol. I .* Hillsdale, NJ: Erlbaum.

Bruce, R. (1993). Women and Islam. *Current Affairs Bulletin,* March, pp. 11-17.

Buescher, T. M. (1985). A framework for understanding the social and emotional development of gifted and talented adolescents. *Roeper Review, 8,* 10-15.

Buescher, T.M. (1991). Gifted adolescents. In N. Colangelo and G.A. Davis (Eds.). *Handbook of gifted education* (pp. 382 - 401). Boston: Allyn and Bacon.

Buescher, T. M. & Higham, S. J. (1989). A developmental study of adjustment among gifted adolescents. In Van Tassel-Baska, J. & Olszewski-Kubilius (Eds.). *Patterns of influence on gifted learners* (pp. 102-124). New York: Teachers College Press.

Butler-Por, N. (1983). Giftedness across cultures. In B. M. Shore, F. Gagne, S. Larivee, R. H. Tali & R. E. Tremblay (Eds.). *Face to face with giftedness* (pp. 250-270). New York: Trillium Press. (Available through Hawker Brownlow Education.)

Caplan, N., Choy, M.H. & Whitmore, J.K. (1992). Indochinese refugee families and academic achievement. *Scientific American, 266* (2), 18-24.

Callahan, C. M., Cunningham, C. M. & Plucker, J. A. (1994). Foundations for the future: The socio-emotional development of gifted, adolescent women. *Roeper Review, 17,*

99-105.

Clark, B. (1986). *Optimizing learning*. Columbus, Ohio: Charles E. Merrill.

Clark, B. (1988). *Growing up gifted*. (3rd ed.). Columbus, OH: Charles E. Merrill.

Clark, B. (1992). *Growing up gifted*. (4th ed.). Columbus, OH: Charles E. Merrill.

Cohen, L. M. (1985). *Towards a theory for gifted education*. Unpublished doctoral dissertation, Temple University, Philadelphia. University Microfilms International, #8509318.

Cohen, L.M. (1987). 13 tips for teaching gifted children. *Teaching Exceptional Children, 20*(1), 34-38.

Cohen, L. M. (1988). Developing children's creativity, thinking and interests: Strategies for the district, school and classroom. *OSSC Bulletin Monograph, 31*, (6), 1-70.

Cohen, L. M. (1989a). A continuum of adaptive creative behaviours. *Creativity Research Journal, 2*, 169-183.

Cohen, L. M. (1989b). What the children taught me: Comments on the purpose of education for gifted black students. In J. Maker & S. Schiever (Eds.), *Critical issues in gifted education: Defensible programs for cultural and ethnic minorities* (Vol. 2). (pp. 246-254). Austin, TX: Pro-Ed.

Cohen, L. M. (1989c). Understanding the interests and themes of the very young gifted child. *Gifted Child Today, 12,* (4), 6-9.

Cohen, L. M. (1991/1992). A gifted education for all children. *Our Gifted Children, 6*, 22-30.

Cohen, L. M. (1992a). Differentiating the curriculum for gifted students. *Our Gifted Children, 8*, 2-18.

Cohen, L. M. (1992b). Ownership to allship: Building a conceptual framework for educating of the gifted and creative. In N. Colangelo, S. G. Assouline and D. L. Ambroson *Developing talent: Proceedings from the 1991 Henry B. and Jocelyn Wallace National Research Symposium on Talent Development* (p. 204-222). Unionville, NY: Trillium Press.

Cohen, L. M. (1994). Mode-switching strategies. In J. Edwards (Ed.), *Thinking: International interdisciplinary perspectives* (pp. 230-240). Melbourne: Hawker-Brownlow.

Cohen, L. M., Tomchin, E., Frydenberg, E. & Smutny, J (1995). *A comparison of coping concerns and strategies between affluent and impoverished gifted 10-15 year olds*. Work in progress.

Colangelo, N. (1991). Counseling gifted students. In N. Colangelo & G. A. Davis (Eds.). *Handbook of gifted education* (pp. 273-284). Boston: Allyn & Bacon.

Colangelo, N. and Davis, G. A. (Eds.). (1991). *Handbook of gifted education. Boston, MA: Allyn and Bacon.*

Colangelo, N., Kerr, B., Christensen, P. & Maxey, J. (1993). A comparison of gifted underachievers and gifted high achievers. *Gifted Child Quarterly, 37,*155-160.

Coleman, J.M. & Fults, B.A. (1983). Self-concept and the gifted child. *Roeper Review, 5, (4),* 44-47.

Compas, B.E. (1987). Coping with stress during childhood and adolescence. *Psychological Bulletin, 101*(3), 393-403.

Connors, N. A. (1992). Teacher advisory: The fourth R. In J. L. Irvin (Ed.), *Transforming middle level education* (pp. 162-178). Boston: Allyn & Bacon.

Cornell, D.G. (1989). Child adjustment and parent use of the term "gifted". *Gifted Child Quarterly, 33*, 59-64.

Cornell, D. G. (1990). High ability students who are unpopular with their peers. *Gifted Child Quarterly, 34*, 155-160.

Cornell, D. G. , Pelton, G. M., Bassin, L. E., Landrum, M., Ramsay, S. G., Cooley, M. R., Lynch, K. A. and Hamrick, E. (1990). Self-concept and peer status among gifted program youth. *Journal of Educational Psychology, 82*, 456-463.

Costa, A. L (1984). Mediating the metacognitive. *Educational Leasdership, 42*, 57-62.

Covey, S. R. (1989). *The 7 habits of highly effective people*. Melbourne: The Business Library.

Covington, J. W. (1985). Strategic thinking and the fear of failure. In J.W. Segal, S.F Chipman, & R. Glaser (Eds.). *Thinking and learning skills Vol. 1: Relating instruction to research* (pp. 389-415). Hillsdale, N.J.: Earlbaum.

Coxhead, P. & Gupta, R. (Eds.). (1988). *Cultural diversity and learning efficiency*. London: MacMillan.

Cross, T. L., Coleman, L. J. & Stewart, R. A. (1993). The social cognition of gifted adolescents: An exploration of the stigma of giftedness paradigm. *Roeper Review, 16*, 37-40.

Cross, T. L., Dixon, D. N., & Cook, R. (1995). *Psychological autopsies of three gifted student suicides: A work in progress*. Paper presented at the Esther Katz Rosen Symposium, Lawrence, KS, September 9.

Csikszentmihalyi, M. & Larson, R. (1984). *Being adolescent*. New York: Basic Books.

Csikszentmihalyi, M. (1990). *Flow: The psychology of optimal experience*. New York: Harper Perennial.

Csikszentmihalyi, M., Rathunde , K., & Whalen (1993). *Talented teen-agers*. New York: Cambridge University Press.

Cummins, J. (1984). *Bilingualism and special education: Issues in assessment and pedagogy*. Avon, G.B.: Multilingual matters.

Curwin, R. L. & Mendler, A. N. (1988). *Discipline with dignity*. Alexandria, VA: ASCD.

Dalton J. & Smith, D. (1987). *Extending children's special abilities. Strategies for primary classrooms*. Melbourne: Ministry of Education.

Daniels, P.R. (1983). *Teaching the gifted / learning disabled child*. Rockville, MD: Aspen Systems.

Davidson, G. (Ed.). (1988). *Ethnicity and cognitive assessment: Australian perspectives. Darwin: DIT Press*.

Davidson, G.C. & Neale, J.M. (1982). *Abnormal psychology: An experimental clinical approach*. New York: John Wiley & Sons.

Davidson, J. E. (1986). The role of insight in giftedness. R. J. Sternberg & J. E. Davidson (Eds.). *Conceptions of giftedness* (pp. 201-222). New York: Cambridge University Press.

Davis, G. A. & Rimm, S. B. (1989). *Education of the gifted and talented*. Englewood Cliffs, NJ: Prentice-Hall.

deBono, E. (1992). *Six thinking hats for schools. Books 1-4*. Melbourne: Hawker Brownlow Education. (Series can be used in primary and secondary schools.)

DeLacy, P.R. & Poole, M.E. (Eds.). (1975). *Mosaic or melting pot: Cultural evolution in Australia*. Sydney: Harcourt, Brace Jovanovich.

Delisle, J. R. (1986). Death with honours: Suicide among gifted adolescents. *Journal of Counseling and Development, 64*, 558-560.

Delisle, J.R. (1990). The gifted adolescent at risk: Strategies and resources for suicide prevention among gifted youth. *Journal for the Education of the Gifted, 13*,(3), 212-229.

Delisle, J.R. (1992). *Guiding the social and emotional development of gifted youth: A practical guide for educators and counselors*. New York: Longman.

Dembo, M.H. (1991). *Applying educational psychology in the classroom*. New York: Longman.

Demick, J. & Wapner, S. (1991). *Field dependence-independence: Cognitive style across the life span*. New Jersey: Lawrence Erbaum Associates.

Demo, D.H., Small, S.A. & Savin-Williams, R.C. (1987). Family relations and self-esteem of adolescents and parents. *Journal of Marriage and the Family, 49*, 705-716.

Derevensky, J. and Coleman, E.B. (1989). Gifted children's fears. *Gifted Child Quarterly,*

33, 65-68.

DeVos, G. A. & Sofue, T. (Eds.). (1986). *Religion and the family in East Asia.* Berkeley, CA: University of California Press.

Dirks, J. (1979). Parents" reactions to identification of the gifted. *Roeper Review, 2* (2), 9-10.

Dirkes, M.A. (1983). Anxiety in the gifted, pluses and minuses. *Roeper Review. 6,* 68-70.

Douthitt, V.L. (1992). A comparison of adaptive behavior in gifted and nongifted children. *Roeper Review, 14* (3),149-150.

Duerk, J. (1989). *Circle of stones: Woman's journey to herself.* San Diego, CA: Lura Media.

Dusek, J. (Ed.). (1985). *Teacher expectancies.* Hillsdale, NJ: Erlbaum.

Dweck, C. S. (1995). *Students" theories about their intelligence: Implications for the gifted.* Paper presented at the Esther Katz Rosen Symposium. Lawrence, KS: September 8.

Dweck, C. S. & Leggert, E. L. (1988). A social-cognitive approach to motivation and personality. *Psychological Review, 95* (2), 256-273.

Elmore, R. F. & Zenus, V. (1994). Enhancing social-emotional development of middle school gifted students. *Roeper Review, 16,* 182-185.

Erikson, E.H. (1963). *Childhood and Society* (2nd edition). New York: Norton.

Erikson, E. H. (1985). *The life cycle completed.* New York: Norton.

Fallon, B., Frydenberg, E. & Boldero, J. (1993, September). *Perceptions of family climate and adolescent coping.* Paper presented at the 28th Annual Conference of the Australian Psychological Society, Gold Coast, Australia.

Farrell, D. M. (1989). Suicide among gifted students. *Roeper Review, 11* (3), 134-138.

Feldhusen, J. F. & Treffinger, D. J. (1985). *Creative thinking and problem solving in gfted education.* Dubuque, Iowa: Kendall Hunt.

Feldman, D.H., (1980). *Beyond universals in cognitive development.* Norwood, NJ: Ablex.

Feldman, D. H. (1986). *Nature's gambit.* Basic Books: New York.

Fetterman, D. M. (1988). *Excellence & equity: A qualitatively different perspective on gifted and talented education.* Albany, NY: State University of New York Press.

Feuerstein, R. (1979). *Instrumental enrichment: An intervention program for cognitive modifiability.* Baltimore, MD: University Park Press.

Flannery, D. J., Vazsony, A. T., Torquati, J. & Fredrich, A. (1993). Ethnic and gender differences In risk for early adolescent substance use. *Journal of Youth and Adolescence, 23,* 195-213.

Flavell, J.H. (1976). Metacognitive aspects of problem-solving. In L.B. Resnick (Ed.). *The nature of intelligence.* Hillsdale, NJ: Lawrence Earlbaum.

Flavell, J. H. (1981). Monitoring social cognitive enterprises: something else that may develop in the area of social cognition. In J. H. Flavell & L. Ross (Eds.). *Social cognitive development: Frontiers and possible futures* (pp.272-287). New York: Cambridge University Press.

Folkman, S., Chesney, M., McKusick, L., Ironson, G., Johnson, D.S. & Coates, T.J. (1991). Translating coping theory into an intervention. In Eckenrode, J. (Ed.). *The social context of coping.* New York and London: Plenum Press.

Folkman, S. & Lazarus, R.S. (1988a). Coping as a mediator of emotion. *Journal of Personality and Social Psychology, 54*(3), 466-475.

Folkman, S. & Lazarus, R.S. (1988b). The relationship between coping and emotion: Implications for theory and research. Special issue: Stress and coping in relation to health and disease. *Social Science and Medicine, 26*(3), 309-317.

Ford, M. (1989). Students" perceptions of affective issues impacting the social emotional development and school performance of gifted/talented youngsters. *Roeper Review, 11,* 131-134.

Ford, D. Y. (1994). Nurturing resilience in gifted black youth. *Roeper Review, 17,* 80-85.

Ford-Harris, D. Y. (1995). Respondent to C. Dweck, *Students" theories about their intelli-*

gence: Implications for the gifted. Esther Katz Rosen Symposium on the Psychological Development of Gifted Children. Lawrence, KS: September 8.

Foster, W. (1983). Self-concept, intimacy and the attainment of excellence. *Journal for the Education of the Gifted, 6,* 20-29.

Foster, W. & Mengel, H. (1987). Work and love: The interaction of intimacy, self-esteem, and productive excellence. In T. Buescher (Ed.), *Understanding gifted and talented adolescents* (pp. 11-16). Evanston, IL: Northwestern University, Center for Talent Development.

Freeman, J. (1985). Emotional aspects of giftedness. In Freeman, J. (Ed.). *The psychology of gifted children* (pp. 247-264). Chichester, GB: J.Wiley & Sons.

Frydenberg, E. (1993). The coping strategies used by capable adolescents. *Australian Journal of Guidance and Counselling, 3* (1), 1-9.

Frydenberg, E., & Lewis, R. (1990). How adolescents cope with different concerns: The development of the adolescent coping checklist (ACC). *Psychological Test Bulletin,* Australian Council for Educational Research, November, pp. 63-73.

Frydenberg, E. & Lewis, R. (1991a). Adolescent coping in the Australian context. *Australian Educational Researcher,18,* 65-82.

Frydenberg, E. & Lewis, R. (1991b). Adolescent coping styles and strategies: Is there functional and dysfunctional coping? *Australian Journal of Guidance and Counselling, 1*(1), 1-8.

Frydenberg, E. & Lewis, R. (1991c). Adolescent coping: The different ways in which boys and girls cope. *Journal of Adolescence,* 14,119-133.

Frydenberg, E. & Lewis, R. (1993a). *Manual: the adolescent coping scale.* Australian Council for Educational Research.

Frydenberg, E. & Lewis, R. (1993b). Boys play sport and girls turn to others: age, gender and ethnicity as determinants of coping. *Journal of Adolescence,16,* 253-266

Frydenberg, E. & Lewis, R. (1993c, September). *Stress in the family: How adolescents cope?* Paper presented at the 28th Annual Conference of the Australian Psychological Society, Gold Coast, Australia.

Frydenberg, E. Saljo. R & Anderson, P. (1993). *Conflict: Continuity and discontinuity of conflict during family discourse.* Paper presented at III European Congress of Psychology, Finland.

Fullan, M. (1991). *The new meaning of educational change.* London: Castell Educational Ltd.

Galbraith, J. (1991). *The gifted kids" survival guide* (for 10 and under). Melbourne: Hawker Brownlow Education.

Galbraith, J. (1991). *The gifted kids" survival guide* (for ages 11-18). Melbourne: Hawker Brownlow Education.

Gallagher, J. J. (1986). Equity vs excellence: An educational drama. *Roeper Review, 8,* 233-239.

Gallagher, J. J. & Kirk, S.A. (1989). *Education of exceptional children.* Boston: Houghton Mifflin Company.

Gardner, H. (1983). *Frames of mind.* New York: Basic Books.

Garfinkel, B. & Northrup, G. (Eds). (1989). *Adolescent suicide: recognition, treatment and prevention.* New York: The Haworth Press.

Gaston, R. B. (1993). *Effects of parental alcoholism on gifted children.* Unpublished Masters thesis, University of Texas-Pan American. Edinburg, TX.

George, W.C. (1983). Research issues in educating America's gifted. *G/C/T,* Mar/April, pp. 20-21.

Gilligan, C. (1982). *In a different voice: Psychological theory and women's development.* Lexington, MA: Harvard University Press.

Ginsburg, H. (1972). *The myth of the deprived child.* Englewood Cliffs, NJ: Prentice-Hall.

Ginsburg-Riggs, G. (1981). .C/C/T goes to England. *G/C/T,* October, pp. 38-39.

Glasser, W. (1986). *Control theory in the classroom*. New York: Harper & Row.

Gordon, T. (1975). *P.E.T. Parent effectiveness training*. New York: Plume.

Gordon, W. J. J. & Poze, T. (1972). *Strange and familiar*. Cambridge, MA: SES Associates.

Gordon, W. J. J. & Poze, T. (1980). *The new art of the possible*. Cambridge, MA: Porpoise Books.

Gordon, W. J. J. (1961). *Synectics*. New York: Harper & Row.

Gordon, W. J. J. (1974). *Making it strange*. Books 1-4. New York: Harper & Row.

Gowan, J. C. (1972). *The development of the creative individual*. San Diego: Robert R. Knapp.

Gowan, J. C. (1979). Differentiated guidance for the gifted: A developmental view. In J. C. Gowan, J. Khatena, & E. P. Torrance (Eds.), *Educating the ablest* (2nd ed.). (pp. 190-199). Itaska, IL: F. E. Peacock.

Gregory, S. & Hartley, G.M. (Eds.). (1991). *Constructing deafness*. London: Open University.

Gross, M. (1989). The pursuit of excellence or the search for intimacy? The forced-choice dilemma of gifted youth. *Roeper Review. 11*, 189-194.

Gross, M. U. M. (1993). *Exceptionally gifted children*. New York: Routledge.

Gruber, H. E. (1981). *Darwin on man: A psychological study of creativity*. Chicago, IL: University of Chicago Press. (Originally published by Gruber and Barrett, 1974).

Gruber, H. E. (1982). On the hypothesised relationship between giftedness and creativity. In D. H. Feldman (Ed.). *Developmental approaches to giftedness and creativity* (pp. 7-30). San Francisco: Jossey-Bass.

Gruber, H. E. & Voneche, J. J. (Eds.). (1977). *The essential Piaget*. New York: Basic Books.

Halsted, J. (1988). *Guiding gifted readers from pre-school to high school: A handbook for parents, teachers, counselors and librarians*. Columbus: Ohio Publishing.

Hamilton, L. (1995). Respondent to N. Kogan, *Motivational and personality patterns in performing artists*. Presentation at the Esther Katz Rosen Symposium on the Psychological Development of Gifted Children. Lawrence, KS: September 9.

Harris, I. D. & Howard, K. I. (1984). Parental criticism and the adolescent experience. *Journal of Youth and Adolescence, 13*, 113-121.

Harris, S. (1990). Walking through cultural doors: Aborigines, communication, schooling and cultural continuity in C. Hedrich & R. Holton (Eds.). *Cross-cultural communication and professional education* (pp. 127-138). Adelaide, S.A.: Centre for Cross Cultural Studies, Flinders University.

Hauser, P. & Nelson, G. A. (1988). *Books for the gifted child*. New York: R. R. Bowker.

Hauser, S. & Bowlds, M. (1990). Stress, coping and adaptation. In S. Feldman & G. Eliott (Eds.). *At the threshhold: The developing adolescent* (pp. 388-413). Cambridge, MA: Harvard University Press.

Hayes, M. & Sloat, R. (1989). Gifted students at risk for suicide. *Roeper Review, 11*, 102-107.

Hayes, M. & Sloat, R. (1990). Suicide and the gifted adolescent. *Journal for the Education of the Gifted, 13*, 229-244.

Heaven, P. & Callan, P. (1990). *Adolescence: An Australian perspective*. Sydney: Harcourt, Brace Jovanovich.

Herman, J. L., Aschbacher, P. R., & Winters, L. (1992). *A Practical Guide to Alternative Assessment*. Alexandria, VA: ASCD

Herald-Sun (1995). *Signs of drug dependency*. Melbourne: author.

Hewitt, P. L. & Dyck, D. G. (1986). Perfectionism, stress and vulnerability to depression. *Cognitive Therapy Research, 10*, 137-142.

Hoge, R.D. & Renzulli, J.S. (1991). *Self-concept and the gifted child: Executive summary*. Storrs, Ct: NRC/GT.

Holley, C. D. & Dansereau, D. F. (1984). *Spatial learning strategies*. New York: Academic Press.

Hollingworth, l. (1942). *Children above 180 I.Q. Stanford Binet: Origin and development.* Yonkers-on-Hudson, NY: World Book.

Holt, D. G. (1993). *Humor as a coping mechanism: Dealing with manifestations of stress associated with children identified as gifted and talented.* Unpublished dissertation, Purdue University, Lafayette, IN.

Hoodbhoy, P. (1991). *Islam and science: Religious orthodoxy and the battle for rationality.* London: Zed Books.

Horowitz, F. D. & O'Brien, M. (1985). Epilogue: Perspectives on research and development. In F.D. Horowitz & M. O'Brien (Eds.). *The gifted and talented: Developmental perspectives.* (pp. 437-454). Washington, DC: American Psychological Association.

Howard-Hamilton, M. F. (1994). An assessment of moral development in gifted adolescents. *Roeper Review, 17,* 57-59.

Howard-Hamilton, M. F. & Franks, B. A. (1995). Gifted adolescents: Psychological behaviors, values, and developmental implications. *Roeper Review, 17,* 186-191.

Hull, J.M. (1990). *Touching the rock: An experience of blindness.* Melbourne: Lovell Publishing.

Janos, P. M., Marwood, K. A. & Robinson, N. M. (1985). Friendship patterns in highly intelligent children. *Roeper Review, 8,* 46-49.

Janos, P.M. & Robinson, N.M. (1985). Psychosocial development in intellectually gifted children. In F.D. Horowitz & M. O'Brien (Eds.). *The gifted and talented: Developmental Perspectives* (pp. 149-195). American Psychological Association, Washington, D.C.

Janos, P.M., Fung, H.C., & Robinson, N.M. (1985). Self-concept, self-esteem and peer relations among gifted children who feel "different". *Gifted Child Quarterly, 29,* 78-82

Jenkins-Friedman, R. (1989). Families of gifted children and youth. In M. J. Fine & C. I. Carlson (Eds.). *A handbook of family, school problems and interventions: A systems perspective* (pp. 175-187). New York: Grune & Stratton.

Jenkins-Friedman, R. & Murphy, D.L. (1988). The Mary Poppins effect: Relationships between gifted students" self-concept and adjustment. *Roeper Review, 11,* 26-30.

Jenkins-Friedman, R. & Murphy, D. M. (1990). Advice from a caterpillar: Ameliorating diminished self-concept among newly placed gifted students through systematic teaching about abilities. C. Taylor (Ed.). *Perspectives on talent: Proceedings of the 7th World Conference on Gifted and Talented Students.* Monroe, NY: Trillium Press.

Jenkins-Friedman, R. & Tollefson, N. (1992). Resiliency in cognition and motivation. In N. Colangelo, S. G. Assouline, and D. L. Ambroson (Eds.). *Talent development: Proceedings form the 1991 Henry B. and Jocelyn Wallace National Research Symposium on Talent Development* (pp. 325-333). Unionville, NY: Trillium.

Johnson, E. M. (1993). *Concerns and coping strategies of gifted adolescent girls.* Unpublished Masters essay, University of Melbourne, DEPSE, CHIP Unit: Melbourne, Australia.

John-Steiner, V. (1985). *Notebooks of the mind.* New York: Harper & Row.

Jones, B. F. (1986). Quality and equality through cognitive instruction. *Educational Leadership, 43* (7), 4-11.

Kantor, M. (1990). *When ants learn to dance.* New York: Simon & Schuster.

Kaplan, R.B. (1972). Cultural thought patterns in inter-cultural education, in K. Crott (Ed.). *Readings on English as a second language* (pp. 245-262). New York: Cambridge University Press.

Karnes, M. B. (1979). Young disabled children can be gifted and talented. *Journal for the Education of the Gifted, 2,* 157-172.

Karnes, M.; Shwedel, A. & Lewis, K. G. (1983). Long-term effects of early programming for the gifted/talented disabled. *Journal for the Education of the Gifted, 6,* 266-278.

Kaufmann, F. (1992). *Yes, you can: Using synectics in your classroom.* Paper presented at

AAEGT National Conference, Melbourne, September.

Kerr, B. (1991). *A handbook for counselling the gifted and talented.* Alexandria, VA: American Association for Counselling and Development.

Kerr, B. A. (1985). *Smart girls, gifted women.* Columbus, OH: Ohio Publishing. (Re-published by Hawker Brownlow Education).

Kerr, B. A. (1995). Respondent to J. Eccles, *Not you! not here! not now!* Presentation at the Esther Katz Rosen Symposium on the Psychological Development of Gifted Children. Lawrence, KS: September 8.

Kerr, B. A., Colangelo, N. and Gaeth, J. (1988). Gifted adolescents" attitudes toward their giftedness. *Gifted Child Quarterly, 32*, 245-247.

Khatena, J. (1979). Creativity, general systems and the gifted. *Gifted Child Quarterly, 23*, 698-715.

Khatena, J. (1992). *Gifted: Challenge and response for education.* Itaska, IL: F. E. Peacock.

Kitano, M. K. & Kirby, D. (1986). *Gifted education: A comprehensive view.* Boston: Little, Brown.

Klein, R. (1984). *Hating Alison Ashley.* New York: Penguin Books.

Kline, B. E. & Meckstroth, E. O. (1985). Understanding and encouraging the exceptionally gifted. *Roeper Review, 8* (1), 24-30.

Kline, B.E. & Short, E.B. (1991). Changes in emotional resilience: gifted adolescent boys. *Roeper Review, 4*, 184-187.

Kolb, K. J. & Jussim, L. (1994). Teacher expectations and underachieving gifted children. *Roeper Review, 17*, 26-30.

Kohlberg, L. (1963). The development of children's orientations toward a moral order: Sequence in the development of moral thought. *Vita humana 6*, 11-33.

Kohlberg, L. (1981). *The philosophy of moral development.* San Francisco: Harper and Row.

Kosky, R., Silburn, S. & Zubrick, S. R. (1990). Are children and adolescents who have suicidal thoughts different from those who attempt suicide? *The Journal of Nervous and Mental Diseases, 78*, 38-43.

Krueger, M. L. (1978). *On being gifted.* New York: Walker and Company.

LaFrance, E. B. (1995). Creative thinking differences in three groups of exceptional children as expressed though completion of figural forms. *Roeper Review, 17*, 248-252.

Land, G. T. & Kenneally, C. (1977). Creativity, reality and general systems: A personal viewpoint. *Journal of Creative Behavior, 11*, 12-35.

Lazarus, R. S. & Launier, R. (1978). Stress-related transactions between person and environment. In A. Pervin & M. Lewis (Eds.). *Perspectives in international psychology* (pp. 287-327). New York: Plenum.

Lebra, T.S. & Lebra, W.P. (Eds.). (1986). *Japanese culture and behavior: Selected readings.* Honolulu: University of Hawaii Press.

L'Engle, M. (1973). *A wind in the door.* New York: Farrar, Straus and Giroux.

Lewis, M. (1986). Foreword. In C. R. Pfeffer *The suicidal child.* New York: Guilford Press.

Lockhead, J. (1985). Teaching analytic reasoning skills through pair problem-solving. In J.W. Segal, S. F. Chipman & R. Glaser (Eds.), *Thinking and learning skills, vol. 1: Relating instruction to research* (pp.109-131). Hillsdale, NJ: Earlbaum.

Loeb, R.C. & Jay, G. (1987). Self-concept in gifted children: Differential impact in boys and girls. *Gifted Child Ouarterly, 31*, 9- 14.

Lovecky, D. V. (1993). The quest for meaning: Counseling issues with gifted children and adolescents. In L. K. Silverman (Ed.), *Counseling the gifted and talented* (pp. 29-50). Denver: Love Publishing.

Lovecky, D. V. (1994). Exceptionally gifted children: Different minds. *Roeper Review, 17*, 116-120.

Luftig, R. L. & Nichols, M. L. (1990). Assessing the social status of gifted students by their age peers. *Gifted Child Quarterly, 34,* 111- 115.

Maccoby, E.E. & Martin, J.A. (1983). Social Development in Context of the Family: Prent-Child Interaction. IN E.M. Heatherton (Ed.), Handbook of Child Psychology: Vol. 4. *Social, Personality & Social Development* (pp. 1-102). New York: Wiley.

Maker, C.J. (1977). *Providing programs for the gifted handicapped.* Reston, VA: The Council for Exceptional Children.

Maker, C.J. & Shiever, S.W. (Eds.). (1989). *Critical issues in gifted education: Defensible programs for cultural and ethnic minorities.* Austin, TX: Pro-Ed.

Maker, C.J. & Whitmore, J.R. (1985). *Intellectual giftedness in disabled persons.* Rockville, MD: Aspen Systems.

Manaster, G. J., Chan, J. C., Watt, C., & Wiehe, J. (1994). Gifted adolescents" attitudes toward their giftedness: A partial replication. *Gifted Child Quarterly, 38,* 176-178.

Margulies, N. (1992). *Mapping inner space.* Melbourne: Hawker Brownlow Education.

Marzano, R. J. & Arredondo, D. E. (1986). *Tactics for thinking.* Alexandria, VA: ASCD.

Matters, P. N. (1989). *A meeting of minds: The mentor program.* Unpublished Masters thesis. Melbourne: Monash University.

Matthews, J. L., Golin, A. K., Moore, M. W., & Baker, C. (1992). Use of SOMPA in identification of gifted African-American children. *Journal for the Education of the Gifted, 15,* 344-356.

May, K. M. (1994). A developmental view of a gifted child's social and emotional adjustment. *Roeper Review, 17,* 105-109.

McCowan, K. (1995). Depression still misunderstood. *Register Guard,* September 7.

McCubbin, H.I., Cauble, A.E. & Patterson, J.M. (Eds.). (1982). *Family stress, coping, and social support.* Springfield, Illinois: Charles C.Thomas.

McCubbin, H.I., Needle, R.H., Wilson, M. (1985). Adolescent health risk behaviors: Family stress and adolescent coping as critical factors. Special issue: The family and health care. Family Relations. *Journal of Applied Family and Child Studies, 34*(1), 51-62.

Meichenbaum, D. (1977). *Cognitive behavior modification: An integrative approach.* New York: Plenum.

Mendaglio, S. (1995). Sensitivity among gifted persons: A multi-faceted perspective. *Roeper Review 17,* 169-172.

Merrell, K. W. & Gill, S. J. (1994). Using teacher ratings of social behavior to differentiate gifted from non-gifted students. *Roeper Review, 16,* 286-289.

Messibov, F.B. & Schopler, E. (Eds.). (1992). *High-functioning individuals with autism.* New York: Plenum Press.

Miller, A. (1981). *The drama of the gifted child: The search for the true self.* New York: Basic Books.

Moore, S. & Rosenthal, D. (1993). *Sexuality in adolescence.* London: Routledge.

Morelock, M. J. & Feldman, D. H. (1991). Extreme precocity. In N. Colangelo & G. A. Davis (Eds.), *Handbook of gifted education* (pp. 347-364). Boston: Allyn & Bacon

Morgan, V. (1992). The biggest secret of all. *A Different Drummer, 9* (1), 17-18.

Morgan, V. A. (1992). *Intervention strategies for gifted children at risk: Finding the angel in the marble.* Unpublished doctoral dissertation. Eugene, OR: University of Oregon.

Morrissey, C. & Hannah, T. E. (1987). Measurement of psychological hardiness in adolescents. *Journal of Genetic Psychology, 148,* 393-397.

Moss, E. (1990). Social interaction and metacognitive development in gifted preschoolers. *Gifted Child Quarterly, 34,* 16-20.

Nelson, J. , Lott, L, & Glenn, H. S. (1993). *Positive discipline in the classroom.* Rocklin, CA: Prima Publishing.

Noller, P. & Callan, V. (1986). Adolescents and parents" perceptions of family cohesion and adaptability. *Journal of Adolescence, 9,* 97-106.

Noller, P. & Callan, V. (1991). *The adolescent in the family*. London: Routledge.

Novak, J.D. & Gowin, D.B. (1984). *Learning how to learn*. New York: Cambridge University Press.

Olszewski-Kubilius, P., Grant, B., & Seibert, C. (1994). Social support systems and the disadvantaged gifted: A framework for developing programs and services. *Roeper Review, 17*, 20-25.

Olszewski P, Kulieke M. and Buescher T. (1987). The influence of the family environment on the development of talent: A literature review. *Journal for the Education of the Gifted, 2*, 6-28.

Overton, W. F. (1975). General systems, structure and development. In F. Riegel and G. C. Rosenwald (Eds.). *Structure and transformation: Developmental and historical aspects* (vol. 3), (pp. 61-81). New York: Wiley.

Palmer, R. (1989). *Anorexia nervosa: A guide for sufferers and their families*. London: Penguin.

Parker, J. G. & Asher, S. R. (1987). Peer relations and later personal adjustment: Are low-accepted children at risk? *Psychological Bulletin, 102* , 357-389.

Parker, W. D. & Adkins, K. K. (1995). Perfectionism and the gifted. *Roeper Review, 17*, 173-176.

Parsons, G. (1986). *The language of caring*. Unpublished manuscript for a pilot study at Phoenix School. Roseburg, Oregon (cited in Morgan, 1992).

Passow, A.H. (1988). Educating gifted persons who are caring and concerned. *Roeper Review, 11*, 13-15.

Patai, R. (1976). *The Arab mind*. New York: Charles Scribner's Sons.

Pataki, C. & Carlson, G. (1990). Affective disorders in children and adolescents. In B. Tong and G. Burrows (Eds). *Handbook of Studies on Child Psychiatry* (pp. 137-160). Amsterdam: Elsevier Press.

Patterson, J.M. & McCubbin, H.I. (1987). Adolescent coping style and behaviors: Conceptualisation and measurement. *Journal of Adolescence, 10*(2), 163-186.

Perkins, D.N. (1981). *The mind's best work*. Cambridge, MA: Harvard University Press.

Peterson, C., Peterson, J. & Skevington, S. (1986). Heated argument and adolescent development. *Journal of Social and Personal Relationships, 3*, 229-240.

Piaget, J. (1980). *Adaptation and intelligence: Organic selection and phenocopy*. Chicago: University of Chicago Press (Originally published in French, 1974).

Piechowski, M. M. (1986). The concept of developmental potential. *Roeper Review, 8*, 190-197.

Piechowski, M. M. (1991). Emotional development and emotional giftedness. In N. Colangelo & G. A. Davis (Eds.). *Handbook of gifted education* (pp. 285-306). Sydney: Allyn and Bacon.

Plucker, J. A. (1994). Issues in the social and emotional adjustment and development of a gifted, Chinese American student. *Roeper Review, 17*, 89-94.

Poland, S. (1989). *Suicide prevention in the schools*. New York: The Guilford Press.

Polette, N. (1984). *Books and real life: A guide for gifted students and teachers*. Jefferson, NC: McFarland.

Presseisen, B. (1987). *Thinking skills throughout the curriculum: A conceptual design*. Bloomington, IN: Pi Lamda Theta.

Pringle, K. M. (1970). *Able misfits. The educational and behavioral difficulties of intelligent children*. London: Longman Group Limited.

Purkey, W. (1970). *Self-concept and school achievement*. Englewood Cliffs, NJ: Prentice Hall.

Reed, D. F., McMillan, J. H., & McBee, R. H. (1995). Defying the odds: Midle schoolers in high risk circumstances who succeed. *Middle School Journal, 27* (1), 3-10.

Reichart, S. (1982, August). Sexuality and the gifted child. *Gifted Children Monthly*, pp. 1-2.

Reid, L. (1990). *Thinking skills resource book*. Mansfield Center, CT: Creative Learning Press.

Renzulli, J. S. (1991). The National Research Center on the Gifted and Talented: The dream, the design, and the destination. *Gifted Child Quarterly, 35,* 73-80.

Renzulli, J. S. (1994). *Schools for talent development: A practial plan for total school improvement*. Mansfield Center, CT: Creative Learning Press.

Renzulli, J. S., Smith, L. H., White, A. J., Callahan, C. M., & Hartman, R. K. (1976). *Scale for rating the behavioral characteristics of superior students*. Mansfield, CT: Creative Learning Press.

Rimm, S. B. (1985). Identifying underachievement: The characteristics approach. *Gifted Child Today 41*, 2-5.

Rimm, S.B. (1986). *Underachievement syndrome: Causes and cures*. Watertown, WI: Apple Publishing.

Rimm, S. & Lowe, B. (1988). Family environment of underachieving gifted students. *Gifted Child Quarterly, 32,* 353-359.

Rimm, S. B. (1991). Underachievement and superachievement: Flip sides of the same psychological coin. In N. Colangelo & G. Davis (Eds.). *Handbook of gifted education* (pp. 328-343). Boston: Allyn & Bacon.

Robbins, S. (1989). *Organisational behavior: Concepts, controversies and applications*. Sydney: Prentice-Hall.

Robinson, G.L. (1985). *Cross-cultural understanding: Processes and approaches for foreign language, English as a second language and bilingual educators*. New York: Pergamon Institute of English.

Roedell, W. C. (1984). Vulnerabilities of highly gifted children. *Roeper Review, 6,* 127-130.

Roedell, W. C., Jackson, N. E. & Robinson, H. B. (1980). *Gifted young children*. New York: Teachers College Press.

Roeper, A. (1982). How the gifted cope with their emotions. *Roeper Review, 5,* 21-24.

Roeper, A. (1988). Should educators of the gifted and talented be more concerned with world issues? *Roeper Review, 11,* 12-13.

Rosenthal, D.A. (1984). Intergenerational conflict and culture: a study of immigrant and nonimmigrant adolescents and their parents. *Genetic Psychology Monographs, 109,* 53-75.

Rosenthal, R. & Jacobson, L. (1968). *Pygmalion in the classroom: Teacher expectations and pupils" intellectual development*. New York: Holt, Rinehart & Winston.

Runions, T. (1980). The mentor academy program: Educating the gifted/talented for the 80's. *Gifted Child Quarterly, 24,* 152-157.

Runions, T. & Smyth, E. (1985). Gifted adolescents as co-learners in mentorships. *Journal for the Education of the Gifted, 8,* 127-133.

Rutter, M. (1979). Protective factors in children's responses to stress and disadvantage. In M. W. Kent & J. E. Rolf (Eds.), *Social competence in children* (pp. 49-74). Hanover, NH: University Press of New England.

Rutter, M. (1985). Resilience in the face of adversity: Protective factors and resistance to psychiatric disorder. *British Hournal of Psychiatry, 147,* 598-611.

Rutter, M. (1987). Psychosocial resilience and protective mechanisms. *American Journal of Orthopsychiatry, 57,* 316-331.

Rutter, M. & Rutter, M. (1992). *Developing minds: Challenge and continuity across the life-span*. London: Penguin.

Sachs, O. (1989). *Seeing voices: A journey into the world of the deaf*. New York: Picador.

Sayers, B. (1988). Left or right brain: Is there a neurological relationship to traditional aboriginal learning styles? In B. Harvey & S. McGinty (Eds.). *Learning my way: Papers from the National Conference on Adult Aboriginal Learning* (pp. 238-248). Mt. Lawley, W.A.: Institute of Applied Aboriginal Studies.

Schlegel, A. & Barry, I. H. (1991). *Adolescence, an anthropological inquiry*. New York:

Free Press.

Schmeck, R.R., Geisler-Brenstein, & Cercy, S.P. (1991). Self-concept and learning: The revised inventory of learning processes. *Educational Psychology, 11*, 343-362.

Schmitz, C. & Galbraith, J. (1985). *Managing the social and emotional needs of the gifted. A teacher's survival guide.* Minneapolis, MN: Free Spirit Publishing.

Schneider, B. H. (1987). *The gifted child in peer group perspective.* New York: Springer-Verlag.

Seligman, M. (1992). *Learned Optimism.* Sydney: Random House.

Shaffer, D. (1986). Developmental factors in child and adolescent suicide. In M. Rutter, G. Tizzard and P. Reid. (Eds). *Depression in young people* (pp. 383-399). New York: Guilford Press.

Shore, B. M. & Dover, A. C. (1987). Metacognition, intelligence, and giftedness. *Gifted Child Quarterly, 31*, 37-39.

Shulman, S., Sieffge-Krenke, I., Samet, N. (1987). Adolescent coping style as a function of perceived family climate. *Journal of Adolescent Research, 2* (4), 367-381.

Sieffge-Krenke, I. (1990). Developmental processes in self-concept and coping behavior. In Bosma, H. & Jackson, S. (Eds.). *Coping and self-concept in adolescence* (pp. 49-68). New York: Springer-Verlag.

Silverman, L. K. (1988). Affective curriculum for the gifted. In Van Tassel-Baska, J., Feldhusen, J., Seeley, K., Wheatley, G., Silverman, L. & Foster, W. (Eds.). *Comprehensive curriculum for gifted learners* (pp. 335-355). Boston, MA: Allyn & Bacon.

Silverman, L.K. (1991). Family counselling. In N. Colangelo and G.A. Davis (Eds.). *Handbook of gifted education.* (pp. 307 - 320). Boston: Allyn and Bacon.

Silverman, L. K. (Ed.). (1993a). *Counseling the gifted and talented.* Denver: Love Publishing.

Silverman, L. K. (1993b). A developmental model for counseling the gifted. In L. K. Silverman (Ed.), *Counseling the gifted and talented* (pp. 51-78). Denver: Love Publishing.

Silverman, L. K. (1993c). Techniques for preventative counseling. In L. K. Silverman (Ed.), *Counseling the gifted and talented* (pp. 81-109). Denver: Love Publishing.

Silverman, L. K. (1993d). Social development, leadership, and gender issues. In L. K. Silverman (Ed.), *Counseling the gifted and talented* (pp. 291-336). Denver: Love Publishing.

Silverman, L. K. (1993e). Counseling families. In L. K. Silverman (Ed.), *Counseling the gifted and talented* (pp. 151-178). Denver: Love Publishing.

Simonton, D. K. (1978). The eminent genius in history: The critical role of creative development. *Gifted Child Quarterly, 22*, 187-195.

Sisk, D.A. (1982). Caring and sharing: moral development of gifted students. *Elementary School Journal, 28* (3), 221-229.

Smilansky, M. (1991). *Friendship in adolescence and young adulthood.* Gaithersburg, MD: Psychosocial & Educational Publications.

Snyder, C. R. (1995). *Children and the price of excellence: Hope for the few or the many.* Paper presented at the Esther Katz Rosen Symposium. Lawrence, KS: September 9.

Sowa, C. J., McIntire, J., May, K. M., & Bland, L. (1994). Social and emotional adjustment themes across gifted children. *Roeper Review, 17*, 95-98.

Sternberg, R. J. (1985). Beyond IQ: *A triarchic theory of human intelligence.* New York: Cambridge University Press.

Sternberg, R. J. (1986). Intelligence, wisdom and creativity: Three is better than one. *Educational Psychologist, 21*, 175-190.

Sternberg, R. J. (Ed.). (1988). *The nature of creativity.* New York: Cambridge University Press.

Sternberg, R. J. (1990). *Metaphors of mind: Conceptions of the nature of intelligence.* New York: Cambridge University Press.

Sternberg, R. J. (1991). Giftedness according to the triarchic theory of human intelligence. In N. Colangelo & G. A. Davis (Eds.), *Handbook of gifted education* (pp. 45-54). Boston: Allyn & Bacon.

Sternberg, R. J. & Clinkenbeard, P. R. (1995). The triarchic model applied to identifying, teaching, and assessing gifted children. *Roeper Review, 17,* 255-260.

Storfer, M. D. (1990). *Intelligence and giftedness: The contributions of heredity and early environment.* San Franscisco: Jossey-Bass.

Supplee, P. L. (1990). *Reaching the gifted underachiever.* New York: Teachers College Press.

Suter, D. & Wolf, J. (1987). Issues in the identification and programming of the gifted learning/disabled child. *Journal for the Education of the Gifted,10,* 227-237.

Swanson, J. D. (1995). Gifted African-American children in rural schools: Searching for the answers. *Roeper Review, 17,* 261-266.

Swassing, R.J. (1985). *Teaching gifted children and adolescents.* Columbus, OH: Merill.

Swicegood, P.R. & Parsons, J. L. (1989). Better questions and answers equal success. *Teaching Exceptional Children, 2* (3), 4-8.

Tallent-Runnels, M. K. & Sigler, E. A. (1995). The status of the selection of gifted students with learning disabilities for gifted programs. *Roeper Review, 17,* 246-248.

Tannenbaum, A.J. (1983). *Gifted children: Psychological and educational perspectives.* New York: Macmillan.

Tannenbaum, A. (1991). The social psychology of giftedness. In N. Colangelo & G. A. Davis (Eds.). *Handbook of gifted education* (pp. 27-44). Sydney: Allyn and Bacon.

Terman, L. M. (Ed.). (1925). *Genetic studies of genius (Vol. 1): Mental and physical traits of a thousand gifted children.* Palo Alto, CA: Stanford University Press.

Terrassier, J. C. (1985). Dyssynchrony: Uneven development. In J. Freeman (Ed.), *The psychology of gifted children* (pp. 265-274). Chichester, GB: J. Wiley & Sons.

Tomchin, E., Callahan, C., Sowa, C., May, K., Taylor, J. l. & Plucker, J. (1995, April). *Adolescents social and emotional adjustment: Patterns in gifted populations.* Paper presented at the Annual Meeting of the American Educational Research Association, San Francisco, CA.

Torrance, E. P. (1962). *Guiding creative talent.* Englewood Cliffs, NJ: Prentice-Hall.

Torrance, E.P. (1977). *Discovery and nurturance of giftedness in the culturally different.* Reston, VA: The Council for Exceptional Children.

Torrance, E. P. (1980). What we can learn from the Japanese about giftedness and creativity. *G/C/T,* May/June, pp. 4-9.

Treffinger, D. J. ((1992). *Volume I, II, III: The programming for giftedness series.* Sarasota, FL: Center for Creative Learning, Inc.

Trueba, H. T. (1989). *Raising silent voices: Educating the linguistic minorities for the 21st century.* New York: Newbury House.

Tye, K. B. & Bireley, M. (1991). Moral and spiritual development of the gifted adolescent. In M. Bireley & J. Genshaft (Eds.). *Understanding the gifted adolescent* (pp. 215-227). New York: Teachers College Press.

Ury, W. (1991). *Getting past no: Negotiating with difficult people.* Sydney: Bantam Books.

Van Tassel-Baska, J. (1991). Serving the disabled gifted through educational collaboration. *Journal for the Education of the Gifted, 14,* 227-237.

Van Tassel-Baska, J. (1992). *Planning effective curriculum for gifted learners.* Denver: Love Publishing.

Van Tassel-Baska, J. & Olszewski-Kubilius (Eds.). (1989). *Patterns of influence on gifted learners.* New York: Teachers College Press.

Van Tassel-Baska, J., Olszewski-Kubilius, P., &Kulieke, M. (1994). A study of self-concept and social support in advantaged and disadvantaged seventh and eighth grade gifted students. *Roeper Review, 16,* 186-191.

Van Tassel-Baska, J. with Feldhusen, J., Seeley, K., Wheatley, G., Silverman, L. & Foster, W. (1988). *Comprehensive curriculum for gifted learners.* Boston: Allyn & Bacon.

Vail, P. L. (1987). *Smart kids with school problems: Things to know and ways to help.* New York: Plume.

Vuchinich, S. (1987). Starting and stopping spontaneous family conflict. *Journal of Marriage and the Family, 49,* 591-601.

Webb, J.T.; Meckstroth, E.A. and Tolan, S.S. (1982). *Guiding the gifted child. A practical source for parents and teachers.* Columbus, OH: Ohio Psychology Press.

Wechsler, D. (1975). Intelligence defined and undefined: A realistic appraisal. *American Psychologist, 30,* 135-139.

West, T.W. (1991). *In the mind's eye: Visual thinkers, gifted people with learning difficulties, computer images and theories of creativity.* New York: Prometheus.

Whimby, A. & Lockhead, J. (1980). *Problem solving and comprehension: A short course in analytical reasoning* (2nd ed.). Philadelphia: Franklin Institute Press.

Whitmore, J.R. (1980). *Giftedness, conflict, and underachievement.* Boston: Allyn and Bacon.

Whitmore, J. R. (1987). *Conflict and the underachiever.* Keynote presentation at the meeting of Oregon Association for Talented and Gifted (OATAG), Spring Conference, Pendleton, Oregon.

Whitmore, J. R. (1989). Re-examining the concept of underachievement. *Understanding Our Gifted, 2* (1), 1-9.

Wilks, J. (1986). The relative importance of parents and friends in adolescent decision making. *Journal of Youth and Adolescence, 15,* 323-335.

Williams, D. (1992). *Nobody nowhere - The extraordinary autobiography of an autistic child.* New York: Times Books.

Williams, F.E. (1986). The cognitive-affective interaction model for enriching gifted programs, in J. Renzulli (Ed.). *Systems and models for developing programs for the gifted and talented* (pp. 461-484). Mansfield Center, CT: Creative Learning Press.

Wolfgang, A. (Ed.), (1984). *Towards nonverbal behavior: Perspectives, applications, intercultural insights.* New York: C. J. Hogrefe, Inc.

World Health Organization (1994). *World health statistics annual.* New York: Author.

Yewchuk, C.R. (1985). Gifted/learning disabled children: problems of assessment, in Cropley, A. J., Urban, K. K., Wagner, H. & Wierczerkowski, W. (Eds.). *Giftedness: A continuing worldwide challenge* (pp.40-48). New York: Trillium Press.

Zimpher, N. L. & Rieger, S. R. (1988). Mentoring teachers - What are the issues? *Theory into Practice,* Summer, pp. 175-182.

Resources for Teachers

Bloom, B. S. (Ed.). (1985). *Developing talent in young people*. New York: Ballentine.

Brody, L., Fox, L.H. & Tobin, D. (Eds.). (1983). *Learning-disabled/gifted children*. Baltimore, MD: University Park Press.

Clark, B. (1986). *Optimizing learning*. Columbus, OH: Charles E. Merrill.

Clark, B. (1992). *Growing up gifted*. (4th Ed.). Columbus, OH: Charles E. Merrill.

Cohen, L. M. (1992a). Differentiating the curriculum for gifted students. *Our Gifted Children, 8*, 2-18.

Colangelo, N. & Davis, G. A. (Eds.). (1991). *Handbook of gifted education*. Boston, MA: Allyn and Bacon.

Coleman, M.R. (1995). *Educating Gifted Students with Learning Disabilites*. Waco, TX: Prufrock Press.

Dalton J. & Smith, D. (1987). *Extending children's special abilities. Strategies for primary classrooms*. Melbourne: Ministry of Education.

Daniels, P.R. (1983). *Teaching the gifted/learning disabled child*. Rockville, MD: Aspen Systems.

Davis, G. A. & Rimm, S. B. (1989). *Education of the gifted and talented*. Englewood Cliffs, NJ: Prentice-Hall.

Delisle, J.R. (1992). *Guiding the social and emotional development of gifted youth: A practical guide for educators and counselors*. New York: Longman.

Elwell, P.A. (1994). *Creative Problem Solving for Teens*. Waco, TX: Prufrock Press.

Feldhusen, J. F. (1992). *Talent identification and development in education (TIDE)*. Sarasota FL: Center for Creative Learning.

Feldhusen, J. F. & Treffinger, D. J. (1985). *Creative thinking and problem solving in gifted education*. Dubuque, Iowa: Kendall Hunt.

Freeman, J. (Ed.). (1986). *The psychology of gifted children*. Chichester, GB: J. Wiley & Sons.

Frydenberg. E. and Lewis, R. (1993). *Manual: The Adolescent Coping Scale*. Melbourne: Australian Council for Educational Research.

Gallagher, J. J. (1985). *Teaching the gifted child* (3rd ed.). Boston: Houghton Mifflin.

Heacox, D. (1993). *Up from underachievement*. Minneapolis: Free Spirit Publishing.

Horowitz, F. D. & O'Brien, M. (Eds.). (1985). *The gifted and talented: Developmental perspectives* (pp. 437-454). Washington, DC: American Psychological Association.

Johnsen, S. & Johnson, K. (1995). *Independent Study Program*. Waco, TX: Prufrock Press.

Karnes, M.B. (Ed.). (1983). *The underserved: Our young gifted children*. Reston, VA: ERIC Clearinghouse.

Kelly, L. (1995). Challenging Minds. Waco, TX: Prufrock Press.

Kerr, B. (1991). *A handbook for counselling the gifted and talented*. Alexandria, VA: American Association for Counselling and Development.

Kerr, B. A. (1985). *Smart girls, gifted women*. Columbus, OH: Ohio Publishing.

Kerr, B. (1991). *A handbook for counselling the gifted and talented*. Alexandria, VA: American Association for Counselling and Development.

Khatena, J. (1992). *Gifted: Challenge and response for education*. Itaska, IL: F. E. Peacock.

Maker, C. J. (1982). *Teaching models in education of the gifted*. Rockville, MD: Aspen Systems.

Maker, C.J. (1977). *Providing programs for the gifted handicapped*. Reston, VA: The Council for Exceptional Children.

Maker, C.J. Shiever, S.W. (Eds.). (1989). *Critical issues in gifted education: Defensible programs for cultural and ethnic minorities*. Austin, TX: Pro-Ed.

Maker, C.J. & Whitmore, J. R. (1985). *Intellectual giftedness in disabled persons.* Rockville, MD: Aspen Systems.

Mares, L. (1991). *Young Gifted Children: From Potential to Achievement.* Melbourne: Hawker Brownlow Education.

Mares, L. (1991). *Adolescence and Giftedness.* Melbourne: Hawker Brownlow Education.

Marjorum, T. (1988). *Teaching able children.* London: Kogan Page Limited.

McIntosh, J. & Meacham, A. (1992). *Creative Problem Solving in the Classroom.* Waco, TX: Prufrock Press.

McIntosh, J. (1991). *20 Ideas for Teaching Gifted Kids in the Middle School and High School.* Waco, TX: Prufrock Press.

McIntosh, J. (1991). *20 More Ideas for Teaching Gifted Kids in the Middle School and High School.* Waco, TX: Prufrock Press.

Miller, A. (1981). *The drama of the gifted child*: The search for the true self. New York: Basic Books.

Nash, D. & Treffinger, D. (1993). *The Mentor Kit.* Waco, TX: Prufrock Press.

Renzulli, J. S. (Ed.). (1986). *Systems and models for developing programs for the gifted and talented* (pp. 461-484). Mansfield Center, CT: Creative Learning Press.

Renzulli, J. S. (1993). *The enrichment triad model: A guide for developing defensible programs for the gifted and talented.* Mansfield Center, CT: Creative Learning Press.

Renzulli, J. S. (1994). *Schools for talent development: A practial plan for total school improvement.* Mansfield Center, CT: Creative Learning Press.

Renzulli, J. S. & Reiss, S. M. (1985). *The schoolwide enrichment model: A comprehensive plan for educational excellence.* Mansfield Center, CT: Creative Learning Press.

Renzulli, J. S. & Reiss. (1993). *The complete triad trainers" inservice manual.* Mansfield Center, CT: Creative Learning Press.

Renzulli, J. S., Reiss, S. M. & Smith, L. H. (1993). *The revolving door identification model.* Mansfield Center, CT: Creative Learning Press.

Rimm, S.B. (1986). *Underachievement syndrome: Causes and cures.* Watertown, WI: Apple Publishing.

Schmitz, C. & Galbraith, J. (1985). *Managing the social and emotional needs of the gifted. A teacher's survival guide.* Minneapolis, MN: Free Spirit Publishing.

Schneider, B. H. (1987). *The gifted child in peer group perspective.* New York: Springer-Verlag.

Silverman, L. K. (Ed.). (1993a). *Counseling the gifted and talented.* Denver: Love Publishing.

Supplee, P. L. (1990). *Reaching the gifted underachiever.* New York: Teachers College Press.

Swassing, R.J. (1985). *Teaching gifted children and adolescents.* Columbus, OH: Merill.

Tannenbaum, A.J. (1983). *Gifted children: Psychological and educational perspectives.* New York: Macmillan.

Treffinger, D. J. & Sortore, M. R. (1992). *Volume I, II, III: The programming for giftedness series.* Sarasota, FL: Center for Creative Learning, Inc.

Van Tassel-Baska, J. (1990). *A practical guide to counseling the gifted in a school setting* (2nd ed.). Reston, VA: ERIC Clearinghouse, Council for Exceptional Children.

Van Tassel-Baska, J. & Olszewski-Kubilius (Eds.). (1989). *Patterns of influence on gifted learners.* New York: Teachers College Press.

Van Tassel-Baska, J. with Feldhusen, J., Seeley, K., Wheatley, G., Silverman, L. & Foster, W. (1988). *Comprehensive curriculum for gifted learners.* Boston: Allyn & Bacon.

Whitmore, J.R. (1980). *Giftedness, conflict, and underachievement.* Boston: Allyn and Bacon.

Winebrenner, S. (1993). *Teaching gifted kids in the regular classroom.* Minneapolis: Free Spirit Publishing.

RESOURCES FOR PARENTS

Books

Adderholdt-Elliott, M. (1987). *Perfectionism: What's bad about being too good.* Minneapolis, MN: Free Spirit Publishing.

Alvino, J. (Ed.). (1985). *Parents" guide to raising a gifted child.* New York: Ballentine Books.

Culross, R. (1991). *Counselling the gifted: developing the whole child.* Melbourne: Hawker Brownlow Education.

Dunn, R., Dunn, K. & Treffinger, D. (1992). *Bringing out the giftedness in your child.* New York: John Wiley.

Ellis, J. L. & Willinsky, J. M. (1992). *Girls, women and giftedness.* Melbourne: Hawker Brownlow Education.

Heacox, D. (1993). *Up from underachievement.* Minneapolis, MN: Free Spirit Publishing.

Kerr, B. A. (1985). *Smart girls, gifted women.* Columbus, OH: Ohio Publishing.

Landau, E. (1991). *The courage to be gifted.* Melbourne: Hawker Brownlow Education.

Lewis, G. (1990). *Bringing up your talented child.* Kensington, NSW: Bay Books.

Mares, L. (1991). *Young gifted children: From potential to achievement.* Melbourne: Hawker Brownlow Education.

Mares, L. (1991). *Adolescence and giftedness.* Melbourne: Hawker Brownlow Education.

Perino S. C. & Perino, J. (1981). *Parenting the gifted. Developing the promise.* New York: Bowker.

Perry, K. (1992). *Playing smart.* Minneapolis, MN: Free Spirit Publishing.

Saunders, J. & Espeland, P. (1986). *Bringing out the best.* Minneapolis, MN: Free Spirit Publishing.

Smutny, J. F., Veenker, K. & Veenker, S. (1989). *Your gifted child.* New York: Facts on File.

Journals

Gifted Child Today Magazine, Prufrock Press, P.O. Box 8813, Waco, TX 78714-8813.

The Journal of Secondary Gifted Education, Prufrock Press, P.O. Box 8813, Waco, TX 78714-8813.

The Roeper Review A Journal on Gifted Education, Editor: Ruthan Brodsky, Roeper School, P.O. Box 329, Bloomfield Hills, MI, 48013.

Gifted Child Quarterly National Association for GIfted Children, 1155 15th Street, Suite 1002, Washington D.C. 20005.

Understanding Our Gifted, Open Space Communications, 1900 Folsom, Suite 108, Boulder, CO 80302

ABOUT THE AUTHORS

LeoNora Cohen

Dr. Nora Cohen has worked in the field of gifted education for more than 27 years as a teacher, parent, initiator, coordinator for the Mentally Gifted Program for Philadelphia Schools, reseracher, and professor. She has published more than 50 articles, books, and chapters related to the development of gifted young people. She was an associate professor in the TAG Institute at the University of Oregon, senior lecturer at the CHIP Unit at the University of Melbourne, and is presently an associate professor inthe School of Education at Oregon State University. She is interested in a wide range of concerns related to able young people. She founded the Conceptual Foundations Divsion of the National Assocation for Gifted CHildren and served as president of the state assocations for gifted in Pennsylvania and Oregon. She is the mother of Max and Elizabeth Cohen.

Erica Frydenberg

Dr. Erica Frydenberg is an educational and clinical psychologist and senior secturer in psychology in the Department of Learning, Assessment, and Sepcial Education, in the Faculty of Education at the University of Melbourne. Her main areas of research relate to understanding what concerns young people and how they cope. She has authored or co-autohored more than 30 publichations relating to adolescent concerns and coping. She and Ramon Lewis developed the Adolescent Coping Scale, an instrument designed for research and for use by counselors. The Coping Scale for Adults is scheduled for publication in 1996. She has served as a foundation member of the Psychologists Registration Board and is a fellow for the Australian Psychological Society. She is the mother of Joshua and Lexi Frydenberg.

KIDS' SECTION:
COPING FOR CAPABLE KIDS

by
LeoNora M. Cohen and Erica Frydenberg

Contents

Introduction

Will the Real Problem Please Stand Up?

"I worry about school, environment, family, getting good grades, disappointing my parents, what will happen in the year 2000."

—Meridith, 16

"I've discovered that once you have a good relationship with teachers you automatically get a bad name with a lot of your peers."
—Catherine, 13

"I can't stand the dumb rules at school, marching into assembly, the childish behavior of the kids, detention as a class because the kids are being stupid, having to do group work with the kids when I do all the work and they try to bother me."

—Neil, 14

Coping and Capable Kids

From the scripts of thousands of young people describing how they cope, we have been able to draw up some general principles that apply to coping. Keep these in mind. The stories of particular young people ("Is This Like You: Case Studies of Capable Kids") are also helpful when you reflect on your own coping practices.

1. Coping is your way of dealing with your world and the problems that life dishes out. There is no formula for coping, no single way of dealing with problems. The type of problem, the particular circumstance and the unique needs of the person mean that every problem situation (difficulty) must be addressed by drawing on a range of strategies which we have called the coping repertoire or coping vocabulary.

2. Drawing on your own experience, reflecting on the experience of others, examining your own resources and calling on the support of others can assist to deal with circumstances effectively. Some strategies deal directly with the problem, others just alleviate the stress for a time but do not lead to a solution. Some strategies work better than others. A few may even be harmful, like taking drugs or alcohol to try to forget about problems.

3. Even when there are situations in which we cannot control the problem, such as the death of a parent or grandparent, or separation of parents, there are some strategies that can help you cope more effectively. Sharing grief with a counselor or friends or writing about your pain, are examples. You are in control. You can make choices about how you deal with circumstances. If you work out what the real problem is, it is easier to choose the most effective strategies. You have the resources, you choose how to deal with problems and you can expand your repertoire of strategies.

4. Adaptation is a two-way street. You can change yourself to fit the environment or fit in with what others want; or you can change the environment to fit you. Worrying is wait-

ing; often it means waiting for the world around you to change. Alternatively, you can go about changing the world. For example, painting or reorganizing one's room or notebooks or getting involved in social action changes one's environment a little. It often brings order to a chaotic situation.

Who Are Capable Kids?

This is a test. What do we mean by *capable*?

1. Is it a state of mind in which you believe that you can do it, you can be effective and competent, whatever comes your way?
2. Is it that you are able to sort out and cope with the stresses of everyday life?
3. Is it that you are gifted, that you have the potential to learn easily, master material rapidly, think productively, use your talents in very high levels of performance or creative work?

4. Is it that you can read this book and apply it to yourself?

5. Is it any or all of the above?

The answer of course is number 5.

For number 1, a positive state of mind, you need self-confidence and a positive self-concept, that is, a view of yourself as capable. This may come about as a result of encouragement and positive attitudes towards you as well as successful experiences in dealing with mistakes and problems from the time you were very small. You might be a good athlete, be popular and have a lot of friends, and use your abilities to succeed. You probably look at yourself as physically and/or socially able, and your concept of how you compare with others (your real self) and your aspirations for yourself (your ideal self) are not too far apart. If you do not view yourself as capable, this book can help you find strategies and ways of thinking to build your self-confidence.

For competence in coping, it helps to have the ingredients for a healthy self-concept, plus experiences in coping that lead you to believe you can handle your problems. Sometimes this confidence comes from successfully handling stressful situations, like testing yourself on a difficult mountain climb, taking a lead role in a theater performance, playing a musical solo, or working and studying very hard to master a subject like physics or psychology. It might come from working out problems with friends, handling a sticky situation with a teacher or traveling somewhere alone. Sometimes you develop competence in coping from dealing with serious difficulties, like losing a parent or dealing with family problems like divorce or alcohol abuse. For example, 16-year-old Tuan lost his mother on the boat trip escaping from an internment camp in Vietnam when he was 7 years old. He had to deal with many hardships including shouldering responsibility for the education of his two younger siblings and coping with a different country and new language. Yet he is at the top of his class and is determined to keep the promise he made to his mother, before she died, to become a doctor. You could say that Tuan is *resilient*, because he has been able to bounce back and recover from some very difficult situations.

Sometimes you have overcome a physical disability or have to deal with a serious illness, loss of family income or even homelessness. 11 year-old Denise, for example, is responsible for caring for her three younger siblings and cooking dinner for her family of nine because her parents must work in the evening to supplement their meager income. She has had to learn to manage the demands of running a household and still get her schoolwork done. If you have difficulties coping but you want to learn to cope better, this book can help you.

If you are gifted (some people feel uncomfortable with the term), you may have the self-confidence and experience in coping with difficulties that make you feel capable and let you cope competently, as in the first two options. On the other hand, you may be experiencing a lot of pain and find that coping with the various stresses that come your way is very difficult. You may believe that you have to prove how bright you are over and over again, and you are not sure that you really are that able. You usually may be able to cope successfully with learning new things, especially when you find them interesting; however, your heightened sensitivity, intensity, perfectionist tendencies and desire to do things your own way may get in the way of successful coping, especially with personal problems. These characteristics may also get in the way of feeling like you "fit in" with other kids. If you want more information about these emotional and social aspects of giftedness, please read "Giftedness" in the teacher/parent section. This book can be especially helpful for bright kids who are having difficulty coping.

Of course, if you read this book, either because the title catches your interest or it was given to you by a caring parent, teacher, or counselor, you are probably a bright, capable kid who wants to find better ways to cope with stresses.

You can either read the other part of this book to find out what adults are learning about kids like you, or you can start with this section written for you and go the other way. Please note that comments from students are their exact words, but names have been changed to maintain confidentiality. If you feel that you need further help to solve your problems, talk to a parent; the school counselor, homeroom teacher, a coach, or other trusted person in the school; or priest, minister or other adult. They can help you locate community-based resources or can work with you on solving your difficulties.

DEALING WITH CONCERNS AND WORRIES

When you identify some of the things that concern you, it is some-times difficult to sort out what the real problem is when there may appear to be a **flood of worries.** You first need to get your head above water, then wade to the safety of the shore. Once on firm ground you can dig in the sand, **burrowing in different directions** till you work out the real concern. Is the problem that you have too much work? Is the problem that you do not know where to go for help? Or is the problem perhaps that you have too many commitments? Once you have the facts you can put them through a **problem sifter** to get to the real prob-lem. It is worth spending some time thinking or talking the concerns over with others to establish what the real problem is. School and other worries may involve many parts. It is most helpful to get the problem down to its tangible, concrete components before you tackle it. For example, if you are worried that others are teasing you, what is it they are saying and can you work out whether there is something different that you can do in a particular circumstance?

Is the work too easy for you and too difficult for others? Is there too much work and not enough help? Are you helping others and not feeling appreciated for it? Are you lonely at school and have nobody to share your experiences with? Is there a problem at home that is making it hard to concentrate on schoolwork? If you do your best work will the others give you a difficult time? Are you covering up and others see through it? Are you much younger than the rest of the group but see their actions as childish? Would you like your class to be different? Would you like your school to be different? Or would you like the world to be different? What are the things that you can change, who can help you, and how can you go about making the changes? Are there things that you could do differently? Are there things that you could ask others, like teachers or peers, to do differently?

It is okay to have two feelings at once. For example, you may be happy that you have been accepted to a group or school or class but worried that you may not succeed or fit in. But you need to work out what is the real concern. Identifying the right problem is important before you **sift through the sand of solutions**. For example, if it is a concern about an aspect of the environment, get some information about the issue and follow this with some information about what others are doing about the problem. If it is about disappointing your parents, ask them what they expect and work out if it is achievable and how it is best achieved.

Once you have your real problem you can select solutions until you come up with the best strategy to use under the circumstances. Then try it out or put it into practice. See if it works. If it does not, rework the problem. You may need to determine whether you are tackling the real problem. Or it may be that you need to explore other strategies and try them out.

Even though you may sometimes feel helpless and hopeless when facing difficulties, **you do have the resources to cope**. You can find the courage to change what you do or how you think. You can use your wonderful mind to come up with creative and flexible ways to deal with any problems that you may encounter with friends, family, school or work.

Give yourself permission to extend your strategies for coping. There is no single solution for any problem. Evaluating your strategies will encourage you to be flexible and expand your coping repertoire.

Oceans of Emotion

Underlying many of the other emotions that we experience is *fear*. Fear is the basis of many of our worries. We spend much of our time afraid of failure, loss, rejection, losing control, and so on. We are afraid of what we don't know and things we have not yet experienced. "How will I manage?" or "Will I have the resources to cope?" are some of the questions we ask ourselves. There are the stresses of going for an important exam, giving a talk in front of the class, dealing with an unfamiliar situation like going to a new school. We are afraid of what others will think or do if we get things wrong. What might we lose? Usually it is not much, just an opportunity and at worst we might get a rebuke or reminder of what to do next time. Will we have the strategies to cope? Will there be anyone else there to help us?

Here is a poem by Scott Lascelles, age 15, that expresses this notion:

Deep Ocean
There is a sea
Inside my soul,
A deep dark ocean;
Where sharks swim,
And dolphins cry,
Full of emotion.
There is a sea
Inside my soul,
There is something moving under;
Trying to escape and being seen,
I can already hear the thunder.
There is a sea
Inside my soul,
I am swamped by emotion;
I have to break free
Of the cold, cold ocean.
There was a sea
Inside my soul,
But you made waves in my ocean;
I have finally escaped,
From the cold,
From the dark, from the emotion.

Most of us have an infinite number of resources or strategies with which to cope. They are our "bag of tricks" that we have collected along the way. Not all of them are productive. We can ask for help along the way. One's coping repertoire should be a constantly developing "store of strategies" that we accumulate as we go through life, learning what works well and what does not.

Separating the Facts from the Feelings

It is important to be able to separate the feeling from the facts and know how you feel. This can be difficult for some people and easy for others. Jessica, a very able 13-year-old speaking about her upset at the divorce of her parents and how she dealt with this at school, had worked out the difference between "knowing the facts and knowing the feelings."

"Knowing the feelings is a lot better because you can always find out the facts later. It's better to be able to say well I'm not sure what's really going on but at least I know what I'm feeling and I can understand that. Then being able to say, well I know it's happening and there is not much I can do about it. It is not my fault."

Impediments to Coping

Self-stresses

The guilt and shame that put us under pressure and make us feel bad are stresses that we put on ourselves. Sometimes they are called *irrational beliefs* and are the things that go on in our heads. They sometimes immobilize us or prevent us from exploring our range of options within our coping repertoire.

The Shoulds, Have Tos and Musts

♦ Others should know what's in my head that I am feeling or wanting.
♦ I shouldn't have problems.
♦ Everyone has to love me.
♦ I've got to get it right.
♦ I'm supposed to know it.
♦ I have to be perfect.

- ◆ I can't make a fool of myself.
- ◆ I can't make mistakes.
- ◆ I can't let the team down.
- ◆ I won't try till I'm sure that I can do it.
- ◆ Everyone can see my faults—everyone can see what I am thinking and feeling.
- ◆ They can see right through me and I have to hide.
- ◆ I'm a good person but why don't others see it?
- ◆ I'm not as good or as smart as they think.
- ◆ I look, act and feel so stupid (like an idiot).
- ◆ Everyone else is better than I am—they know more and are more popular even though I do well at school.

A lot of people think like that some of the time and run "non-productive" messages through their heads which then inhibit them from utilizing productive coping strategies. There are ways to change the scripts or messages that we send to our brains that enable us to be effective in our coping.

I Can Change the Way I Think

Give Yourself Permission:

- ◆ It's okay to have problems, most people do.
- ◆ It's okay if everyone doesn't love me.
- ◆ It's okay not to get it right all the time.
- ◆ It's okay for me not to know everything, nobody does.
- ◆ It's okay for me not to be perfect.
- ◆ It's okay to make a fool of myself sometimes.
- ◆ It's okay to make mistakes.
- ◆ It's okay if our team loses, as long as I've tried my best.
- ◆ It's okay to make a mistake, that is, try before I am sure that I have it perfect.
- ◆ It's okay for others to see my faults. I am living with them and working on changing some of them.
- ◆ It's okay if others can't see that I am a good person but I feel good about the things that I do.
- ◆ It's okay not to be as good or smart as others think.

♦ It's okay to be myself. Even though at times I feel that I look and act like a "dork," others may not see it that way.

♦ It's okay if others are better than I am at some things. I have my strengths and they have theirs.

♦ It's okay for others not to know what's in my head or what I am feeling or wanting. I need to tell them if I want them to know.

♦ *And finally there is the belief or the self-statement:*

**I can learn new ways to cope and
expand my repertoire of coping!**

COPING STRATEGIES USED BY CAPABLE KIDS

From all the thousands of individual descriptions of coping, we have been able to group the coping actions of young people into 18 strategies which more or less capture the coping behaviors of most young people. Some of the descriptions of coping that a population of capable young people provided for us do not fit readily into the 18 categories but describe additional coping behaviors. Here are some coping behaviors that represent the 18 strategies:

1. Seek Social Support

"It helps to talk to friends or relatives to help me sort it out."
—Beth, 15

"I have discovered that talking to somebody really helps."
—John, 13

"I discuss the problem with my sister, an aunt, or an uncle who is understanding."
—Amanda, 12

"I talk to my friends to see how they coped with the same problem."
—Maria, 14

2. Focus on Solving the Problem

"I use lots of self-assessment to evaluate where I am at the moment to achieve what I want in the future."
—Jamie, 16

"I read as much as I can to find ways to solve the problem."
—Jim, 15

"I analyze the problem, formulate ideas to attack the problem and find sensible solutions."
—Brian, 16

"I look at all the possible ways I could overcome this worry, then I work out a plan to cope with it."
—Ruth, 17

"I write down my problems and see my alternatives."
—Sherron, 15

"If I'm having problems with a friend, I think about what I want to say and then I call that friend and talk it out."
—Darcy, 10

3. Work Hard and Achieve

"I have a problem making speeches so I rehearse the speech as often as I can and hope that I do not forget the lines."
—Sam, 12

"I try to work very hard and efficiently on schoolwork, aiming for high grades."
—Eddie, 16

"It's best to space out your study."
—Chris, 12

"I am working hard to the best of my ability at school."
—Chen, 14

4. Worry

I 'm a bit of a worry wart. I worry about school, I worry about the behavior of kids. I feel responsible."
—Robert, 13

"I worry a lot and when I worry I eat a lot. I don't sleep well when things are worrying me."
—Amber, 12

5. Invest in Close Friends

"I spend as much time as I can with my boyfriend."
—Pam, 16

"I find a friendship to compensate for the loss of family love."
—Andy, 15

6. Seek to Belong

"I am friends with anybody who wants to be my friend. When you are new you have to be."
—Adam, 15

"If I talk to people about what they like they accept me. It's better than in the past when people mostly ignored me and I wasn't popular."
—Lourdes, 12

"It's better to make up with my friends by going over to them and asking them for forgiveness."
—Tom, 11

"Staying friends is easier than fighting."
—Annie, 13

7. Wishful Thinking
"I keep hoping that nothing goes wrong in my life."
—Jared, 12

"I daydream a lot."
—Sonya, 13

"I imagine a new world where I create a story that comes out happily, but sometimes I neglect problems."
—Jeremy, 11

8. Social Action
"I support the peace movement by going to peace rallies."
—Julia, 15

"I try to make people realize that war does not solve problems."
—Gabriel, 16

"I got people to sign a petition and sent a letter to the government."
—Marco, 15

9. Tension Reduction

"I've discovered that slamming the door at home or telling the people at school to stop annoying me soothes me."
—Drew, 10

"Eating relieves tension but sometimes I can't sleep because things get on top of me."
—Demetrious, 12

"I smoke, take valium or get drunk to forget my worries."
—Jasper, 16

"If something bad has happened I go and write it down, I have a cry and then I feel a lot better."
—Astrid, 16

"I get rid of frustration by yelling or fighting with my brother or parents."
—Austin, 14

"If you tell a loved pet the problem on your mind and get your emotions out you feel a lot better."
—Sarah, 10

10. Not Coping

"I don't cope very well. I just worry more."
—Lynne, 14

"There's nothing I can do about it."
—Tony, 11

"I don't do anything. There's nothing I can do about war and nuclear weapons."
—Natasha, 14

"I don't cope with my problems. I lock them up."
—Anna, 10

"I don't have any strategies. I just battle on taking each day as it comes."
—Jason, 16

11. Ignore the Problems

"I relax, take things as they come, and don't worry too much."
—Cory, 14

"I try to forget about my concerns."
—Beth, 12

"I keep coming up with excuses not to do something."
—Jamal, 12

"I keep my mind occupied by other things."
—Jeff, 14

"I over-involve myself in club activities to forget my worries."
—Jenny, 15

12. Self-blame

"I let my parents down so I have to face the consequences."
—John, 15

"I have no self-discipline, so I don't make time to do my studies."
—Charlie, 14

"Often I find that I just don't care. I feel guilty because I don't care."
—Tiffany, 13

13. Keep to Self

"I shut myself off from family problems to keep from getting hurt."
—Amy, 16

"I spend a lot of time in my room and don't discuss my problems."
—Ravi, 16

"I try to keep to myself about anything I have done."
—Cara, 13

"I don't show my feelings. Instead I deal with things myself."
—Elizabeth, 14

14. Seek Spiritual Support

"I'm taking bible studies in order to learn what I am to do in the future."
—Jake, 15

"I find that meditation is useful in preventing over-anxiety and depression."
—Lynne, 16

"I pray to the Lord to take care of all my worries."
—Aisha, 14

"I lie awake at night and have conversations with myself, talking to something like a God."
—Denise, 16

15. Focus on the Positive

"I attempt to look on the better side of things and make comparisons with those less fortunate."
—Dana, 16

"It helps if you look at positive things."
—Jacki, 12

"I try to find the best in everyone and everything. Even when I fail at something, I try to see what I can learn from it."
—Hilmir, 16

"I think about all the good things that might happen to me."
—Nina, 12

16. Seek Professional Help

"I've discovered that asking for help helps."
—Rhonda, 12

"*I seek help from my tutor and sometimes talk to teachers.*"
—Erin, 14

"*I see a teacher or get help from my friend's parents.*"
—Brianna, 14

"*I go to the counselor to get help in dealing with the kids. It's hard when you're new in a school and everyone else has their group.*"
—Ben, 16.

"*Go to the teachers and ask for help.*"
—Rob, 17

17. Seek Relaxing Diversions

"*I escape with music, either listening to it or playing my guitar.*"
—Rick, 15

"*To help me cope I draw. I always have a sketch pad and pencils at hand.*"
—Dave, 10

"*To cope I vegetate on the computer and invent things in my room.*"
—Doug, 15

"*I've discovered that pressure is relieved when I draw.*"
—Jesse, 14

"*When I feel frustrated it can help to read a book or play a game.*"
—Pat, 12

"*I relax by reading autobiographies or watching sports on TV.*"
—Nick, 15

18. Physical Recreation

"Playing sports or just keeping fit can really help me to have a positive attitude."
—Hillary, 16

"Playing sports is a big factor in staying in touch with reality."
—Max, 17

"Running helps me relax."
—Kate, 13

"I take it out on a soccer ball and physically tire myself out."
—Mario, 17

"It obviously requires a balanced diet and many physically demanding activities."
—Anna, 16

"I go to the gymnasium, jog and work out until I am exhausted. Then I usually feel relaxed."
—Cliff, 17

Not all strategies fall neatly within the 18 conceptual areas but they do represent the thoughts and actions of capable young people. Some of these are actually a combination of more than one strategy. Here are some additional coping strategies that might help you understand the variety and range of coping options that are available. No list is exhaustive. We would like to learn of the strategies that you use and in which circumstances. At the back of the book are the names of the authors and where to send any correspondence. We would like to hear from you.

Additional Coping Strategies

"I find everything fascinating but I prefer to observe from outside. It'd be nice to be invisible to watch people. I wish I could see inside their minds too."
—Helen, 16

"If there is something I don't like doing I make myself try doing it."
—Peter, 15

"When I disagree with my parents and get angry I go to my room and read."
—Joel, 11

"I close off, breathe deeply and count to ten when teachers only give partial answers or my peers are immature."
—Dan, 16

"If I'm being put down I don't class it as being put down, just as an act of an insecure person."
—Jeff, 16

"It's best to do things that cover up your perfection so that it doesn't show."
—Heather, 16

"If I work my head off I forget my problems."
—Chris, 15

"I'm not really like other kids so I have learned to mess around by myself."
—Dave, 16

"I just talk to people I WANT to talk to."
—Chirpa, 14

"After a quarrel, I apologize in public. If the person accepts the apology, that's great. If not, the others will defend you."
__Ben, 12

"It's easier to change yourself than others if they are annoying you."
—Julio, 12

"I can learn more about myself when I think about it. I get it into my head to cope subconsciously so now I can remember what to do on the test."
—Ed, 11

"When the teacher is repetitious and boring it helps to translate what the teacher says in English into Spanish. This keeps me awake."
  Ryan, 13

"I find that when I'm teased, I try to turn the problem around into humor. I might agree about my big nose or big feet, or use a friendly comeback, like 'my big nose really helps me to smell how sweet you are."
—Darren, 12

"I've discovered that walking away from those who tease me and playing with those that accept me works."
—Josh, 11

"It is better to work things out for yourself than just be given the formula."
—Dustin, 15

"I have discovered that people don't call me a dork if I hide my grades."
—Tatiana, 14

"When threatened by a bully, I say 'I'm not going to fight you, 'cause I know you'll win and you'll slaughter me.' That meets their needs for power and keeps me out of trouble."
—Ben, 12

"You go through times when you get really worried then it turns out okay. You wonder why it even worried you. It always turns out okay in the end."
—Reo, 13

"I've discovered that drugs and alcohol don't fix problems, EVER."
—Luke, 17

"Martial arts helps you gain confidence, but only for defense, not attack. It improves the status of a small person."
—Emmy, 9

"To deal with my depression I try to get out more and get more sleep."
—Jocelyn, 15

"I find it's better to stop trying to 'be cool' and just do what I like doing with people who are nice."
Michael, 14

"When I'm at a new place where I don't know anybody, I find someone who looks more nervous than I feel and I start a conversation and make them feel good. This makes me feel more comfortable too."
—Ben, 12

"When I am firm with people I feel good—like one of the boys tried to make me smoke but I said no. They sort of tried to convince me to smoke but I didn't. I felt good after that."
—Dennis, 13

"I remember that I am in control and my future depends on me to achieve."
—Carmen, 17

"I use personal success as a locomotive. This eliminates worry and I get good test grades."
—Emile, 16

"I establish security that people are not so stupid to blow up the world and I will survive."
—Lauren, 14

"I don't let a bad grade get me down. I learn from a mistake and don't let it reoccur."
—Chris, 15

"I rehearse things in my mind to help me plan what to say."
—Meadow, 13

"To stay out of trouble, I avoid gangs and make friends with kids who want to be somebody."
—Teal, 14

"I keep my thoughts and worries in a diary. It really helps to get out my troubles on paper."
—Kamaria, 15

"Sometimes it's worth it to take some risks, like when I'm not good at a sport, but I try anyway."
—Nathan, 14

Coping Strategies Checklist

Check to see what your pattern of coping strategies is. Use the number system below to mark how you cope.

The C.O.P.E.

*This is not a test. It's just a quick way of checking how you cope.

Don't use 0	Use a little 1	Use somewhat 2	Use a great deal 3

____ 1. I find that talking to somebody really helps.

____ 2. I look at all the possible ways I could overcome this problem, then I work out a plan to cope with it.

____ 3. I am working hard to the best of my ability at school.

____ 4. I worry about things at school or at home. I feel responsible.

____ 5. I spend as much time as I can with my boyfriend or girlfriend.

____ 6. If I talk to people about what they like they accept me. It's better than in the past when people mostly ignored me and I wasn't popular.

____ 7. I daydream about things being different.

____ 8. I get people to sign a petition or join a group.

____ 9. If something bad has happened I cry or scream or eat or drink to make myself feel better.

____ 10. I don't have any strategies. I just battle on taking each day as it comes.

____ 11. I try to forget about my concerns.

____ 12. It is my fault that this has happened.

____ 13. I don't show others my feelings. Instead I deal with things myself.

____ 14. I pray to the Lord to take care of all my worries.

____ 15. I try to keep positive when things are difficult.

____ 16. I go to the teacher or counselor and ask for help.

____ 17. I relax with music, reading or TV.

____ 18. Playing sports helps me to deal with things.

Scoring Key—The C.O.P.E.

Find your **O** score by adding your score on items **1, 5, 6, 8, 14, 16**
Maximum **O** score (high usage) **18**
Interacting with <u>Other</u> people and remaining socially connected. (O = <u>Other</u>)

Find your **P** score by adding your score on items **2, 3, 15, 17, 18**
Maximum **P** score (high usage) **15**
Attempt to remain <u>Positive</u> while solving the <u>Problem</u>.
(P = <u>Positive</u> <u>Problem</u> Solving)

Find your **E** score by adding your score on items **4, 7, 9, 10, 11, 12, 13**
Maximum **E** score (high usage) **21**
Less productive in reaching a solution; have an <u>Emotional</u> focus (E = <u>Emotional</u>)

The eighteen coping strategies can be meaningfully grouped into three styles of coping. One group of strategies **(O)** relates to interacting with other people and remaining socially connected. These strategies are: Seeking Social Support, Investing in Close Friends (a strategy which involves engaging in an intimate relationship, like having a boyfriend or girlfriend), Seeking to Belong (which denotes a concern for others and in particular what others think), the Seeking of Spiritual Support, the use of Professional Help and the recourse to Social Action. Then there are those strategies **(P)** that represent an attempt to remain positive while solving the problem. These strategies are: Focus on the Positive, Focus on Solving the Problem, Physical Recreation, Seek Relaxing Diversions and Working Hard to Achieve.

The third group of strategies **(E)** is less productive in reaching a solution and has an emotional focus. These strategies are Worry (in particular about the individual's personal future), Wishful Thinking, Ignoring the Problem, the use of Tension Reduction strategies (such as crying, smoking, eating or drinking), Keeping Problems to Oneself, Self-blame and Not Coping, which is a declaration of an inability to cope. Some problems cannot be solved by an individual, such as violence in one's community or wars in another country, so emotional coping is appropriate.

A high **P** score would indicate that you use the strategies related to attempts to remain positive while solving the problem. Similarly a low **P** score would indicate little usage of these strategies.

A high **O** score would indicate that you use the strategies related to interacting with other people and remaining socially connected. Similarly a low **O** score would indicate little usage of these strategies.

A high **E** score would indicate that you use the strategies that are less productive in reaching a solution and have an emotional focus. Similarly a low **E** score would indicate little usage of these strategies.

The important question to ask yourself is "Do I like it as it is?" or "Do I want to increase my usage of some strategies and reduce my usage of others?" Look at the range of strategies recorded by young people (pp. 21-33) and read the stories of some young people's experiences in the next chapter to get some good ideas of what to do and what not to do. You can turn to the activities suggested in "Some Tried and True Activities to Develop Your Coping Skills" to develop some areas of coping. You might choose to discuss coping with your friends, what strategies work for them in particular circumstances (but remember that you are an individual and your circumstances may be unique).

The Adolescent Coping Scale is a comprehensive instrument that allows you to identify your coping patterns and develop a coping profile. It is discussed in greater detail in the Adult Section, "Some Definitions," pp. 25-40. If you feel that you would like help with your coping but have been unsuccessful in discussing your concerns with a parent, consider finding a counselor so that you can discuss your particular needs in the framework of a confidential professional relationship. You can talk to your school counselor or a trusted teacher about getting the help you need. If you feel you are in a crisis situation, you can look for help in the phone book. Often there is a Community Services page that has listings, sometimes under "Crisis Hotlines." Look also in the yellow or white pages under "Crisis Intervention," "Alcoholism," "Suicide Hotline," or "Drug Abuse" (see pp. 146-147 in the Adult section.)

You might also feel that you and other students in your school would benefit from discussing coping strategies together. Perhaps you and your friends might talk to a teacher, school counselor or administrator to suggest ways your school could offer such a program.

IS THIS LIKE YOU?
CASE STUDIES
OF CAPABLE KIDS

A group of young people (9- to 17-year-olds), identified by their teachers as highly talented and "able" students, were asked how they managed different aspects of their lives, their attitudes toward school, their frustrations and the coping strategies they used.

Do you recognize yourself among them? Do they share some of your problems? Are these some of the solutions you would use? While each person and each circumstance is unique, it is helpful to know what others are experiencing. We are not alone in our concerns. Some people use different strategies, with different outcomes. We can learn from their experience. Some of these interviews and questionnaire responses are recorded below so that their comments might perhaps help you to discover that your own frustrations are not unique.

The teachers and parents of these students were also interviewed, and some of their comments have been included. Sometimes we do not see ourselves as others do. Each person's perception helps to complete the picture. After all, parents and teachers respond to students according to how they perceive them. Mostly we are not aware of how others see us. If we were, in some circumstances we might do things differently. It is good to compare your own view of things with those of others. You might choose to change what you do. The teachers' and parents' stories give some insights as to what are some of the effective strategies used and some that are not so effective.

ALEX: "I Just Don't See the Point of School."

I just don't see the point of school. The courses I do I don't want to do half of them. I don't mind doing the classes I'm interested in. I mean, they don't have a massive choice of subjects you can do here.

My Dad picked my courses for me. I'm stuck with those subjects and just don't like it. Up to about eighth grade everything came so easy. There was nothing I couldn't do. And then from ninth grade upwards things became fractionally more difficult and if there was something I didn't understand I just blocked it out of my mind and just didn't do it. I was rebelling against boredom and I just messed around. I felt everything I was doing there was irrelevant. So I just didn't want to do it. I just blew it. I wasn't going to school that often and it took me ages to get there. I was always confident in myself up to eighth grade After that—you know: just like growing up, self-doubt and everything.

[About the other school serving the gifted] The school functioned pretty well—the students were largely White and Asian, there were no problems with students. The teaching standards were not that big. There's some with really low standards—there's no really shining teachers, they're all pretty ordinary. A good teacher is one who won't be sort of like totally dominant, who can relate to his or her students, like who can talk to the kids. If we had the latitude, we'd have our own pace and would get it done without being pressured. In class, generally, it's not going to have a bearing on future life, but if they could help get it more realistic—the sort of stuff that would be useful in the future, that would help. You need some classes, and then an essay after.

My ideal school would be ... where you can just join in when you feel like it—the more relaxed it is the more eager you are to get to class. This year the English teacher is just so old fashioned and she doesn't try to bring anything new into the class. It just gets tiresome the way she does things.

I don't want to be different. I just want to be like everyone else. Sometimes the other kids resent me for being what I am. They'll pick on me, discriminate against me because of being smart. They'll shy away from me—they think I'm a freak. I'm alienated, I'm not like anyone else. I'm not artistically creative or anything but in the way I deal with things it's different. Oh, I try to make myself popular, I'm generally a clown: a lot of times it is defensive. If there's a group I don't want to get into but everyone else is wanting to get into it, I'm not going to try to please everyone else. I'll just do what I want.

I'd like to change my appearance and my will, my commitment—I haven't a commitment to stick to any one thing. I've always wanted to be an athlete but I just haven't got the body for it. Oh, I'm not like mega puny. I used to play baseball, and I think I could have really become good at baseball, but my parents never wanted me to play baseball so I just didn't get any support for it. I don't get much more from my parents in comparison with other kids.

Oh God, at home it's just my parents, hassling, hassling me all the time. You don't cross my dad. My mother doesn't punish me or anything—she doesn't spoil me like buying stuff for me. My mother does most of the nagging.

I want to be a journalist or maybe work in a zoo. I like animals: I can associate with animals better than people. I don't like to hang 'round with dumb people. I sort of like people of my intellect, but there are not that many around, and the ones that are similar to my intellect don't want to associate with me. I don't fit in with my own age group; older people I don't fit in with because I can't do the stuff they're doing. I do whatever I do to have fun. If it gets me away from the house I'll do it: I just want to get away really soon.

Alex is a junior in a low income urban high school. He was considered to be the most exceptionally able child in his middle school. In eighth grade he was given a scholarship to a special school for gifted students, but he scored at only passing level for all his classes and largely mixed with 'skin heads'. He returned to his current school and has proceeded to do no work.He therefore failed in classes he has not liked and succeeded only indifferently in other subjects. He has suffered as well from teachers' assumptions that he could do his work without any trouble and from busy work. Alex is an underachiever.

Alex's teacher says:

In terms of schoolwork he's got all of the typical avoidance techniques, like: he's ill; he turns up late; he complains of headaches or stomach aches to try to get sent home. And then the thing that worries me most is that he expects that if you like him you will be manipulated into assisting him in avoiding whatever it is ... I think he's quite miserable at school; I don't think he can see much purpose to being here. I don't think he sees any sense of achievement in anything he does.

ANDREW: "You've Got to Show Them You're Not Just a Blind Kid."

I'm happy at school, though one of my best friends has just left and I've had to find other friends. It is difficult finding friends in a way because you can't just join in with what the other kids are doing most of the time and you've got to find other ways to show them you're not just a blind kid. You can show them you're not just scared to do things, that you climb and rappel down a cliff, you're in the scouts and stuff, and do anything really. My friends have got a sense of humor, and have interests that I have. Some do like books but not many. Sometimes they say jokingly, 'you're a nerd,' but that happens to everyone and I don't really mind. I try to make myself popular with those I like, but I don't try to be popular with those I don't like. I find that as I had a bit of sight before, I've got a similar personality to other kids around me. I think I came to terms with going blind before it actually happened. My friends helped a lot. Others helped me in another way: they didn't comment on my blindness they just sort of accepted it and helped me go on as a normal person and give me experiences that I wouldn't have had without them.

I get frustrated with things that get moved into the corridor at school or home. I just trip over them. I get frustrated at P.E. I don't run fast because I think I'll run into things. I don't feel insecure in the way that I don't want to put a foot forward in case there might be a hole or something. But I'm really quite fast at my best. I don't really like graphics because I can't do it. I want to do more art, but I have to do homework during that time. The school tries to make it work for me, but can't see how. Being blind has just added more problems: you always need someone else around because you trip over things. In the classroom you can't do everything yourself—you can't read off the board, so you need people for that. I don't really finish work that quickly. Sometimes I get to do work for homework and that's how I deal with the load. It's definitely a drag; it definitely takes longer. I really need Mrs. S. [his aide] in class. I couldn't do classwork otherwise. I'm good friends in that I can crack jokes which I can't do with other teachers.

The only thing I want changed is what everybody else wants changed: that teachers aren't so grumpy. Last year I had good classes. This year a couple are not so good—the way they're taught, or they're extremely uninteresting. If I don't like the subject, I mess around because I want something to do, and if I haven't got something to do I get into trouble.

My dad thinks that I use language very well—I don't think I do that much. My mom, she hasn't really commented that much but I think she's quite pleased with what I'm doing at the moment.

I hope to get a good job and be busy, but not too busy. Maybe working with computers, or being a translator in a hospital or airport. Languages interest me a lot. I admire people with disabilities who can get on with life and it doesn't really worry them—especially people without sight who can do art. I like art a lot. I want to play in a jazz group very soon. Maybe later on I'd like to invent my own pieces, but I don't think I'd like to become a composer.

Andrew is 14 years old in grade 8 in the regular classes at an urban middle school. At birth, he had a hydrocephalic-shaped cranium, malformed bones suggesting brain damage, potentially physically disabling characteristics, and what appeared to be profound deafness for the first six months. These difficulties seemed to lessen in his early years. However, Andrew suffered a stroke at the age of 9 when undergoing an angiogram to find out why his optic nerves were atrophying. Among the difficulties that resulted, Andrew lost the use of his left hand and became totally blind. His elementary school principal fought to provide the equipment necessary for his disability. His teachers were firm and supportive in their expectations and encouraged his fine writing talent. In middle school he has achieved near the top of his class. He is motivated to earn good grades and is assisted by a fine teachers' aide in an inclusion format where his needs are monitored.

Andrew's Teacher's Aide says:

Andrew has problems with organization and planning skills, knowing landmarks around the school, and where his personal belongings, cane and bag are. He will walk away and tends to forget about them. It's easier to rely on other kids to help him. But he has learned there are no exceptions made. Oh, he tried it! It was good for the other kids because they could see he couldn't get away with it. Blind students are taught early on not to be too dependent. Yet he is prepared to try anything. Despite his having had sight, it is difficult for him to get an idea of the visual, and even now, so soon after loosing his sight he thinks in terms of Braille.

There is some awkwardness with other children who don't know how to approach him. Integration in the regular school program helps that. He shares when appropriate. He can come out with adverse comments. He has a pretty good relationships with his peers: he is very personable with a sense of humor and has no problems socially.

Andrew's Father says:

He learned braille only from sixth grade, but remarkably quickly. Because he has only one hand, to put anything on the brailler or on the computer takes time. To do math with a calculator and brailler requires a series of cumbersome movements. He will have to learn to do much more mental arithmetic and to memorize much more efficiently. It is difficult to get a balance between the necessity to foster independence on the one hand and to maintain motivation when so much of the physical awkwardness is burdensome. It can take much time for parents to transcribe some homework from dictation in order not to stultify creativity. His extracurricular writing demonstrates a willingness to keep going over long periods. We try to encourage creative achievements by setting his writing up in print. He gets very disappointed when his English teachers, while praising his abilities, do not find time to read these productions which mean so much to him. When lauded by an overseas visitor, he accused us of not having praised him for his special talent. This was not quite correct, but the perception was interesting.

He loves art and woodwork but may have to curtail subjects like these in order to cope with the volume of work in core subjects. I think this entails efforts on our part to supply the experiences outside of school, such as enabling him to be involved in scouts. He has joined the school's book club and plays trumpet in the school band.

It is very pleasurable to read to him, and with the availability of talking books, an extraordinarily rich variety of literature is available to him. His 9-year-old brother is a marvelous companion, teasing him, but without malice. Andrew is a conciliator in a marriage that endures considerable strain. The problem of finding enough hours in the day to accommodate our own needs may make it difficult to coax him to perform outside of the comfortable and doubtlessly rich imaginative world that he has created for himself. It is a balancing act to weigh up the needs of the various family members, especially with a diabetic older daughter in a very rebellious stage.

CATHERINE: "School is Tedious ... and I Have Eternal Underlying Depression."

I am not very happy at school because school life becomes very tedious and work drones on. Never-ending work frustrates me. I usually do my homework at school the next morning or lunchtime, though I do important things like projects at home.

My "enemies" also frustrate me. These are people who think I'm nobody and think they're superior, probably because they have boyfriends. My group of friends share the same kind of enemies, so we score points by making smart comments about them. One of my aims in life is to prove to people who don't like me that I am some- one. To do this I'll have to become very famous. I'd like to be an author.

I don't like the way the P.E. department hates my group of friends. They need to organize fun sports for people who aren't very good at it and not look down on us.

Also, I don't like my friends getting jealous. One says that if we both handed in the same essay I'd get a better mark. I know that at times it is true, but the way I look at it is that if Picasso painted a stripe on a bit of canvas he'd get millions for it; if someone unknown did the same, he'd get nothing. It's the same idea.

I am happy, though, with the way the teachers treat me. One day, for example, a teacher asked my advice on what was making another teacher unpopular. She said I would take an "objective" view on such a matter. There is always mutual respect between a teacher and a student who takes her work seriously. I realize teach- ers are there to help so I listen to them. The problem here, though, is that once you have a good relationship with teachers, you auto- matically get a bad one with a lot of peers. I hate being called a "dork" because I do well. I don't want to start getting bad marks just to be liked by a whole lot of people who are only interested in boys. I've had a few detentions in my life so I'm not a "goody-goody" anyway.

You asked me what is different about me, and all that I know is that I can achieve good grades without doing as much work as everyone else. I don't act differently than anyone else. I don't talk about being "a brain." I don't have a boyfriend, never have had one, but the same goes for a lot of people, and I don't really mind. I am respected by people who care about schoolwork and ridiculed by those who don't.

My biggest worry is the state I am in at the moment: eternal, underlying depression. Even when I'm having fun I sometimes feel dreary inside. To cope, I try to go out more and get more sleep. Sometimes I feel under pressure to do well, e.g. I "made it" into the

Alliance Francaise finals twice, and everyone expects you to achieve this a third time. I was scared of not getting in.

Catherine is in grade 9 in a suburban high school. She is 13.

Catherine's Mother says:
One of Catherine's biggest problems is dealing with unpleasant classmates. This seems to be a recurrent problem among the girls this age and she is getting more proficient at handling it. Apart from suggesting she ignore them, or stand up for herself according to the situation, there is not a lot I feel I could or should do to help her with this difficulty.

I feel that her intellectual ability has been an asset rather than a liability to her. I can't think of anything more that could be provided to help Catherine. The school has a counselor whom she has not used. For a while I felt she lacked confidence, especially socially, but she seems to be mastering that. I don't feel she has many problems and those she has she handles well.

DANIEL: "I hate sports."
I'd prefer it if teachers were less strict. If they have something to tell us, they should say it in a gentle way. For example, instead of saying 'You've got lots of homework tonight,' they could say 'this is your homework, kids, it's not too much.' It makes it seem less even if it's the same amount. But it's better here than at my old school. At that school I hated most of the classes. Now, I've found I like the subjects, it was the teachers I hated.

One of the things I hate, though, is the repetition of math facts and adjectives. When you've finished, the teacher just gives you more. To improve things I would find a fun way to do it—like in a game. Or, let us work it out for ourselves instead of telling us the formula.

I hate sports. I prefer chess to sports any day. I'm sort of regarded as being in the "dorky" group because my group of friends aren't interested in physical activity. We'd prefer to sit and tell jokes rather than get muddy playing football.

I wish the guys would stop teasing me and stop saying I have a funny laugh. They tease me because I'm small. When they do this I usually walk away, or I tell them something about them that they're not aware of.

The way I have found to make friends is to find someone who does the same sort of things. I found one of my closest friends because he was reading the same series I was, and no-one else I know has read it: David Eddings' The Malloreon *and* The Belgariad.

There are problems in not fitting in with everyone else if you don't read the same things or if you haven't seen a movie they've seen. I try to watch the films they see. Otherwise I just ignore them or find someone who's seen a film I've seen. Or else start the discussion on something I'm interested in.

My interests? I draw lots of things—imaginary things. Like machines to do my homework or catch the teacher and hide her so I won't have to hand it in! I design computer games. Sometimes I think up names for them.

I'm not a leader. I'm not tall, or good at sports. But I'm good academically. I try not to make fun of people. The only people I make fun of are my friends.

Daniel is 12 years old and attends 7th grade in a suburban middle school.

Daniel's Teacher says:

Daniel seems to be very happy. He especially enjoys new, challenging things. He doesn't seem to be too worried about anything in particular, as he is very confident. Perhaps he's a bit "laid back" in his attitude—especially towards work. He doesn't need help from me on the whole except that he needs some guidance as he can be a bit pushy and adamant that he is right! Generally, he feels he hasn't done anything wrong, and shrugs things off a bit because of this. Sometimes he says the wrong thing without thinking about the consequences and therefore can be hurtful to others—he's a bit immature in this respect. He's also a bit of a "tattletale"—he enjoys getting others into trouble for fun.

Erik: "My biggest problems are peer pressure from my friends to smoke pot or drink with them."

I am very happy at school because I am learning lots of new things that can help me a lot when I'm older. Last year, I liked calculator math best at school because I know some people don't have the opportunities to take calculator math like me. I like science and I like to read.

At home sometimes my brother or sister frustrates me. I deal with the frustrations by walking away from them, telling them to stop frustrating me, and if it fails, I call on an adult to make them stop. My parents frustrate me. They don't trust me to not do drugs or be with gangs.

I would like peers, teachers, and my parents to treat me with more respect because I have all the respect in the world for them. I could ask them to treat me better if situations are bad. At home, I don't think my parents understand me. I would like it if people would let me solve my problems on my own and I could obtain this by proving to them that I can solve my own problems.

My parents think I'm very gifted and smart like my father and that I should not waste the gift like he did because I can be something when I'm older. My dreams and hopes are to find a cure for a lot of incurable diseases like AIDS, some cancers, and some sex-related diseases.

I'm different by not following people to go outside. I would rather play chess, do homework, or read a book. And my friends call me lazy because I don't want to get drunk or blown on drugs. I try to stay out of trouble. I wish my parents would realize that I'm trying really hard. I used to smoke weed or get drunk, but not any more. I just say, "No, I have to stay in the house if you know you are going to do those things. You could kill yourself, someone else, and fry your brain cells."

I don't try to "fit in," because if people don't accept me for who I am, forget them. I select friends by trust, love, popularity, friendly, cool to hang with, a good person to be with around the girls. I also try to find people who are on my level of intelligence. What good is a friend if they don't know what you're talking about?

My biggest problems are peer pressure from my friends to smoke pot or drink with them. But I just say, "No, I can't. My mom will be able to tell, plus I have to take a drug test soon for school." I'm concerned about the gangs and violence in the world that we live in. I confront it head on by saying no to gangs, drugs, violence, and hate in the world. I try not to worry. Life's too short to worry.

I don't have any role models. No one at all except myself. I set my own standards. When there is a problem, I face the problem because if I don't, it will always be there because a problem can't dissolve or be solved all by itself.

I have many friends. I'm a very good friend. When I have problems with a friend, I talk with them face to face to solve the problems we're having. I don't relate to my parents and I don't talk to them with a problem. I find a friend or someone to talk to who will listen to what I'm saying and give me suggestions.

Erik is 14 years old in ninth grade. He is Native American and goes to a large, urban high school.

HECTOR: "Sometimes it's hard to live between two cultures."

I mostly like school because I learn interesting things and I like the fun activities that we do. My friends are there and I know it will help me to be somebody. I like meeting new friends most. I don't like the tons of homework I get. I deal with it by getting over with it once I get home. I don't like strict teachers. Teachers should remember when they were kids. Some teachers scream in your ear like my seventh grade social studies teacher last year and some people tell the principal, but she doesn't do anything. Other things I don't like at school are the food and the bad students. I wish my peers would stop being so rude (not all of them). I try to act good, be good. I like to play basketball. I am trying to get elected class president. I never give up.

At home my sister doesn't do her chores when we are alone (I am the oldest), so I tell on her. Sometimes my mom doesn't do anything. My mom thinks I'm intelligent since I love math and science and get good grades on those subjects. (I think fast). Also, that my teacher says I share my education with my peers.

One of my goals is to make people realize that we only have one home, earth, because if we don't take care of our world, then we'll destroy ourselves too. I'd like to change a lot of things in the world but it'll probably be impossible. I hope to be valedictorian. I'm going to work hard in school and get a good job, make a lot of money honestly, and live peacefully. I am doing my best in school to reach these goals.

Nothing is different about me. I'm normal like everybody, even though we speak Spanish at home. Sometimes it's hard to live between two cultures because you're considered different if you don't talk or act like others around you. But if you try to fit in, the people from my culture say you're a fake or sellout. I try to take pride in my Latino heritage and I also try to blend in while I'm in school. But I'm into politics. It doesn't cause me any problems. My friends don't think I'm weird or anything. I study real hard. I study more than my friends, but I tell them I don't study much. I don't do anything I don't like just to fit in, except maybe not let on that I'm smart. I wish I could be a fast runner so I could play basketball better. I practice, practice, practice. But I don't really want to change anything about myself.

I like honesty a lot in a friend and also friendliness and trustfulness, because I think that a friend that doesn't have these qualities is not a true friend. I like friends who have something in common, like concern about the world or basketball. My biggest concern is the future of our planet. That's why I'm into politics. I figure if I get elected, maybe I can get people to take better care of the Earth. I also am worried about doing bad in school.

I admire my mother because she has stood by herself and works her heart out just for me and my sister. I love my Mom and I talk to her when I have problems, but I try not to trouble her too much. She has enough to cope with! I admire people who are organized and successful, a person who lives up to their standards and achieves their dreams. I think I am that kind of person.

I have many close friends. I'm a good friend. We don't have many problems because I don't hang with gang kids or others who would keep me from my goals.

Hector is 13 years old in 8th grade in a large, urban middle school.

Hector's mother says:

Hector is a good boy. He tries hard and he is very smart. I think he will be somebody. It is not easy when you are poor and there is much temptation with easy money from drugs, but he has goals. I hope he can get a scholarship to a good high school and to college.

Hector's science teacher:

Hector is a born leader. He has been instrumental in getting a recycling center going in the school yard as part of his eighth grade community service project. He is socially responsible and a serious student. He has a great "can do" attitude. His peers accept and respect him, perhaps because he doesn't flaunt his abilities. His social "smarts" will take him far.

Helen: "I'm Introspective … and I Worry What People Are Going to Think."

I don't really have any trouble with the other kids although I don't have much to do with them. They don't have the same sort of interests: all they want to do is get out of school as quickly as they can and get a job, then live some sort of inane existence. Most of my peers I don't find admirable. They don't seem to care—they're just interested in getting drunk on a Friday night. They're valid in a sense—but their aspirations are not the same as mine. I don't think along the same lines as most people of my age. They do not understand that I want to know everything.

I'm introspective—I think that's good actually. I think you've got to solve things yourself. I don't think I'm totally independent— I'm afraid of doing things the wrong way. I try not to get abusive or offensive so I'm not banned from society. It's not that I don't like people; on the contrary I find everyone fascinating. It'd be nice to be invisible and to watch people. I wish I could see inside people's minds too. I don't really think it's fair of me: it can't be one sided— you have to open up to others as well! But I prefer to observe from the outside. I want to help them but I don't want them to interfere with my goals (which is what most of them end up doing!).

I don't try to make friends, but if I see someone who worries about things other than sex, hair dyes and popularity, I get more interested. I can't relate to people my own age and older ones think, 'Oh no!' when they find out I'm only sixteen. More than 50% of my friends have been exchange students. I do have friends, but not many and none of them are really close.

I wish I knew more. I love learning stuff that is mentally stimulating. I hate it at school if I can't understand something because then I feel even dumber than usual. It's infuriating the way they treat you, especially boys. They say, "Shut up Helen," and that drives me insane. I suppose it's because if I don't know something I'll grill the teacher until I get the answer I like. If I don't understand something I just panic. I know it's counterproductive. I can't stand it if people just give you a formula. When I was in France a lot of learning was rote learn-

ing, and the students didn't understand the reason behind it. I didn't speak for the first four months in France until I could speak with understanding. I didn't like my chem. teacher at all—if I wanted to know something he'd say, "Wait until next year!" I'm always behind in math because I have to do mountains and mountains of problems before I understand it. I try to read around a subject to get a full understanding. For history, in the holidays, I read a lot of documents. I like my history teacher—he gets into it and gets you interested in it—you can tell he really loves history and his enthusiasm is really great.

I find it impossible to judge—I'm always worried about being emotionally violated. I hate people who leer at me. I hate going into a crowd: when I was ten I used to cry—it's like your stomach has dropped out. I find it hard to be objective about myself. A couple of years ago I was anorexic. In France I was put into a psychiatric hospital because of it. I think I thrive on stress. Over the holidays I got so bored my brain just atrophied. I don't sleep that much. I'll read a book a day, and I'm up till four in the morning. I'm always in a bookshop and dress like a peasant. I'm reading Tess of the D'Urbervilles *at the moment which I read at eleven or twelve. I read a book four or five times until I understand it thoroughly.*

I get annoyed at home if people won't leave me alone. To deal with this I swear a lot in French and lock myself in my room. I think I am a big disappointment to my parents: they are both art teachers. I don't think I'm a creative person. I like science because a lot of it is precise; that and math don't offer much scope for creativity. I guess problem solving worries me a bit. English freaks me out, because there are so many interpretations and I don't know if I'm right or wrong. Most of the things I write are for myself and I don't like others to read it; I put off doing portfolio work because I don't want someone to pull it to shreds. My marks are good. It's just that I write something 15,000 times! I worry what people are going to think. I hate having to submit work in the humanities.

I want to become a doctor. I don't want to do anything radical. If I worked in medicine I'd be helping people. A lot of people say, "Why not medical research?" But if I did, I'd not be directly involved with people. I don't really get deeply involved with people: if I were a doctor I'd be dissecting them in a peculiar way—not physically, but trying to figure out how they function. It's a worthwhile job (not like some others!), so I try to get good grades and I talk to people in the business.

Helen is an 11th grade student at a suburban high school. She spent a year in France as an exchange student and has elected to study French, as well as do an independent study in Renaissance History. Her parents are divorced and she lives with her mother and 14-year-old brother with whom she says she has little in common.

JADA: "I Want the World to Live in Peace."

I like everything about school. Everyone makes me feel welcomed and loved right away and it's a great learning environment. I have kind friends. I love to learn and I do well, but I don't like it when teachers get used to me doing well and look at me like I'm stupid when I mess up. I think my teachers have high expectations of me. I think I could talk to them and tell them how I feel. I also hate it when kids try to mess up classes for teachers. They should be considerate of all of us so we can learn.

There's nothing different about me, except maybe that I'm small. I wish I was a little taller. I'm a quiet person. I like things calm and peaceful. But my brother has other ideas. He's always nosing into my business and he plays music too loud. We live in a pretty small apartment, so it's hard, but most of the time we get along.

My biggest worries are all the violence and fighting here and all over the world. I just want the world to learn to live in peace. I think peace begins with me. We each have to try to be more peaceful and less angry. That's what I learned at church and I try to live it. When I see someone being mad, I think about what could be making them unhappy and I get them to talk about it. I like my friends to be happy. When there is some big problem in the world, I try to talk about it with the class in Current Events. I sometimes see racism. That worries me too. Although I'm Black, I personally haven't experienced it. But sometimes one group gets on another, just because of skin color. We have to get over these prejudices. God made us all and wants us to love one another.

My dream is to help people. I'm not sure how, yet. I want to go to college. Maybe I'll become a social worker or a doctor. I work hard at school and try to stay focused on my goal. I want to be a good mother and have a happy family like mine.

My parents think I bring joy to their faces and I have the gift of being able to stand up for what I believe in. They are my role models, because they are the ones who have guided me to the right path. They are very loving and encouraging to me.. I admire Mahatma Gandhi for his non-violent way of helping poor people of India and his willingness to starve himself to improve their conditions. Actually I admire everybody. Everybody has something little I admire. Of course, my chief role model is Jesus Christ.

My parents are very brave. My Dad's a minister. He's in the middle of gangs all the time and he works with the homeless. He and my mother work together to try to get young people to stop fighting. My dad is trying to get fathers to be more responsible. He meets with a group of fathers every week and helps them to be better dads. When I was little before I went to school, I used to go out into the community with my parents. Most people aren't afraid of little kids, so sometimes maybe I helped a little in getting people to talk about their troubles. I liked to help give blankets and socks to homeless people. They weren't afraid of taking them from me. When I have a problem, I talk to my mom with a people question and my dad with a knowledge question.

I have lots of good friends. I choose friends who are honest and moral. A moral person is someone who is responsible and does all they can to help any and everyone including themselves, to the best of their abilities. A moral person respects each one you meet and lives by the scriptures. I think I am moral a person and a good friend. When my friends and I disagree, we talk it out.

Jada, age 12, is a sixth grader in a middle school in a large city.

Jada's homeroom teacher:

I have never met such a child as Jada. She is a quiet, gentle girl, a peacemaker, a balm on troubled water. Although she's a good student and very bright, I wish we could bottle this gift of hers! Whenever there's a fight, I can ask her to help them settle it. I'm not quite sure how she does it, but she is successful. The smallest child in the class manages to calm some of the biggest, toughest kids. Wherever she is, kids around her are calm and friendly.

Jada's Mother:

We couldn't have had a greater blessing than our daughter, Jada. She is kind, considerate, and stands up for her beliefs.

Sometimes I worry that maybe she is too serious, that she doesn't play enough. It's as if she has the weight of the world on her shoulders. But perhaps that is our fault, because of our ministering and all.

Jill: "I Worry More about People and the World."

School is okay, though I don't love it. I like the arts subjects, and English: writing and reading. I don't like math much or sports—at least I like playing sports but not P.E. I wish the teachers would treat us more like friends. I wish they didn't see themselves as being in charge so much, but would treat us more normally, with respect.

What is different about me? Well, I think I worry more about other people around the world, the starving people and people who are treated unfairly. It makes me really angry but no one else seems to get upset about it. But I just sit here and think about it and hear about it and it makes me really upset. Some scary or sad movies have that effect on me but they don't seem to have that effect on anyone else. That makes me feel different. I plan how I am going to help people, like become somebody important and then make a lot of money that way, because, you know, everything is money now. I'd give a lot to charities and go around the world and help that way somehow. And if I get people to listen to me, they'll do it too, and that's how I can help.

Sometimes I eat a lot when I'm worried. For example, when I worry about friends or about my parents or brother or sister, or I have fights, I eat a lot. Sometimes I worry about my brother being kidnapped so I eat a lot. Plus I don't sleep very well because things worry me.

Jill is 12 years old, and in 7th grade at a middle school with a good reputation for quality education. She is particularly concerned about and sensitive to social issues.

Jill's Teacher says:
Jill internalizes everything to a great degree and her idea of trying to understand where it comes from and what it's all about is really quite remarkable for a child of her age. She is very serious and conscientious. She is also a deep thinker about what you are actually saying and what it's going to mean in the long term. She

never makes an off-the-cuff statement. It's always thought out, it's always logically put into its place, and it's always on target.

She's very independent, she knows her place, and she knows she must obey and live within the rules. I think in the future Jill will be a real world-beater because she won't be held back by boundaries. She knows that she has to obey rules but barriers will not be a problem—she will jump everything.

She gets along well with other children. She's athletic, musical, very talented in everything she does. Once again, when it comes to sports, it's sports on her terms and her rules. When she feels like playing, she plays to her utmost, and if she doesn't feel like playing then she doesn't play!

Jill's Father says:

Jill seems to be very happy at school. She seems to get along quite well with the other kids right now. At the moment there is no division or competition between the girls at school—you know how cliquey they can be. I think it would be very helpful if there was someone at school for the children to talk to about their social problems. A school counselor is necessary to nip problems in the bud.

MATTHEW: "A Non-stop Thinker" Whose Parents Say "Don't Wind up in a Factory Like Us."

I know that I am a non-stop thinker, as my brain just about works nine to five or more, for sure. I am considerate and also independent, as I rarely rely on others. I like to do things on my own and depend on myself most of the time. I always like to be doing something, and if I'm not, I get angry and frustrated.

I wasn't 100 percent happy at school because the atmosphere was stupid. It was the teachers. In ninth grade we had one absolutely pathetic teacher—it was routine, all structured. We'd do the same thing every day and it was boring. Every day he'd just tell us stories we didn't really care about and at the end he'd give us a sheet of questions that were absolutely pointless. We just hated our history teacher—she was really stubborn, and always thought she was right; on some occasions she was wrong. I like teaching that develops a working environment, but in my math class the environment was so tense, you were afraid to say anything. Most of my other teachers gave me room to maneuver.

The things I hate are people who are unreasonable, uncoopera- tive and I hate being like anyone else. There are times when you can be outgoing, but there's a limit. We're not here to distract the teacher. We're here to learn—and that really gets to me. I like to be different and I hate being put into a type of group.

Because they are working in factories there is a high expectation from my parents. My dad's always complaining about the sort of life we're living. My mom will say, "Dad is expecting you to get into a good university, and if you don't he'll feel bad. If you do he'll be the happiest person!" I'm proud of them actually. My younger sister feels the same way as I do. They have the same expectations for her, though not for my older sister who's never around. There's a sense of pressure on her as well. My younger sister is trying to hide it, trying to say she'd like to get into different subjects. I try to weaken the pressure on her like telling them there are other universities. I get along well with her. My parents have this one thing that there's only one university in our city. That's tradition I guess. I tell them every once in awhile it depends where you want to go, which school offers you the best. They are working as hard as they can just to give us a good education. They will say, "Try to work as hard as you can, because you don't want to land in a factory like us." It's about time I gave them something back, made them happy. If I didn't succeed I would probably feel a big let down and non-satisfaction, a sense that you'd have worked as hard as you could for nothing.

They believe I have gifts: they are always carrying on about it. I share my school grades with them when I get marks below what I expect. But I don't talk to my parents much about my problems. There's this one person now I share most with, I'm more comfort- able talking to her about them.

The Vietnamese community in my city accepts each other as one big family. The Vietnamese family is an extended family. My main role model is my cousin doing a Ph.D. in chemistry. He was the first person to get into an American university and the relatives then said, "Oh, Stanford's the place to go." He set the standard; I've sort of taken things from him. We're just close: there's a sort of bond.

Our nights are not as structured as an American family. Where they always seem to have dinner together, we can have it at differ- ent times. That was one thing that didn't limit me—like the home- work situation when I came home. I didn't have to do homework, eat with my parents and then go back and do homework. I could eat and do homework whenever I felt like it and that gave me more freedom. That's more or less a Vietnamese sort of family.

I've no idea where my sense of moral values comes from. Probably my mom, she often tells me to do things. But mostly it's self-motivation. My mom only told me to pray once in awhile, and then it was the sort of thing I did every night, and faith brought me to believe about God. The Vietnamese experience inspired me to think about other things. I just saw people having bad lives. It didn't start with that, that just strengthened it.

Matthew is 17 in 12th grade in an urban high school for academically talented students. He is Vietnamese and his parents were "boat people," staying at a refugee camp for three years until they could immigrate to the United States. His mother was a primary teacher in Vietnam and his father was a businessman. Both parents have factory jobs in America, his father being a foreman at his plant. Matthew did not speak English before attending elementary school shortly after coming to the United States. He is the second of three children, each a year apart in school, although his older sister dropped out after 11th grade. Although standardized testing revealed only normal abilities (not atypical for culturally different students whose native language is other than English), he had one of the highest grade point averages at his school and has earned several scholarships to a top university.

Matthew's English Teacher

Matthew is fortunate in being in classes and a grade level with a cohort of motivated, able peers. There is an extraordinary sense of sharing, and even if the kids question the sense of the busy work they are given, there is never any sense of not doing it to the best of their ability. All the students are physically active in the yard, the boys invariably sharing a basketball court. Matthew shows a fascination for the possibilities of language—different structures and styles, such as satire and metaphor—a sure sign of interest in novel and challenging ideas. It is interesting to me how few of his other teachers observe more than a dutifully bright boy, and yet his physical coordination and sense of fair play seems symptomatic of his whole personality.

His strong sense of responsibility towards his family is an important element in giving purpose to his zest for learning. He has a real empathy for others and his choice of psychology as a major for college seems a particularly happy one.

There is never any sense of self-consciousness about his faith or moral values. He would not be swayed from his behavior by peer pressure. He is a popular boy and there is no invidious sense of competitiveness-at-all-costs. He has true leadership qualities, although the school gives little real outlet for these. He leads group discussions and is a motivating force for the group's achievement, not being afraid to ask probing questions.

MEGAN: "I Feel Like an Idiot...and I'm Interested in a Lot of Different Things Than My Friends."

Sometimes I am really happy at school, if I have kept up with my work and have had a good social day. Usually I feel like an idiot, both academically and socially, and I feel as though I'm always saying and doing the wrong thing. I often feel like I can't communicate when I'm talking, as I do this best in writing.

I like learning—facts to me are usually interesting. The thing I like least is the amount of paperwork we have to do before we learn anything. I call this the learning to crap ratio—for example Mr. Smith has a high one, at least ten paperwork units to one learning.

I enjoy reading—but many of my peers think that I am driven to this by an absence of friends, and I hate having their sympathy because I don't have a boyfriend. For people that think like this I can do little to change their opinion, other than keep on reading.

Socially, at school, I talk about things that don't interest me, because if I only talked about the things that are of interest to me I would be a bore. My main problem is that I am interested in a lot of different things than my friends. If I were in a more popular group I would have to conform a lot more. I don't know if I am a good friend—I try to be sympathetic and understanding, but I don't think I am much fun to be with. I try to be as little involved as possible in fights between my friends, and if I am involved, which is rarely, I usually apologize first.

As to role models, I admire people who are intelligent and have a strong personality. But I don't really have anyone I would model myself upon. I just want to be myself.

My biggest problem in life is my relationship with my mother. She gets angry with me when I disagree with her, but her argument on these subjects is always illogical. We have no common ground on which to talk, but she is offended when I read. When I am frustrated I usually read, dream up stories or pace up and down. She has an annoying habit of telling everyone I'm gifted which usually makes them dislike me from the start. Then she goes on about how I get it from her. Dad thinks I'm intelligent, but dislikes the connotations of the "gifted" children, the pushy mothers, etc.

Megan is 15 years old and in tenth grade at a rural school. She is a highly talented student, particularly in the humanities subjects, with a passion for literature, history, language and social studies. Her father is the one person with whom she can share her interests. Megan's parents are separated and she lives with her mother, with whom she currently has a great deal of conflict over many issues.

Megan's Mother says:

Megan is a lot happier than at the elementary school where she went until sixth grade. When she got to high school, she spent most of her free periods alone or talking with the teachers—at least she talked about her interests, which was more than occurred at the elementary school. Since seventh grade she has had a friend, although she says she wishes her friend shared her interests in history and literature. As to coping—well, her marks are reasonably high in her interest areas.

I think she needs friends she can discuss her interests with: humanities subjects. There is no one, other than maybe her father, with whom she can share these interests.

She doesn't cope with people not sharing these matters, but in turn she doesn't tolerate the interests of most of her peers—or even adults—whom she considers have 'garbage' literature tastes, immature interests (especially boys and lack of appropriate ambition—marriage being the lowest of the low!). I think she is marking time until she goes to college—and I hope that it isn't a disappointment—where she'll find people with similar interests. I'm worried that by then she may have lost the ability to listen to other people's opinions.

Megan's Teacher says:

Megan seems to be happy. She achieves this by almost total withdrawal from peers. She copes by escaping into books and an imaginary world. Her major problem seems to be her relationship with her mother, who is quite the opposite of Megan. She doesn't appear to cope very well with this problem, other than by trying to ignore it. She socializes with me—e.g. comes to writing groups. I have organized Ancient Greek lessons, etc. and accept her as she is. I liaise between Megan and other members of staff. Megan doesn't communicate with staff or peers. This is not arrogance—just insecurity because she is so different. She is, however, a model student.

NEIL: "I'm Basically 'Not Acceptable' to Most Kids at School."

I've been at this school a long time. I've wanted to leave. The dumb rules they have! Standing in line marching into assembly. The childish behavior of most of the other kids in the class. Having detentions as a class because they're being stupid. I get bored. Most of the English work we get is boring. The teachers don't bother me. They're busy with the kids who can't do the work or who are messing around. They always put me with the dumb kids in groups to work. They use me to help explain math to people I hate. The other students are beyond help. I get chosen last for groups or teams—unless it's math games when they want the 'brain' on the team. Orchestra's pretty weak: but my piano teacher is great. I like helping out with plays and stuff. I like art—you get free choice in most things.

Where do I start with the things I least like? The kids—being with guys who are total idiots. They choose one person, who doesn't want to follow their group like a sheep, then they just victimize them. The way they perform in front of the girls! I feel older than them. I don't care about them—I don't do what other people do. The older friends I have out of school and my cousins are humorous, interesting, interested in music, intelligent, not interested in girls / sports too much. I'm not very popular, but I suppose I've done that. Sometimes I wish I had more friends, but not at this school. I'd like them to leave me alone, and the other people who are into music like me. I'm basically "not acceptable" to most kids at school.

I hate them calling out across the street "Faggot," and they have even written graffiti with my name in it at the subway station. I don't want to go and see the counselor about this. My mom goes to see her and I hate it. I do see her but not about punishing the jerks in my class. It'd be a lot worse for me if this happened.

I worry about it! Then I play music. I compose. I talk to myself. I might talk to an adult. I try to forget it. I fight back at them, I laugh at them ("You don't have to punch me, I know you're the toughest / strongest and you want everyone to see your muscles—take your shirt off! Flex those biceps!"). At home there's not enough to do. Mom and Dad won't let me go into the city. I wish people (like my dad) wouldn't say I've got a big head. I wish I had a bigger body, I'm pretty puny. I wish I was older. I wish I knew what lay ahead in my future. I hope to be able to leave the school. I'm going to take music and maybe drama at a school where they specialize in the arts. I'd like to be a jazz pianist. I'd like to do TV or comedy. I want to get out of this city and study music in L.A. or London.

Neil is in 9th grade at a private school with a good music program. His music teacher has described his particular class as "being less than popular, with lots of bullies and troublemakers. Neil does not perform to his potential—except in test conditions.

Neil's Father says:

I'm well aware he's not happy. He accepts that he has to see through this year at least. He's mature in that way. I suppose I support him in avoiding uncomfortable situations. I write notes excusing him from some sports days and allowing him to miss school for some musical events. He's not too enthusiastic about showing what he can do in terms of proper schoolwork. I think he's got a superior front he puts on to hide himself—this probably puts people off. He's a real show-off on the piano and he is very good, so I suppose he's chosen which ability he wants to develop. He has a tremendous amount of self-discipline and doesn't have tantrums like other adolescents, but he resents my disciplining him. We share our music, but not his feelings. He talks more to his mother. He's more sensitive to how she feels, whereas he tends to resent me for worrying or making rules, for instance. He has a 16-year-old sister, and they fight like cats and dogs. He's actually got a few more brains than her and it's a bad combination: she teases him unmercifully. His younger brother has cerebral palsy, and Neil really can't do enough for him. He's patient and spends time after school and weekends with him. We're very proud of him in that respect. He needs help really in being tolerant of other people. He doesn't seem to show any respect for the school or the staff, and it's an excellent school. They've really made allowances for his music and encouraged him.

Neil's Music Teacher says:
He is somewhat of a loner. It's difficult to judge whether this is by choice or by necessity. He has a sharp wit, and can cut others down, and if some boys push him too far I can see he has trouble coping. He is a music teacher's delight because he genuinely loves to play and improve. He tells me more than I'm comfortable with knowing about other students and his family life. He is well past any course I teach at this school. I try to find new challenges and follow up his suggestions. He plays a big part in the orchestra, he writes pieces for school productions, concerts, etc. It's such a shame he doesn't get the appreciation, or rather the recognition from the other students. If he played football or baseball—well it would be a different story! I don't see any evidence of a big head, although other staff have described him as being boastful or full of himself. I'm surprised at that. Neil's very advanced and mature; he has a high IQ, and he's very gifted in music.

NIKKI: "I'm a Black Girl and I'm Smart and Most People Put Black Girls in a Stereotype."

I usually like school. I love to learn and I love to talk and hang out with my friends. We learn new and interesting things and have fun. I also have some teachers who help me out in difficult situations, but some who are really mean. I hate boring long reprimands from teachers or the principal. I like sports and Language Arts, especially writing.

Homework sometimes frustrates me, but I just try my best to finish it. At school, I don't like the focus on boys and clothes, not on school work. Those kids will not know anything when they get to high school. I hate it when people constantly talk about me for no reason, but I try to sit away from the problem and calm down. This happens at school on the phone to people I don't even know by my "so-called friends" who are really acquaintances. I hate it when people label me as smart and then make a big deal of a bad grade. This boy Steve used to clap when I got a bad grade. I try to act average and always do good so people won't do it so much. I want for my peers to see me for who I really am, not just a nerd. I just be myself. I hate it when people make fun of me.

Teachers shouldn't compare me to my peers because it may cause something between me and that person. I wish some teachers would stop treating me like I'm two years old. I wish they would treat me with respect as they would want to be treated. I will be responsible. I will also watch my attitude.

I'm different because I'm a black girl and smart and most people put black girls in a stereotype that they just have babies. I have a different outlook on things. I am studying, staying out of gangs and drugs, and not having sex before I marry. My shape has changed from skinny to athletic, so I have to put some jerk guys in check before they start anything.

I'm extremely loud and love to be noticed, but my friends and family get upset. They say I draw too much attention to myself, so I try to be more quiet and think before I act. Sometimes I treat people mean when I get mad, so I work on controlling my anger. I don't try to fit in. If my friends don't like me the way I am, that's their problem. Some people think that because I talk proper, I speak like a white girl. I just try to be myself, but I try to be nice to people. I don't really want to change anything about myself. I do try to be less loud, but I'm happy the way I am. I would change people's ideas about me.

At home, my little brother does something to me and when I say something to him I get in trouble or when I tell on him, he doesn't get in trouble. My mom and dad are divorced. I live with my brother, my big sister, my Mom and grandmother, but both my parents think I am smart and have gifts in speech. My mother thinks I have a gift for writing stories and expressing the way I feel.

My goals are to finish college and become a writer and an actress. When I was in fifth grade, I had a teacher who really encouraged me to write. She said I used rich language and metaphors. She had us keep a diary. I still do. It's sort of my secret room that no one else can go in 'cause I've got the key. I can make it look and be however I want. I have to share my real room with my brother and sister, so this is my space. I try to keep a positive *outlook and write whenever the ideas are flowing, even if it's late at night. When I graduate, I want to get a red motorcycle and become an actress in a movie written, directed, and produced by me. I want to finish my book, I also want to have a good husband and a lot of kids, maybe even adopt. I work hard in school. I want to make something of my life.*

I try to find people who have the same interests as I do. My few real friends are honest, understanding, nice and caring. I can laugh with them. I can tell them things and these friends won't go back telling everyone. My "so-called friends" who are really acquaintances sometimes say things. None of my friends do alcohol or drugs.

My biggest worry is safety. I worry about the safety of me and my family. I worry about surviving. I don't want to die young. All that violence, gangs, Black on Black crime with young people shooting up each other. It's a tough world out there!

I try to forget about it and tend to look forward to a new day. I worry about money and will I be able to get a scholarship to go through college so I can meet my goals. I wish my dad would send more money so it wouldn't be so hard at home and I wish he would call me more often. I try to earn money babysitting so I don't have to ask for money for school supplies. Sometimes I'll make up songs or write poems about these problems. My best poems are when I'm upset.

I admire my grandmother because she has overcome so much and my sister because she has her feet on the ground and is intelligent and she knows what she wants to do with her life. But my mother is my role model because she stayed in school, followed through with her goals in life and still is proceeding to get her masters degree even with us three kids.

I try to be a moral person. A moral person is one who doesn't do anything bad or crude. Sometimes my big mouth gets me in trouble, but I try to think before I talk. I'm learning to count to ten when I get mad. I want to get an education. I hope we can get out of the city to someplace nice where I feel safe and I can have my own room.

I relate to my grandmother well. I talk to her when I have a problem. I also talk to my Mom. She helps me with my problems, but I hate to bother her because she's working and studying too. I have a few really close friends. We don't have many problems. If we do, we try to sit down and work them out. I think I am a good friend. They are decent, not mean and they want to be somebody, like me.

Nikki is 13, in 8th grade. She attends middle school in a big city.

Nikki's Language Arts Teacher:

Nikki has a lot of talent as a writer. She's sometimes seeks attention by being loud, but inside I think she's very sensitive. She uses language beautifully, especially her poetry. I try to encourage her to submit her work to various competitions. She won second place for an essay she wrote about Black families. I think she has a lot of good, common sense. Her mother is an inspiration, working on an advanced degree at the same time trying to earn enough to feed her family. Nikki sometimes talks to me about her situation. I wish there were ways to make it easier for single mothers, but Nikki's Mom is an amazing person. I'll try to help Nikki find some teachers that can mentor her next year in high school. This is one young person who will do something with her life with a little support.

SANDRA: "I Want to Be Treated as Normal."

I generally enjoy the one day I go to school. I love doing math, but it's too easy. So when I have finished, I help the other kids at my table. But sometimes the other kids in my class tease me. So sometimes I keep it a secret that the work is so easy—but the kids know!

I want to be treated as normal. Some children treat me as if I'm from another planet. But mostly it's good. I am usually treated like a 10-12-year-old, though some kids treat me as if I shouldn't be in sixth grade.

How do I cope? I cope by trying to ignore it, or I leave the group. This year the teacher thinks I should be in fourth grade and that I shouldn't be home-schooled. I wish the teacher would give me harder work for home. I was allowed to take harder work last year. I cope by finishing my work quickly, then I help others. They seem to like me to help them because then they get the work done. I keep problems to myself until they fade away. I wish I could talk about them, but I find it hard. What is different about me? Well, I have a different brain. I have the brain of a 13-year-old in the body of a 9-

year-old. It is a problem. It makes me mad! I don't deal with my problems. I lock them up.

In a way, I wish I could be like my friends. But then, maybe not. ... I don't know. Sometimes I wish my mom hadn't taught me so much, then I wouldn't be so far ahead and I could be in fourth grade like other 9-year-olds.

I am worried what full-time school will be like when I go next year. As for advice about what would help other bright kids at school, I would suggest you might be able to help schools give children the right work. Don't push, but don't hold back.

Sandra is a 9-year-old in sixth grade in an elementary school. She is 2 years younger than the other students in her grade and has problems in relationships with her classmates. She now has most of her education at home, spending only one day each week at school.

Sandra's Mother says:

Sandra began to speak (single words) at 6 months, and was speaking in sentences at 1 year. She began to recognize words at 18 months, and I taught her to read by reading children's books and emphasizing words. She was reading well by 4 years of age. I don't think my daughter is gifted, but is only advanced because of one-to-one attention and home schooling. We had Sandra tested when she was 4 years of age and were told her reading age was 12 years. Therefore we decided to keep her home because no kindergarten had programs that could accommodate her. Our experiences with the educational system have been negative. Neither my husband nor I finished high school, and I have a brother who cannot read.

SHAWN: "I hate it when adults judge you"

I am happy at school because I have a good education in the gifted program. My classes are fun and my friends are there. I like it when we do fun projects. What I like least is when we do long, boring work. I get frustrated at school and at home when someone ignores me. When this happens, I usually walk away like I didn't want them in the first place. At home, my sisters get me in trouble but I just ignore them.

I like math, computers and gym. I'm going to join debating so I get better at speaking and arguing. I really hate it when teachers and all adults judge you by the color of your skin, the clothes you wear, the people you befriend, or by what your interests are. I think parents should stop teaching their children to think this way. I would like teachers to be looser and not so stiff all the time and have peers not try to look so cool when they're not. I would like for peers to stop messing with me. Because I am smart a few of them call me nerd. I just try to ignore it or I make a joke and agree with them.

My parents think I have a gift in learning, sports, and especially arguing. My dream is to graduate from a well educated college and pursue a football career and then become a lawyer. I am trying to master the art of winning arguments with my parents.

The only thing that's different about me is that I'm Black. There's not many Black people in my class. I don't let this get to me. I don't do anything to fit in. I am the way I am. But I wish I could change my physique. To play football you have to be big and I'm still thin and a little short. I eat a lot, but I guess I burn it off. My mom teases me about my appetite. I'm always hungry cause I'm very energetic. But I'm only 12 so I have to give my body some time to grow. Some kids in my class are much taller than me, but I'm not the smallest. No way. I like myself for what I am except that I stutter sometimes. I'll have to practice public speaking. It's not a problem when I talk to my parents.

I'm a friendly person. If kids have my interests then I think it's real easy to befriend them. I like to be with decent kids—ones who go to church and don't do anything seriously wrong. I have a few really close friends. Others are more acquaintances, but I'm open to friendship if they don't use drugs or alcohol. I don't have many problems with friends, but if I do, I talk it out.

Basically I worry about my future. What occupation will I have after college? I wonder how much my net worth would be. Will I turn out to be somebody, not just some bum on the street? I worry that everything in the world will change before I'm 20. Sometimes you can just hope for the best.

I admire Derrick Thomas for going to college during the NFL off-season to get an education. I admire my parents who are hard working and loving. They encourage me to stay in school and stay out of trouble. I talk to my parents when I have a major problem.

Shawn is a 12 year old boy in seventh grade in a large, urban middle school. He is African American.

These responses were collected through interviews and questionnaires. Students were asked the following questions. You may wish to think about how you would answer these questions and discuss your answers with others. You might also want to interview your friends about these topics:

Interview Questions

1. Are you happy at school? If so, why? If not, why not?
2. What frustrates you at school? At home? How do you deal with these frustrations?
3. What do you like best/least about school?
4. What would you most like changed about ways peers or teachers treat you? What do you do or could you do to improve ways peers or teachers treat you?
5. Do you think your parents believe you have any gifts? If so, what are they?
6. What are your dreams, hopes, goals? What are you doing to reach these goals?
7. What is different about you if anything? Does this cause you any problems? If so, how do you deal with these problems?
8. What do you do to "fit in" that you don't like doing? What alternatives are there and what would the consequences be for doing things differently?
9. What do you wish you could change about yourself?
10. How do you select your friends?
11. What are your biggest problems or worries? How do you cope with these?
12. Whom do you admire and why? Who are your role models?
13. Do you use any different strategies than those described in the Adolescent Coping Scales to help yourself with difficulties?
14. What is your definition of a moral person? Do you fit that definition?
15. Do you have friends? Close ones? Many? Few? Are you a good friend? How do you cope with friendship problems?
16. How do you relate to your parents? Whom do you talk to when you have a problem?

Coping Strategies:
Advice from Capable Adolescents

The following are helpful hints from a group of gifted young people who were asked to put into priority order some strategies that young people like themselves may use. You can look up the reference to the study in the "References" section under Buescher and Higham who reported this study in 1989.

♦ Accept your abilities and use them to help fellow students.

♦ Make friends with other students of exceptional talent.

♦ Develop more relationships with adults, especially those that you would find interesting.

♦ Focus your attention on activities at school other than the academic in which you might achieve.

♦ Develop your talents in areas other than what is possible to do at school.

♦ Become active in community groups that are associated with causes that you feel passionate about, where your age is not a problem for membership.

SOME TRIED AND TRUE ACTIVITIES TO DEVELOP YOUR COPING SKILLS

Worksheets

Following is a series of worksheets that may assist you in becoming a more capable coper.

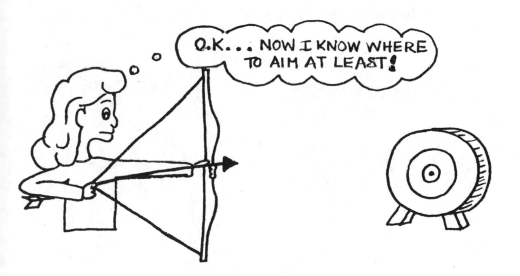

Accentuate the Positive

It is helpful to learn to focus on the positive characteristics of individuals as well as in situations. Find a positive adjective that accurately describes each person and add it as a preface to their name. For example "Helpful Harry," "Smiling Sandra," "Generous Jenny." It is fun to try and think of an adjective that starts with the same letter or sound as the person's name.

First do it with members of your family.

Then try it with people in your class.

Now do it using the names of your friends.

Think about a difficult situation. Perhaps your family has to move to another city and you are sad about losing your friends. Maybe you got mononucleosis and have to stay at home for six weeks to get well.

What positive things can you think of for each situation?

There is a saying, "When one door closes, another opens."

How could this be applied to your case?

DETERMINED DONNA!

CREATIVE CLARE!

Serving Others

One way to feel good about yourself is to make someone else feel good. Here are some suggestions of things that you might do to make someone else feel good.

1. Write to someone to make them feel special.
2. Do a job for someone that would be helpful, such as shopping for an elderly person.
3. Play a game or do something with someone who is lonely.
4. Invite someone to join you and a friend.
5. Ask someone who speaks a different language to teach you a few words.
6. Say hello to someone you don't know at school.
7. Thank someone for being your friend.

Add your own ideas to this list.
1.
2.
3.
4.

**Think about how you feel when you have
made someone else feel good!**

Dealing with Authority Successfully

Have you had to deal with these problems?
1. The subject is boring. You learned it before, did it years ago, it's too easy, no challenge.
2. You're stifled. Your interests are not addressed; there's no room for creativity.
3. The adult in charge is wrong. She or he made a mistake.
4. You feel the adult doesn't like you, picks on you, ignores you or punishes you unjustly.

What Can You Do?
Suppose you say in class:
"This class is so dumb." (or stupid or boring!!!)
"You're wrong, Mr. (or Ms.) So and So!"
"I didn't do it. You always pick on me!"
What are the teacher's usual reactions?
How would you feel if the teacher said to you in front of the class:
"That's a stupid piece of writing!"
"That's wrong. You don't think!"

Suppose you say at home:
"You and your stupid rules! Everyone else is allowed to..."
"It's not my fault. You're always blaming me!"
"You're always controlling me. Just leave me alone!"
What are your parent's usual reactions?

Here are some strategies other capable kids like you used to deal with these problems:
1. Take a trip inside your imagination, think in another way, or see if you can find something new in the same old material.
   "When I'm bored I try to imagine the teacher's words spelled backwards."
   "I slip away between the words into my favorite daydream and force myself to come back every few minutes to be sure I haven't missed anything new."
2. Think up an alternative assignment and ask POLITELY if you may do it.

"When I had done graphing linear equations for the third time in two years in my math class, I asked the teacher if I could try to do an experiment that required use of linear equations to describe my findings instead of just doing the exercises in the book. To my surprise, he was enthusiastic."

3. Make time to talk to the teacher.

   "I asked the teacher after class if I could please have an appointment with her about some alternative assignments."

4. Remember flies are attracted to honey, not vinegar.

   "I tried to remember something positive we had done, expressed an interest in it and asked if I could work more on that topic. My teacher was delighted that I was interested."

   "I've discovered that when I want to disagree with the teacher, I use a 'sweetener' like 'Could it have another explanation?' or 'In my opinion' or 'Have you thought about this possibility?' or 'I respectfully disagree with that statement because ..."

5. Use "I" statements instead of blaming someone else.

   "I feel really angry when you make all my decisions for me, or blame me for something I didn't do!"

6. Offer to take on a responsibility for a favor.

   "I'll wash the car if you'll drive my friends and me to the dance."

Social Skills

Developing social skills is an important part of living happily in a community with others. Think about what these skills are:

In a Friend
1. What skills or characteristics do you feel are most important in a friend?
2. What skills or characteristics do you feel are most important to be a friend?
3. Must all friends bring the same characteristics to a relationship? Why or why not?

In a Member of the Opposite Sex
1. What skills or characteristics are most important in an intimate relationship?
2. Are there particular skills brought to the relationship by females as compared to males? Males as compared to females?
3. What if the person of the opposite sex has or doesn't have those characteristics? Does it matter?
4. Which characteristics that have been considered typically male do females now bring to a relationship and vice versa?
5. Which relationship skills could be used in other situations?

Who Are My Friends?

For each item below think about a specific person:

1. Do you have a close friend with whom you most like to sit or spend time with at school?
2. Do you have a friend with whom you would most like to work on a committee?
3. Is there someone you would like to invite to a party at your house?
4. Is there someone else you would like to have as a friend?
5. Is there someone you feel could help you with your school-work?
6. Is there someone to whom you like to teach something?
7. Is there someone with whom you would enjoy having lunch?
8. Is there someone you would like to choose as a partner for a class project?
9. Do you have someone with whom you would like to go to a dance?
10. Is there someone you would like to know better?

Belonging to a Group

It is important for us to feel that we belong somewhere. Usually the groups that we belong to are the family, community, sports organizations, interest clubs and organizations, churches, and so on.

We all belong to many groups. Think of a group to which you belong.

You can do this activity with pencil and paper but it is best to do it with some friends at school or outside school.

Our Group

1. What motto or slogan would be good for your group? For a motto or slogan to be truly powerful, there must be a rationale behind it. Explain your rationale for creating the slogan.
2. What might be a good name for your group? Create names that are related to your motto or slogan.
3. What code of conduct should your group follow?
4. Identify the forms of support each group member would like from the group.
5. Design a logo, poster or badge that could serve as a symbol for your group.

Conversation Starters

Sometimes it is difficult to strike up a conversation. These are some helpful conversation starters:

1. Ask about someone's pet.
2. Find out where someone lives.
3. Share your interests and hobbies and then ask about the other person's interests or hobbies.
4. Find out if the person watches your favorite TV show.
5. Ask about their favorite sport or sports team. Share information about yours.
6. Find out about the person's favorite or least favorite school subject. Ask about their favorite or least favorite teacher.
7. Ask a question about a school subject or an activity you share.
8. What other conversation starters can you or your friends think of? What has worked for you?

Identifying Your Own Feelings

It is important to recognize some of the feelings and emotions that we have in different circumstances.

Describe a time when you did each of the things below, then describe how the person felt and how you felt.

What happened when you:
1. Interrupted someone?
2. Expressed appreciation to someone?
3. Criticized someone?
4. Said, "I love you"?
5. Remembered a birthday?
6. Forgot a birthday?
7. Offered to help?
8. Refused to help?
9. Lost your temper?
10. Displayed jealousy?
11. Listened attentively?

Dealing with Aggression

What do you do when a bully threatens you or actually hits you?

- ◆ Do you run?
- ◆ Do you hit them back?
- ◆ Do you seek help from an adult?
- ◆ Do you avoid them by taking a different way home or going out a different door at school?
- ◆ Do you tell them how you feel?
- ◆ Do you tell them how they are really feeling deep down inside?

  "You're really not feeling very good about yourself to pick on someone so much smaller than you!"

- ◆ Do you admire their strength and build up their ego to distract them from pounding you?

  "Let's see those muscles. What biceps!"

What do you do when you feel very angry at someone?

- ◆ Do you think before you act?
- ◆ Do you count to 10 and give yourself time to assess the situation?
- ◆ Do you use "I" statements?

  "I'm so mad at you. I hate it when you make a scene in public and everyone stares at us!"

Each situation may require a different response. What works best for you in which particular circumstance? You might want to discuss strategies with your friends or classmates.

SOMETIMES THE BEST WAY TO DEAL WITH A BULLY IS TO AVOID HIM!!

Wishful Thinking

Swap Shop

There is a recycling shop in the neighborhood. You are able to purchase or obtain qualities that you would like to have or increase. In order to do this, you need to swap qualities that you already have that you no longer want to keep in yourself.

What qualities would you like more of, and what qualities are you willing to swap? That is, what would you like to have more of and what would you like to part with?

Qualities I Want More Of	Qualities I Want to Give Up
1.	1.
2.	2.
3.	3.
4.	4.
5.	5.
6.	6.
7.	7.
8.	8
9.	9.
10.	10.

Creating a Positive Climate

Another way to focus on the positive is to try to make a significant impact on the atmosphere in your school or community.

List ten things you, your classmates or friends could do that would improve the environment in your school or community.

Some ideas are:

♦ Planting flowers where others may enjoy them.
♦ Fixing up something that is worn.
♦ Paint welcome or greeting signs.
♦ Design a package of information to welcome new students.
♦ Welcome someone new in your neighborhood.
♦ Welcome someone new in a group that you are associated with.
♦ Clean up a neglected area.

Now write your own ideas in the space below.

1.

2.

3.

4.

5.

6.

7.

8.

9.

10.

Changing Your World

There are lots of things that you would like to change in your world. First, it is important to recognize what these things are. Second, consider who else might be interested in your particular social issue. Third, try to learn as much as you can about these issues. Fourth, identify what you can do about these issues. Fifth, assess what things are possible for you to do. Ideas and dreams may be more significant in our lives than inventions.

1. Talk to a resource person and invite them (if appropriate) to visit your group to talk about the future and how it may be different from the present.
2. What single change would create a difference in your life?
3. Think of some of the important changes that have taken place in our world. Find out how they came about.
4. Think of some ideas that would change your school to make it a better place.

Dealing with Social Issues: Justice, Poverty, Environment, Peace, Safety and Others

These are the things that matter to many people in the world but sometimes it feels that you are alone in your caring. There are like-minded individuals but it often takes time before you meet them. Here are some things that you can do in the meantime.

♦ When the world seems different to you than to others around you, find someone to talk to.

♦ Share your perceptions and thoughts with other people. Others may have similar views or they may start thinking about things differently. You may be bringing new light to their world.

The principles are:

♦ Offload by sharing (packages are lighter when carried with someone else).

♦ Check out what others think. Don't assume you know.

♦ You are not alone—you may just not have met the other individuals who think like you.

♦ Share your perception of things with others. Writing down the problem is a way of sharing.

♦ Review your ideas or add to them. When you meet others with similar interests then you can call on your writings.

♦ Send a letter to the editor of a newspaper.

♦ Join a group or club where your interests are shared by others.

♦ Start a group or club if you already know of others who share your interests or concerns.

What to Do
When all your work's due at the same time

Try to go to
bed early before
a big exam or
test.

Put the problem
in proportion — are
you likely to care
about having done
every task perfectly
when you're 20?

Put the problem
in proportion — are
you likely to care
about having done
every task perfectly
when you're 20?

Do your best, then go and
treat yourself by doing
something FUN!

Organize your mind and study effectively.
Break tasks down into manageable blocks.
Make a work timetable.

Just do your
best, and
promise yourself
a bit more time
next week.

Forgive yourself!

Time Management Strategies

Student Guidelines:

1. Be proactive rather than reactive. Learn to anticipate and plan for stress.

2. Plan your time. Try not to let events or people push you beyond your limits. Tell them what your limits are. Be aware of your own stress signals.

3. Plan quality time. Find some uninterrupted time to focus on a particular task. Only do one thing at a time.

4. Find out your own best time for working. Accept this rhythm in yourself and use it to your best advantage.

5. Be realistic about what you can do. Don't put demands on yourself you cannot cope with. Be honest with yourself and others.

6. Know what you do with your time — make a list of what you do throughout the day. Have you spent time wisely?

7. This is mismanagement of time:
    a. Too much time spent in crisis situations.
    b. Too much time spent on trivia — more than is necessary.
    c. Too many interruptions which ruin planning and momentum.
    d. Too little time spent on important tasks.
    e. Too little quality time spent on tasks requiring creativity and productivity.
8. Set long-term goals as well as short-term goals and prioritize.

Time Management Worksheet

Daily and weekly tasks can be prioritized. List them from most important down to least important. Assess how long each task will take.

	Tasks	Time	Whom to ask if help is needed
1.			
2.			
3.			
4.			
5.			
6.			
7.			

Goal Setting

Worksheet One

1. Establish one area of your school performance that you'd like to improve.

2. Describe how long it will take to achieve this goal. Be reasonable and give a rational estimate.

3. If you feel that you'll be able to achieve this goal within 4 weeks call it a short-term goal. If it will take you over 5 weeks to achieve this goal call it a long-term goal. Check the box below that you feel best describes the type of goal you're trying to achieve.
   ❑ Short-term Goal   ❑ Long-term Goal

4. What steps do you need to take to achieve this goal? (Preferably list the order in which you need to do them.)

5. What reward will you give yourself when you achieve this goal? (This is an important part of goal setting as you probably won't reach your goal without some sort of reward.)

6. Sometimes you might find it necessary to use a contract if your goal is a little hard to achieve. The basic contract is as follows (You may wish to change it as you see necessary).

I _____will reward myself with

_____once I achieve my goal. If I

waste time when I could be working on_____then

 I will be unable to reward myself with _____. By signing

below I realize that it is up to myself to achieve this goal and that

I am only hindering myself when I neglect working towards it.

Signed_____

Goal Setting

Worksheet Two

Below is a more extensive goal-setting list. You should list at least 10 long-term and 10 short-term goals to gain full benefit of the sheet. Use worksheet one to help you in establishing your goals. You do not just have to limit yourself to school-based goals. Sports, social and entertainment-based goals can also be included.

Short-term goals: A few days to four weeks.
Long-term goals: Four weeks to a few years.

Short-term Goals	Long-term Goals
1.	1.
2.	2.
3.	3.
4.	4.
5.	5.
6.	6.
7.	7.
8.	8.
9.	9.
10.	10.
11.	11.
12.	12.
13.	13.
14.	14.
15.	15.

What to Do
When You're Scared of Failing

Visualize! What's the worst that could happen? Failing is never the end of the world. Then visualize success!

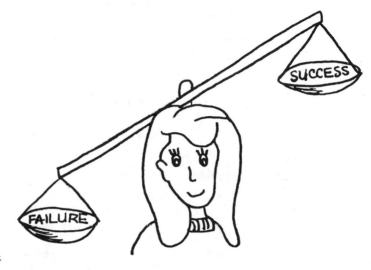

Realize that smart people don't always arrive at the right answer the first time!

Think about your last failure—what did you learn that will help you with the next challenge?

Go to the library and look in the biography section. Your hero or role model must have bombed out sometime in his or her life!

Hey! There's another option other than success and failure—it's called" doing OK" and it feels good!

What to Do
When You Feel Your Work
Just Isn't Good Enough

1. Take a realistic look at the work you're dissatisfied with—try seeing it through someone else's eyes.

2. What exactly is wrong with it?

3. Area there simple changes that could be made to improve it?

4. Are there things you'll keep in mind for next time? What did you learn from this?

5. What are its good qualities?

 MOST IMPORTANTLY

6. Is it of a satisfactory standard and ready to submit?

7. OK. Now push it aside and FORGET it!!

You could use these suggestions for dealing with other problems.
Sometimes we all feel less than perfect—it's because we're HUMAN!

What to Do When Things are Wrong and You Feel Responsible

Share your concerns. Can you get other people interested? Form a group or join a club and you'll make a difference!

Make some realistic goals and pursue them in small, gradual steps.

Remeber, the world can change—but only a little at atime. Just work on a few problems—not all of them.

Release your feelings— don't bottle them up!

Delegate responsiblity and tasks to other people. Don't take everything on yourself.

What to Do
When You're Teased
Because You're Smart

Laugh with them.

Say "Flattery will get you nowhere," or just agree you are brilliant — with a smile!

Answer back.
Tell them something about themselves that they're not aware of!

Don't throw out the baby with the bath water! Remember a certain amount of their rudeness is due to jealousy.

Tell someone what they're doing! If they are made to realize they are acting like childish bullies— they'll feel embarrassed.

Ignore them — they'll grow out of it.

Shake the Feeling

Talk to someone.

Phone a friend.

Get physical.

Ride your bike or jog.

Do something just for fun.

Start a collection.

Reward yourself.

Buy something new, or a special treat.

Lift your mood.

Watch a funny video or play 'up' music.

Fill in some suggestions which might work for YOU.

Up and At Em!

Take a look in the biography section of the library. You might be surprised to know the false starts, mistakes and failures experienced by successful people.

Walt Disney was once fired because he didn't have good ideas!

Read about former President Harry S. Truman. He failed as a farmer and as a small business man and was totally undistinguished as a senator from Missouri. But his grit and determination as President earned him a second term against a highly favored opponent as well as a distinguished place in American History.

CHALLENGE YOUR IDEAS AND GROW!

Famous, well respected people also know that in order to really learn, a process has to be followed. Along this path or process to knowledge, people's philosophies often change. They're not contradicting themselves, they just had the courage to recognize the errors of their thinking and continue! Try looking up the works of some of these people:

Linus Pauling (Vitamin C Expert)
Germaine Greer (Feminist)
Ludvig Van Beethoven (Composer)
Leo Tolstoy (Writer)
Rachel Carson (Writer)
Malcolm X (Political activist)

Paul Robeson (Singer)
Pablo Neruda (Poet)
Kath Walker (Poet)
Albert Einstein (Physicist)
Charles Darwin (Scientist)
Louisa May Alcott (Writer)

How to Get Help When You've Got An Eating Problem

ACCEPT
that sometimes people can see themselves in an unrealistic way. If others don't agree with your judgment about your weight — talk about it.

LOOK
in the front of the phonebook under Crisis or help lines for local numbers. Or call the national hotline for anorexia at (708) 831-3438

ASK
a family friend or teacher to accompany you when you seek help. It's easier to take a friend to help you explain.

EXPLAIN
how you're feeling. If you can't make people understand with words you can use pictures. Send your art or writing to someone who will understand.

REMEMBER
people won't blame you! Professionals understand these problems and can help you recover.

What to Do When Eating Becomes A BIG Problem

Don't get too angry when your parents nag you to eat. Try to tell them how you are feeling rather than telling lies.

If it's harder to tell someone the truth about your problem over the phone, try sending a letter instead.

Would you really like to be healthy again or would you feel like you'd lost if you ate again? Write down your feelings.

Talk to adults about the unstable periods in their lives. Ask about support groups — where other people like you can talk together.

What other areas would you like to be concentrating on? Pursue an interest that has nothing to do with food or how you look.

Spend some 'honest time' thinking alone. There are probably a lot of reasons why you won't/can't eat. Is FEAR one of them? How about REVENGE?

Here are Some of the Good Things about Recovering from Anorexia

✔ You won't feel sick and "tight" inside. You'll be able to relax and smile when you feel well.

✔ You'll *do better* at school because your concentration and motivation will improve.

✔ You won't feel so cold and vulnerable and you'll become more confident.

✔ You won't be nagged or hassled about food.

✔ Dealing with food will become a natural part of life. You'll be able to use your energy and thoughts to make decisions and control your own life.

✔ People will respect you for having the courage to seek help and overcome the problem. You might even end up helping others recover.

✔ You'll feel a lot better about yourself— you'll be able to look in the mirror and like what you see.

What to Do When Everything is Worrying You

It's OK to feel a sense of despair about the tragedies in our world — but you shouldn't feel responsible for them.

A good way to change things is to make suggestions tactfully. Put forward ideas by saying "It seems as if." or "In my opinion."

Try to learn from the mistakes of others, rather than condemning them for doing the wrong thing. Remember to act differently if you're ever in the same situation.

Take responsibility for your behavior and your little piece of the world. You'll make a big difference to those around you.

As humans we must be educated about both sides of life. It's just as important to talk about cruelty, cheating and lying as talking about beauty, fulfillment or love. Understand the importance of the good and the bad in life.

I'D BETTER TALK TO SOMEONE

What to Do When You're Depressed

If you only feel mildly depressed, try associating
with bright, positive people; avoid the situations
which tend to aggravate your depression.

Use humor to improve your day-to-day moods.
Seek help for long-term problems.

Be truthful with yourself and
others. Spend time thinking
about the cause of your feelings.
If you can't change it — don't
dwell on it. If you can change it
— take positive action.

Phone or write to a friend
you trust. Tell someone.
You'll usually feel better
afterwards.

If you need to let your feelings out —
keep a journal. You don't have to show
anyone, it can just be for you.

Remember, you are in control of your future.
You might need help from someone else at times, but you make the final
decisions in your life!

Not All Depression Is the Same

I'm feeling bad today, and the weather's gloomy too. I'll try to snap out of it — maybe see a funny movie.

THESE FEELINGS ARE NATURAL AND HEALTHY — EVERYONE HAS THEM.

Gee, I've been feeling depressed and stressed out for weeks now. It's starting to affect my health. I'd better see the school nurse or my doctor and change my lifestyle — maybe decrease my workload.

THESE FEELINGS CAN BE SERIOUS AND YOU MIGHT GET SICK IF YOU LET THINGS GET WORSE.

I've been feeling this despair for so long. I don't even know what I feel anymore, it's just numb depression. I don't belong anywhere and I don't want to live.

THIS IS REALLY SERIOUS. YOU MUST GET SOME PROFESSIONAL HELP IMMEDIATELY.

What to Do When You Feel Life's Not Worth Living

Tell the truth about how you're feeling. Write a diary and show it to a doctor, teacher or counselor you trust.

Find someone to talk to. If you don't know anyone you trust — ring a crisis line listed in the front of the phone book. The counselors are trained to listen and respond to your needs (You can also call the "Nine-Line". It's free. 1-800-999-9999, but please don't abuse the number with crank calls. Someone else may REALLY need to get through).

Accept that you are only human — you are entitled to make mistakes, be less than perfect, feel overwhelmed and have troubles. Listen to Billy Joel's old song — "You're Only Human".

Read some biographies of successful people; you'll see that every life has some suffering in it. Find out what coping strategies these people use.

Talk to older people. Many have been through suicidal periods in their lives and understand.

How to Recognize
a Suicidal Friend or Student

They might play out their feelings through their writing or art, not just in conversation.

They may have a tendency to feel there's no use trying—they often see themselves as losers.

They tend to lack ways of dealing with life's problems.

They will probably have felt depressed for quite awhile. This long-term, intense depression is a common cause of suicide.

They may withdraw from their schoolmates, families and teachers. They may try to cut themselves off from all outside activities and live in isolation.

They might act out the part of being happy but secretly be isolated and withdrawn. Perhaps someone else in their lives has noticed.

What to Do When You Feel Your Friend is Suicidal

Start by listening even if you think he or she has everything to live for, accept his or her feelings—they are painful.

Ask—if he or she appears very depressed and is hinting at suicide you may have to ask, "Do you ever think of killing yourself?" You won't be putting the idea into his or her head for the first time.

:cept—don't trivial-
e—the problems. What
a small thing to you
ight be devastating to
n or her. Never make fun.

Consult—go to a teacher, doctor, or other concerned adult. Suicidal people don't usually tell a lot of friends—you have a responsibility to ask.

Evaluate—make a judgment—how distressed is this person. Is he or she in Imminent danger? See the next sheet—"Help Must Be Sought When ..."

Support—Be there for him or her. Talk about people and events that have made his or her life worth living. Talk about hopes for the future and remind him or her that life offers lots of choices for the future.

Help Must Be Sought When...

Someone talks or writes about suicide as if it were an option she or he is considering.

Someone answers that they have felt suicidal, when you ask them. (This is a cry for help.)

Someone sees them-selves as never fitting in; or when the depression goes beyond a phase and the person has no sense of belonging to or loving the world.

Someone who was pas-sionate about solving the world's problems (e.g. global warming) and always feels responsible suddenly loses interest and gives up.

Someone's behavior changes rapidly, they claim to have over-come their depression and say "the problem's over". Sudden changes in attitude or personali-ty should be reported to a doc-tor or counselor (Chances are the person has given in, not recovered quickly.).

Someone tells you that they have planned how they might kill themselves. If someone has actually formulated a plan of action they should not be left alone. Help should be sought immediately.

The Exception to the Rule

Suicide is a secret that must not be kept. Promises
of confidentiality are very important, but not nearly
as important as saving a human life.

Some Coping Hints for Capable Kids

Here are a sequence of coping actions than can be stepping stones on the path to success.

- ◆ Clear the muddy waters to locate the real problem.
- ◆ Is it you or the situation that needs to change?
- ◆ Which is easier to change (you or the situation)?
- ◆ What can you do? What are your options? List them.
- ◆ Who can you turn to for help and advice?
- ◆ Draw up a plan of action.
- ◆ If you can't manage the whole, tackle a small part of the problem first.
- ◆ Assess how things are working out. If not, switch gears and try other strategies.
- ◆ Let off steam if necessary.
- ◆ Have a break. Do something relaxing that makes you feel good!
- ◆ Reward yourself for what you have done to date.

Clear the muddy waters ...
What is the problem?

Is it me or the situation
that needs changing?

Which is the easiest to
change?

What can you do? Look
at your options.

Who can you turn to for
help and advice?

Draw up an action plan
and tackle a small part.

Remember to let off
steam if you need to.

Assess how you went
... then try another
strategy.

Have a break and relax.

Then try agan. You can
always alter your plans.

Reward yourself for
what you've done so far.

Different People, Different Strategies, Different Circumstances

When you cope with a difficulty, you may find that you need to let out your emotions, ask for help or work very hard at solving the problem. Or you may need to talk to friends, do some hard physical work or just forget about it for awhile.

Remember, there is no right or wrong way of coping.

Whatever strategy you use to deal with a given situation needs to fit you and the particular circumstances.

Ask yourself and discuss with others:

◆ Is it helping me?
◆ Is it effective in bringing about the results I want?
◆ Is it productive, in that it solves the problem for me?

To develop strategies to cope with the demands of everyday living, use your head! You can reflect on what you are doing, think flexibly, make choices, give yourself permissions and change your ways of both perceiving the problem and your ways of coping.

◆ You can broaden your repertoire of coping strategies
◆ You can use different strategies for different circumstances or purposes.
◆ **You can face the difficulties that come your way with courage and with the knowledge that you CAN COPE.**

You may have discovered ways of coping that are effective for you that we did not mention or issues that you really think need to be discussed. The authors would very much like to collect ideas or suggestions that you may have to put in the next edition of this book (or in other books). You can write or e-mail to Dr. LeoNora Cohen or Dr. Erica Frydenberg. Their addresses are:

Dr. Nora Cohen
School of Education
Education Hall 320b
Oregon State University
Corvallis, OR 97331 USA

Dr. Erica Frydenberg
Dept. of Ed. Psych. & Special Ed.
  Old Pathology
University of Melbourne
Parkville, Victoria 3052
Australia

RESOURCES FOR KIDS

Adderholdt-Elliott, M. (1992) *Perfectionism: What's bad about being too good.* Minneapolis: Free Spirit Press.

Barrett, S.L. (1992) *It's all in your head: A guide to understanding your brain and boosting your brain power.* Minneapolis: Free Spirit Press.

Butler, K.A. (1993) *It's all in your mind: A student's guide to learning styles.* Minneapolis: Free Spirit Press.

Delisle, J.R. (1992). *Gifted kids speak out.* Minneapolis: Free Spirit Press.

Delisle, J. (1991) *Kid stories: Biographies of 20 young people you'd like to know.* Minneapolis: Free Spirit Press.

Delisle, J.R. & Gailbraith, J. (1993) *The gifted kids survival guide II.* Minneapolis: Free Spirit Press.

Dunn, D. & Dunn, J. (1995). *A Kid's Guide to Getting Published.* Waco, TX: Prufrock Press.

Galbraith, J. (1992) *The gifted kids' survival guide (for 10 and under).* Minneapolis: Free Spirit Press.

Galbraith, J. (1992) *The gifted kids' survival guide (for ages 11-18).* Minneapolis: Free Spirit Press.

Hipp, E. (1992) *Fighting invisible tigers.* Minneapolis: Free Spirit Press.

Karnes, F.A. & Bean, S.M. (1995). *Leadership for Young People.* Waco, TX: Prufrock Press.

Lewis, B.A. (1992) *Kids with courage.* Minneapolis: Free Spirit Press.